The Sheffield Gang Wars

J.P. Bean

D. & D. Publications

D & D Publications,
Email: sheffieldgangwars@gmail.com

First Published 1981
Reprinted 1981, 1983, 1984,
1986, 1987, 1988, 1989, 1990,
1992, 1993, 1995, 1999, 2000,
2002, 2003, 2004, 2007, 2009,
2011, 2021

ISBN 0 9507645 0 7

Printed by Cream Creative
Worksop, Nottinghamshire.

Contents

Acknowledgements

The author wishes to thank:

South Yorkshire Police, for their assistance regarding the photographs of those convicted of the murder and manslaughter of William Francis Plommer, and the photographs of Sam and Robert Garvin.

Sheffield City Libraries, for permission to reproduce photographs of courtyards in Cross Smithfields and Duke Street.

Times Newspapers Ltd., for permission to quote from *Cloak Without Dagger* by Sir Percy Sillitoe, published by Cassell & Co. Ltd., in 1955.

The many people without whose help and encouragement this book could not have been written.

Foreword

The slums of Sheffield in the 1920s were as bad as any to be found in England. Cobbled courtyards and dimly lit alleys were lined with row upon row of back-to-back houses: dirty, overcrowded, insanitary hovels where several families might share one outside toilet and those occupying the front of the row had to travel all the way round to the back to use it. There were fifteen thousand back-to-back houses in 1923, and that, according to the *Sheffield Mail*, was a modest estimate.

Accusing the Corporation's Health Committee of being uninterested, as some of the members were themselves owners of such property "in a bad state of repair with atrocious privy middens", the *Mail* commented: "There is probably no city in the country where the housing problem is so acute as in Sheffield, and the menace of insanitation is something the enlightened public are not willing to tolerate much longer."

Unemployment was rife. Out of a total population of 512,052 in June 1921, 69,000 men were out of work. When the Board of Guardians - the body responsible for administering the Poor Law - became nearly £100,000 in the red, the Ministry of Health suggested reductions on the scale of relief. Three years and £1½ million later there was another call for reductions. This time it came from the bank. The Guardians had run out of cash.

The Council's Burden of Debt Committee appealed in vain to the Government for a grant to reduce the city's rates, which had soared to unthinkable heights and led to 28,000 summonses being issued for non-payment. In an attempt to create employment, Sheffield Corporation stepped up relief work projects in road building and municipal constructions like the City Hall which was eventually opened in 1932, but this only added to the ratepayer's burden, crippling the large industrial rate paying concerns who were then forced to increase their overhead charges, consequently driving away much of the trade the city badly needed.

Even drinking habits suffered. In 1915 there were 1473 convictions for drunkenness at Sheffield Police Court, in 1921 there were 241. It was suggested that the undermanned police force was failing in its duty to arrest drunks. The real reason was there were not the drunks to arrest. Thirty shillings a week from the Guardians to keep a wife and family did not leave much for a man to spend on beer.

But if the brewer's business was decreasing, the bookmaker's was booming. To the working classes, without jobs, without prospects, and with very little money, gambling provided perhaps the last vestige of hope. Giving evidence to the Betting Tax Committee in 1923, Supt. Denton of Sheffield City Police said: "Probably 90% of the adult working class population of industrial areas bet or assist others in betting." It was well known to the police, he said, that women and even children were backing to a large extent, subscribing pennies and even halfpennies to put on horses. 25% of the poverty in Sheffield, he said, was due to betting. At the relief stations, eight out of ten men could be seen consulting racing papers.

Mr. W.A. Millership, Labour member of the Guardians, hotly denied Supt. Denton's statement. "If we find anybody gambling with his relief pay we stop his money," he said. Whether the Superintendent's figures were inaccurate or not, the city was certainly gripped in a gambling fever. The dream of a modest coup for a comparatively small outlay was for many people impossible to resist.

The street bookmaker made a fortune: daily. Although off-course cash bookmaking had been illegal since 1853* there was little anyone could do to stop it. One prominent local bookie admitted to taking £75-£100 per day; he paid 'touts' ten shillings a day to keep an eye open for the police. Another employed forty runners to bring in the bets at 1/6d - 2/- in the £ commission. If the runners - some of whom were on a weekly wage - were unlucky enough to get caught, the bookmaker paid their fines. He always asked for time to pay as he reckoned this led the police and magistrates to believe bookmaking was not very profitable. The same man, whose runners collected at nearly every works and factory in Sheffield's East End, said he could make £200 a day and knew a number of other bookmakers who regularly made £100 a day. He did not consider £100 a day a great lot, he said, although bookmaking on this scale brought 35-40% profit after all expenses.

One of twelve officers who were permanently employed watching for street betting explained the difficulties that faced the police. The first time he caught a man with money and slips (the officer was on plain clothes duty) he charged him and the man was taken to court. "There were at least fifty people in court for the purpose of seeing my face," he said "in order that they could identify me in future and thus keep out of my way. There are only forty-six bookmakers in the census figures for Sheffield but I should estimate there are nearer a thousand."

In a street betting prosecution at nearby Rotherham Borough Court, a police constable told how between the hours of 12 noon and

* Credit bets could be telephoned or telegraphed to a commission agent's office.

8p.m. he saw 271 men, 243 women and 197 children - 711 in all - go to the defendant for the purpose of betting. At one point there was a queue of 20 people. The defendant had two large canvas pockets sewn inside his coat. He was fined £12. The same court was told how another bookmaker, having been arrested, was being escorted down the street when a woman came up to him offering a slip and money. Wisely perhaps, he refused.

However, gambling in the early 20s was by no means limited to horse racing. At Hyde Park and Carbrook books were made on men running in handicap races. Heavy wagers were staked on the outcome of bare-knuckle fights. And at strategic points around the city large numbers of men congregated to take part in a highly organised yet illegal game that had flourished in Sheffield since before the First World War. The gatherings were called tossing rings; the game was pitch and toss.

Pitch and toss is one of the simplest forms of gambling. Three coins are placed on the ends of the first two fingers and tossed, spinning, into the air. Bets are made on the proportion of heads to tails - or vice versa - as they fall to the ground.

The principal tossing rings in Sheffield, at Sky Edge, Wadsley, Five Arches and Tinsley, were run on strict business lines. The boss was known as the 'towler' or 'toller', as he collected a toll on bets made. The toll varied from place to place - it could be 2/6d in the pound, or 4/-, or the odd amount on any given sum.

Round the tollers hung a number of satellites, chief of whom were known as the 'ponter' and 'pilners', or scouts. The latter were also known as 'pikers' or 'crows' because, like the sentinel crows on a rookery, they were constantly on the lookout for the approach of danger. The business was known as a 'joint' and the ring itself a 'pitch'. Out of the tolls the toller paid his henchmen and thus virtually guaranteed the ring against police raids. Strategic locations were always chosen and scouts placed at all points of approach to signal danger immediately their suspicions were aroused. When the stakes were high it paid the tollers to maintain a small army of scouts to ensure business would not be interrupted by a police raid. In the event of a raid warning being given, the organisers would have ample time to pocket the money and the crowd to scatter. Unlike bookmaking there was no equipment, no betting slips that could be produced as evidence in court.

The action commenced with the toller shouting "Heads a pound", or whatever the amount might be, and someone coming up with an equivalent sum to 'Tail' it. The stake money was placed in the centre of the ring and the toll - paid only by the person initiating the bet - in the toller's pocket. The coins - at Sky Edge, three halfpennies - would be tossed by a man known simply as 'the tosser', usually an artist at the game. Picking up the coins after they had fallen, the ponter officially announced the result, head or tails; winnings were paid out by the toller and re-betting began. Often a winner would leave his money in the ring, the bets thus doubling each toss. The most common bets were in units of 6, 12 or 24 - shillings or pounds depending on the company – of which I, 2 or 4 were pocketed by the toller and the rest was a round stake to be matched by the ring. There was also many cross-bets between individuals. These were private transactions on which the ring organisers levied no toll.

Generally, the organised tossing rings were run on sound sporting lines - the gambler being expected to take his fate, whatever it may be. If anyone was not happy with the execution of a particular toss* they had the right to protest by shouting "barred", at which the ponter would kick the coins as they fell to the ground and the toss would be retaken. The ponter, armed with a stick, was responsible for maintaining order around the ring, but there was little trouble when gambling was in progress.

However, when quarrels did erupt they were by no means gentle affairs. Out of one, as subsequent chapters will relate, sprang a bitter feud that was to result in one man being killed, two hanged for murder, and many law-abiding citizens reduced to a state of terror.

---

* A common trick was to throw up the coins in such a way that they quivered in the air, giving the impression of spinning. This was known as 'flamming'.

1. Beginnings

In the early hours of Sunday, April 29th, 1923, two men broke into the home of William Furniss, dragged him from his bed, and brutally assaulted him with pokers. Despite being knocked unconscious and requiring medical attention, Furniss refused to say anything to the police. He was adamant that he would not prosecute his attackers, although he almost certainly knew who they were.

William Furniss was thirty-two years old. Until a few months before the attack he had worked underground at Nunnery Colliery after being invalided out of the Army in the First World War. His home was 6 ct. 2, Duke Street Lane, a tenement in the heart of a vast warren of courtyard slums known as the Park District of Sheffield. The incident drew little attention in an area where Saturday night violence was part of the normal way of life. None of the four local papers even mentioned it.

Three weeks later, just after 6 a.m. on Friday, May 18th, police and plain clothes detectives were called to a riotous scene in Corporation Street. Bricks and other missiles were flying as about twenty men indulged in a full scale affray. When the police moved in the two rival factions joined forces to attack them. An elderly spectator, Henry Onley, of nearby West Bar Hostel, was hit on the neck by a flying brick and several policemen received injuries that required medical treatment. Most of the men escaped up passages and alleyways but the police managed to arrest one man, Peter Winsey, and a week later he appeared before the magistrates at Sheffield Police Court.

Winsey, who was thirty-eight, pleaded not guilty, said brick throwing was not a pastime of his and on the night in question he had been drinking at a Licensed Victuallers' Ball in the Cutlers' Hall until 1.15 a.m. Afterwards he had returned to a "certain house" and left, with others, at 6 a.m. He declined to tell the Bench who the others were and was fined £1 for the assault on the old man and £6 for assaulting P. C. Sapsford in the execution of his duty.

Nine days after the Corporation Street affray, on the afternoon of Sunday, May 27th, a householder, digging his garden at the top of Manor Laithe Road, Park, was amazed to see two men dragging a third from the direction of Sky Edge. In the words of the householder, the man who was being dragged, "looked as if he had been in a slaughterhouse." His face and hair were one mass of blood and his skull was battered in at the front. His coat was slashed to ribbons and through a rip in his trousers a wound six inches long was visible. In spite of his injuries the man, Frank Kidnew, aged thirty-nine, was smoking a cigarette.

The two men, who had found Kidnew lying near a disused pit-shaft, helped him to a tram stop, but before a tram arrived he collapsed and had to be taken into a nearby house until an ambulance was called. Kidnew's only concern was his clothes. "Reckon they've spoiled my suit," he said. At the Royal Infirmary a hundred cuts were found on his body and he was detained a month. He refused to breathe a word to the police.

The tossing ring at Sky Edge, an elevated expanse of wasteland high above the city, had for years been the most lucrative in Sheffield. Its ideal position and strategically placed 'pikers' - making it virtually immune against police raids - meant that the Skyring, as it was known, attracted big money gamblers from miles around. In charabanc, tram and train they came from as far away as Rotherham, Chesterfield and Barnsley. Betting began at around 10.30 a.m. and, with a break for lunch, continued right through until dusk. There were often several hundred men in the ring at one time, considerable amounts of money changing hands. A publican from Barnsley, who thought nothing of putting fifty pounds on a single toss, won over three hundred pounds on one occasion. At lunch times, when he retired to the Chequers in Weigh Lane, he threw handfuls of silver and copper to children playing outside.

The Sky Edge tossing ring was started before the First World War by a group of betting men headed by 'Snaps' Jackson, a tic-tac man from one of Sheffield's oldest racing families. A regular in the early days was Bill Foulke, the legendary twenty stone Sheffield United and England goalkeeper. When 'Snaps' Jackson went into the army in 1916 his brothers took over the organisation, but by the end of the war a local bookmaker named William Cowan was in control.

During the War the tossing ring had been a thorn-in-the-flesh of the authorities, with deserters from the services known to be frequenting it. One morning in 1916 a combined force of mounted police and soldiers of the York and Lancs. Regiment sealed off every possible escape route from Sky Edge and, with the aid of a spotter plane hovering above, rounded up over a hundred deserters. Residents of Duke Street, the main street through the Park, were startled to see the soldiers, with fixed bayonets, emerging from a solid-tyred, single decker bus and running towards Sky Edge. No one escaped; those present who were not deserters were later fined for illegal gaming. With the war over William Cowan handed the Skyring over to a man whose name has become synonymous with the Sheffield gangs: George Mooney. Mooney, Sheffield born, of Irish descent, was at this time in his late twenties and living in Trinity Street, West Bar. Since his teens he had led a lawless life resulting in a string of convictions, many for crimes of violence, and several prison sentences. Feared locally as leader of the Mooney Gang, a small band of criminals who terrorised shopkeepers and publicans in West Bar and surrounding areas, Mooney spent much of his time on northern racecourses. Occasionally he stood as a bookmaker in the cheaper enclosures, together with his older brother, John Thomas. At the outbreak of war in 1914, along with several of his followers, George Mooney volunteered with the Hallamshire Battalion of the York and Lancs. Regiment. Despite being promoted to the rank of corporal, Mooney soon became bored with the restrictions of army life. He absconded while stationed at Clipstone, Notts. in 1916, was caught, absconded again, and spent much of the remainder of the war on the run from the military police.

When Mooney took over the Skyring, gambling was at its height. Cash was prolific due to war wages and Sankey money*, crowds flocked to Sky Edge daily, and business was so good it had to be divided into two tossing rings, run side by side. As headman he employed ten to a dozen tollers on upwards of two pounds a day each, and a legion of touts and pikers who were paid about ten shillings a day. With such easy money available it is hardly surprising that George Mooney attracted hangers-on. Nor that those hangers-on were not the most law-abiding and respectable of citizens. By 1919 Mooney was no longer leader of a mere handful of petty crooks and small-time scufflers. As headman in the Skyring he commanded an extremely profitable – if illegal and potentially volatile – large business organisation.

Over the years, like other large cities, Sheffield had had its share of gangs. In the 1840s a band of Sheffield men, along with their Manchester, Nottingham and Liverpool counterparts, gathered to form the Northern Mob, intimidating and extorting at prize fights, cock fights, race meetings and anywhere else where crowds congregated. In the 1860s and 70s there were two main sources of gang trouble in the city – the Gutterpercha gang and one led by Kingy

* A payment of ten shillings a day to miners, in addition to regular wages of 8/6d a day.

Broadhead. The latter hung around the lower end of the Park and had a penchant for knocking tall hats off the heads of gentlemen! Prior to and during the First World War, the Gas Tank Gang of Neepsend, and the Red Silk and White Silk Gangs - so called because of their coloured silk neckscarves - held brief sway in the East End: waylaying pedestrians, following and robbing steelworkers on pay night, and generally making a nuisance of themselves until the police swept them off the streets. Their favourite haunt was Blonk Street fairground where they engaged in brawls and skirmishes with on-leave 'squaddies'. Usually the soldiers, heavily outnumbered, came off worst.

The Mooney Gang was more reminiscent of the Northern Mob than the more recent street gangs. Most of Mooney's henchmen frequented the racecourses. A few described themselves as bookmakers or bookmakers' clerks but in the main their incomes were derived from activities outside the law. Some were bruisers who preyed on genuine bookmakers by demanding 'protection' money, palming betting slips for races that had been run and then claiming their 'winnings', inducing subscriptions to bogus charities, and various other sharp practices. If the bookmaker was reluctant to pay up his stand would be smashed, his satchel snatched and he and his clerk beaten up. Others specialised in picking pockets, though few possessed the skill of the professional 'dip'*. Their style bore more resemblance to the "Stand and deliver" of a Dick Turpin than the dexterous artistry of a Diamond Dick Fisher who, operating on public transport in the days when jewelled tie-pins were the vogue, was reputed to be able to bite the setting off a tie-pin without disturbing the composure of his victim. For members of a gang, backed by muscle, such subtleties were unnecessary. Their 'bottling' as it was then known would today be classed as 'mugging'. Card-sharping on the race trains was another of their nefarious means. The crowded carriage always contained at least one dupe eager to be fleeced in a crooked game of cards or dice. The 'Three Card Trick' or 'Find the Lady', 'Crown and Anchor', and 'E and O' were all methods employed in separating the gullible from their money and, as with the gangs' other villainies, if the victim protested too loudly he ended up being assaulted as well as robbed.

The Mooney Gang was drawn from two main areas of Sheffield - West Bar and the Park. By 1923 George Mooney had left Trinity Street, following the death of his first wife, re-married, and moved to

* The 'profession' of pocket-picking has always had its own special degrees. In the 1920s the person who performed the actual theft was known as a 'dip', 'hook' or 'tool' while the 'stall' or 'eye' distracted the victims attention. Top-class dips worked alone, disdaining the assistance of a stall.

23, Corporation Street, a former beerhouse of which his late mother had been licensee. Round the corner, in Steelhouse Lane, lived 'Spud' Murphy; not far away, in Scotland Street, Peter Winsey; and in Furnace Hill, Tommy Rippon. Mooney's brother, John Thomas, lived in Old Street, Park, in the shadow of Sky Edge and only a stone's throw from Albert Foster in Park Hill Lane. Also from the Park were William Furniss, William Roberts and Sandy Bowler, and from nearer the city centre, George 'Ganner' Wheywell and Frank Kidnew. Another man who was to play a leading role in the events of the next few years had recently left the Park to live in a newly built council house at Walkley. Slipping away before trouble erupted was a tactic Sam Garvin knew well. Even when he had played a major part in the inciting of it.

With the Skyring flourishing in the early post-war years there was no shortage of cash to be shared among the gangmen. The dozen or so principals pocketed more each day than many men could earn in a week of legitimate work. But the days of plenty were not to last. A Government return in December 1921 revealed a 99% fall in the cost of living since 1914, the beginning of the war. Wages dropped accordingly. The miners' Sankey money was withdrawn, leaving them with a bare 8/6d a day. The steel industry, which had enjoyed a wartime boom with the manufacture of munitions, wallowed in an economic slump. The Skyring was as popular as ever but its turnover was drastically reduced.

By the beginning of 1923 profits from the Skyring had fallen to such a degree that there was no longer enough cash to satisfy the principal members. Mooney, seeing the need for a greater share-out for himself and his immediate henchmen, decided to dispense with the services of the Park men who had latched onto him in the boom years. Together with his brother, he would run the ring assisted by Peter Winsey, 'Spud' Murphy, Frank Kidnew and Albert Foster. Mooney had grown up with Winsey, who had been taken in as a boy by Mooney's family when his own mother died. Murphy lived round the corner from Mooney's home in Corporation Street, Kidnew was an old friend, and Foster was a man whose violence would be useful in the not-too-distant future. Small, stocky, born in India, Foster was thirty-three and had convictions stretching back to 1905. He carried a loaded revolver and few doubted his frequent assertion that if necessary he would not be afraid to use it.

But the Park men were not going to give up without a fight. Urged on from the sidelines by Sam Garvin, they believed that the tossing ring on Sky Edge, which loomed above their own doorstep, belonged by rights to them - not Mooney from West Bar. Without further ado Sandy Barlow, aided by William Furniss and William Roberts, toured the street corners, taprooms and billiard parlours of the Park district seeking out likely young men who were ready and willing to fight for control of the Skyring. Barlow, an ex-boxer and Garvin's right-hand man, had no difficulty enlisting recruits. A rival gang to the Mooneys emerged: the Park Brigade.

Greatly outnumbered, the Mooneys were soon ousted from Sky Edge. There were rows and skirmishes but it was not long before Garvin's men had firm control of the tossing ring and its revenue. The Mooneys were out for revenge. As a leading light in the Park Brigade, William Furniss was a natural target. The poker attack on Furniss as he lay in bed on April 29th was carried out by Albert Foster and Frank Kidnew. The subsequent brawl in Corporation Street, on May 18th, occurred when the Park Brigade waylaid Peter Winsey and others as they were leaving the home of George Mooney. The slashing of Frank Kidnew was a direct reprisal for the attack on Furniss. The scores were about level, one each and a draw - in which the police came off worse than either gang. However, bitterness had reached such proportions that matters could not be left at that. The gangs were now at war!

At 1 a.m. on Saturday, June 16th, police at West Bar received an urgent call to go to 23, Corporation Street. As they approached they heard two shots fired and on arrival found the house, home of George Mooney and his family, being stormed by members of the Park Brigade - shouting for Mooney to "come out and fight" and threatening to burn the place down. Windows were broken, iron grating wrenched up, there were bullet holes in the wall and, lying on the pavement suffering from bullet wounds in the arm and shoulder, was George 'Ganner' Wheywell, of the Park Brigade. Inside the barricaded house police found George Mooney in a state of fear and his wife, who had called the police, on the verge of hysterics. Wheywell, who was not seriously injured, was taken to the Royal Infirmary. When his coat was removed a bullet fell to the floor.

The following Monday the police obtained a warrant to search 23, Corporation Street. Inside they found the Mooney Gang in possession of what was later described as a miniature arsenal: a double-barrelled sporting gun, a rifle, a six-chambered revolver, a number of undischarged cartridges and three or four types of life-preserver*. Mooney admitted responsibility for the sporting gun and rifle, but not

---

* A life-preserver, so called because it preserved the life of the person wielding it, was a short, heavy cosh. Sometimes it was a hollowed-out chair leg filled with lead, often a truncheon-type stick with a nail through the end.

the revolver. "I have been forced to defend myself as they have been shooting from the outside for this last three weeks, and to defend my wife and children," he told officers. The next day, Tuesday, June 19th, along with his associates, he appeared at Sheffield Police Court. George Mooney (33), 23, Corporation Street; John Thomas Mooney, (41), 3, Old Street, Park; Peter Winsey, (38), 31, Furnace Hill; John James Murphy, (38), 19, Steelhouse Lane; Albert Ernest Foster, (33), 2 ct. 3 hse. Park Hill Lane; and Thomas Rippon, (34), 31, Furnace Hill, were charged jointly with being in possession of a revolver, rifle and ammunition for which they had no certificate under the Firearms Act. Murphy was also charged with assaulting P. C. Cranswick on May 18th, the occasion of the 6 a.m. affray outside Mooney's. The hearing was adjourned until the following Friday, and court staff were somewhat surprised to hear all the defendants except Rippon asking to be kept in custody. Their requests were granted, and Rippon must have wished he had joined them. No sooner had he left the court building than he was spotted by George Wheywell and other members of the Park Brigade, who gave immediate chase. Rippon ran out of Waingate, up Castle Street, and straight into the Central Police Offices where he asked for police protection. His pursuers chased him all the way into the offices and several of them were promptly taken in. All were later released with the exception of George Wheywell.

Wheywell appeared in court the next morning, charged with assaulting Thomas Rippon. Chief Superintendent Hollis told the magistrates of the considerable disorder which existed in the city through the feuds of the rival gangs, adding that the police were anxious to put a stop to it. "It is in the interests of everyone that this man should be kept in custody," he said. The chairman of the bench replied: "A good idea would be for them to go into a field and clear it up." He then granted Wheywell bail.

On Friday, June 22nd the Police Court was crowded and extra police were brought in when the charges of unlawful possession of firearms were brought against George Mooney, John Thomas Mooney, Peter Winsey, John James Murphy and Albert Foster, who had all been in custody since the previous Tuesday, and Thomas Rippon who had enjoyed the questionable privilege of bail. During the hearing a witness named Pope was called but, although his name was shouted along the corridors and outside in Castle Street, he did not appear. Disappearing witnesses were to become a regular feature of subsequent gang cases.

Mr. J. W. Fenoughty, defending, submitted a guilty plea on behalf of George Mooney. The other five men pleaded not guilty.

Mr. A.W. Forsdike, for the prosecution, told the court that there was no denying that during the preceding few weeks there had apparently been two gangs of men in the city. The gangs were known to have been clashing and there had been assaults by both day and night. This had certainly had a terrorising effect upon a section of the city's population, and the police had been forced to step in—possibly, he suggested, with a view to protecting one gang against the other.

Evidence was given by Detective Inspector Naylor who, in reply to Mr. Fenoughty, agreed that George Mooney had appealed "time and time again" in the preceding three weeks for police protection against the Park Brigade. Another detective told the court of the attack on William Furniss and referred to the assault on Frank Kidnew. Mr. Fenoughty asked: "And there can be no doubt about the assault on Kidnew, and that is the reason that Mr. Mooney and Co. went into retirement?" There was hearty laughter in the public gallery.

In evidence, George Mooney said: "I am in a state of siege and terror." He said he was barricaded in his home and had taken the firearms in to protect himself. The other prisoners had nothing to do with them. He was fined £10 and the firearms ordered to be confiscated. The charges against the others were dismissed.

At the conclusion of the case, John James Murphy was put back in the dock, accused of assaulting P.C. Cranswick on May 18th. The police constable was struck on the head by a brick. Murphy said he never threw at Cranswick and "would have been delighted to have seen a policeman's uniform that day." He was fined £10.

The main case arising out of the storming of George Mooney's home was heard on Monday 25th, when five members of the Park Brigade appeared before the magistrates. The court was again crowded and a number of people were unable to obtain admission. Accused of "unlawfully and tumultuously assembling outside 23, Corporation Street," and of behaving in a disorderly manner were: George Arthur Wheywell, described as a baker, of Duke Street, Park; William Furniss of Duke Street Lane; Gilbert Marsh and Albert Flaherty, both of Hoyle Street; and Ernest Chapman, of Arundel Street.

Mr. A. W. Forsdike again prosecuted and outlined similar facts to those he had told the magistrates on the previous Friday. There could be no doubt, he said, that the defendants were the aggressors. They did not live anywhere near Corporation Street and it was plain that they went to Mooney's house deliberately to attack him. Mooney would tell the court that he was unable to leave his house from the time of the disturbance until the following Monday afternoon.

When George Mooney entered the witness box it was suggested to him by Mr. Irwin Mitchell, defending, that he was appearing in a rather unusual role.

Mr. Mitchell: "Can you suggest how Wheywell was hurt?"

Mooney: "Only that it was a bad shot on their part."

Earlier, a detective sergeant had told the court how he found Wheywell suffering from bullet wounds and was told "George Mooney has done it."

Mr. Mitchell claimed it was a case of "the pot calling the kettle black" which depended entirely on the evidence of Mooney. "It is rather Gilbertian*," he said, "to find the Mooneys here today, in their present capacity, with the police ranged alongside them, and Mr. Forsdike taking up cudgels on their behalf."

After hearing all the evidence the Chairman said the Bench were determined to take every step to prevent a re-occurrence of the events described to them. But any apprehension the defendants might have felt at these words was short-lived. Each of them was bound over in the sum of £20 for twelve months. In addition, George Mooney and his followers were bound over in a similar sum.

With the main case out of the way George Wheywell was then returned to the dock on the charge of assaulting Thomas Rippon outside the court buildings on June 19th. Wheywell was known by the police to have played a leading role in the slashing of Frank Kidnew at Sky Edge, when the latter had received a hundred cuts but had refused to prosecute. The previous Friday he had appeared on the Rippon charge and a witness had complained that he had been threatened by Wheywell that he would be "done in". The case opened with Mr. Forsdike describing George Wheywell as "an extremely dangerous man" and stating: "there is only one way to stop these assaults and that is by making an example of someone." At that point Tommy Rippon suddenly expressed a reluctance to proceed, saying he did not want "anything to do with it". The charges were withdrawn and George 'Ganner' Wheywell left the court, his notorious reputation further enhanced by the prosecutor's description and Rippon's evident fear.

The same afternoon, mounted police were called to a disturbance outside Albert Foster's home in Park Hill Lane, heart of Park Brigade territory. A number of women were standing in the street discussing the morning's cases when a score of men were seen to be heading for Foster's. Warned by the womens' screams he locked himself in the house as the men, shouting threats, tried to break in. Soon, hundreds had flocked to the scene and several scuffles broke out amongst female spectators. One woman's forehead was gashed by a blow from a potato masher. Foster left his house under police protection.

* Referring to W.S. Gilbert, of Gilbert & Sullivan fame.

On June 27, two days after the Park Brigade case, when members of both gangs had been bound over in the sum of £20 each, George Mooney and his five associates made a further, but unexpected, appearance at the Police Court. There were many curious expressions about the court as they sat through two hours of uninteresting proceedings and then, at the conclusion of the morning's business, all got up and approached the magistrates clerk's table. A short conversation took place, in which Albert Foster said some of them could not find the sureties fixed two days earlier. The magistrates' clerk told them to go back to their seats until they knew whether they were going to find them or not. After discussing the matter with the police, Foster said once more that they could not find sureties.

The Clerk: "Get your sureties or it will be three weeks in default, and no one wants that."

Foster: "We don't know what we were bound over for."

The Clerk: "If the other side can find them, you ought to do."

Another of the gang: "There are five hundred on the other side, there are more of them than us."

They were told to produce their sureties by the following morning or go to prison for three weeks in default. As they were leaving, one of the men turned to a solicitor in court and smilingly told him: "Back Carpathus today and you'll be alright."

Whether or not the solicitor took their advice is not certain, but it would appear that the Mooney Gang did. That afternoon at Newcastle in the 3.10 Northumberland Plate, Carpathus won by half a length at 4 to 1. The next morning all the sureties were paid.

2. Reactions

On May 7th, just over a week after the poker attack on William Furniss, the Chief Constable of Sheffield, Lieut. Col. John Hall-Dalwood, issued a grave warning regarding the strength of the local police force and its ability to cope with crime prevalent in the city.

In an interview with the *Sheffield Daily Telegraph*, Col. Hall-Dalwood stated:

"The public of Sheffield is paying rates for police protection which under the circumstances it cannot possibly get. In Sheffield we have to admit we are floating on very thin ice indeed and we have also to admit that, unless more generally helped by punishments to fit crimes, unpalatable as it may be, that Sheffield's police force is utterly inadequate numerically to cope with the wave of crime that must necessarily follow in the wake of the unemployment situation at the present time."

The interview had been prompted by a report made to the Home Secretary by the Inspector of Constabulary, who declared that each year the police were having greater difficulty performing their primary duty of preventing crime and offences against the law, the cause being an increased amount of other duties assigned to them. Courts from the highest to the lowest were convicting less readily, he added. Punishments were less and lighter, prosecutions were no longer so great a deterrent. Col. Hall-Dalwood was in full agreement with these views. He alleged:

"It is the boast of the really bad man that he gets the best run for his money in Sheffield.

He would rather be caught in Sheffield than in any other part of the country because, he says, you have to produce more evidence for the prosecution in a Sheffield court to get a conviction than in any other town in the country.

Moreover, the convicted man in Sheffield is invariably pleasantly surprised by the light character of his sentence.

What is happening is that we are making thieves."

The Chief Constable went on to say that the police might receive more assistance from the magistrates in respect of bail.

"Bail in my own personal opinion, is being so freely granted that what is happening now is that criminals are laughing in the face of the police, saying that when they are arrested the magistrates will give them bail, and in more cases than one they have immediately gone away and committed an offence the very same evening .

....If the Sheffield police is to be made more effective, criminals will have to be far more seriously dealt with by local magistrates, bail will have to be less readily granted, and the Government will have to treat the police less a 'pack horse' for a hundred and one little things which are really outside the province of police duties and inside that of Government departments."

It was an ominous warning by a man who knew both the police and the city well. Lieut. Col. J. Hall-Dalwood had been Chief Constable for eleven years. It was a warning that would be repeated on several occasions over the next three years, but it went unheeded.

That the city force was under strength was indisputable. At the time of the Chief Constable's interview, Sheffield had 556 men to police a population of 512,556. Leeds had 725 men to police 465,500. Bristol had 676 for 377,061. Both Birmingham and Manchester had forces of nearly three times the size of Sheffield's, yet populations of less than double. The city police, stretched to their limits by increased burglaries on houses, shops and warehouses, and by an ever-increasing traffic problem, desperately needed more men.

But the only reaction that the Chief Constable's words received was critical. In their Current Topics column of the same edition in which they had published the interview, the *Sheffield Daily Telegraph* opined that too often innocent men were found guilty and "we are inclined to think that leaning to the side of mercy is not on the whole the worst of faults."

Six weeks later, the same paper observed: "Sheffield people are beginning to show concern as a result of recent happenings in the city." Although there were "a number of local gangs in conflict", they informed readers, such concern was apparently mis-placed. ".....The menace, if such it is," they suggested, "has perhaps been over-exaggerated in some quarters and there is a noticeable tendency to attribute the slightest 'breach of the peace' to activities of one gang or another. It is this difficulty in getting hold of the deliberate promoters of real trouble that has necessarily handicapped police investigations."

So the *Sheffield Daily Telegraph* doubted the existence of a gang menace. A poker and a razor attack, an affray and a shooting had not, apparently, been enough to convince them. They did not seem to realise that the police had, in fact, got hold of at least some of the "deliberate promoters of real trouble" and hauled them before the magistrates - who had punished them as they might errant schoolboys.

If the *Sheffield Daily Telegraph* were prepared to ignore the situation, their rivals at the *Sheffield Mail* were certainly not. On the evening of June 26th, the same day that the Mooneys and Park Brigade had been bound over and Wheywell discharged, the *Mail's* headlines screamed: "SCANDAL OF SHEFFIELD GANG FEUDS". The sub-headlines: "Watch Committee and Police must act"; "Lenient magistrates"; "Citizen's indignation at recent revelations"; "The Sheffield gang vendetta must be stamped out." A leading article thundered:

> "The complete failure of the police authorities in Sheffield to crush the lawlessness of the Mooney Gang and its rival demands the very earnest consideration of (1) The Chief Constable (2) The Watch Committee and (3) the Justices of the Peace. We make no attempt at this stage to apportion responsibility.
>
> As to (1) we assume that the Chief Constable has kept the Watch Committee fully informed about the ramifications of the two gangs. We assume too that he made specific representations to the Committee about the manifest need of a special detective organisation.
>
> As to (2) we assume that the Watch Committee have the fullest confidence in the Chief Constable's ability to create this special organisation and to personally direct it.
>
> And as to (3) we assume that the J.P.s, in the continued and deplorable absence of a virile Stipendiary Magistrate*, are prepared to give the Watch Committee and the Chief Constable the utmost possible support."

The *Mail* went on to say:

> "The people of Sheffield have a right to expect that this difficult but quite unexceptionable piece of work shall be done. If it is not done quietly and efficiently, according to the best traditions of English civil government, then the person or persons executively responsible for the failure must go."

Bold words, but it would be a long time before a special detective organisation hit the Sheffield streets, in the shape of the Flying Squad, and the call for a Stipendiary magistrate was one that would be repeated again and again over the next three years.

---

* The position of Stipendiary magistrate had lapsed in 1915 and was not filled until 1975.

Commenting on the article, the Chief Constable told a *Mail* reporter that the police were doing all they could: "I am of the opinion that we are doing all we possibly can to check this sort of thing. The only thing I can do is either prevent crime being committed, or when it is committed find out the guilty parties. The fact that this is being done is proved by the fact that certain people were brought before the court. What powers we have we are exercising."

The last point was a poignant one. When Furniss and Kidnew refused to prosecute or name their attackers, there was little the police could do. Similarly, when Tommy Rippon said he wanted nothing more to do with the charges against George Wheywell the matter was out of police hands. They were fulfilling their responsibility by delivering troublemakers to court. What happened then was the magistrates' responsibility.

When Alderman Alfred Cattell, chairman of the Watch Committee, was asked to comment on the press reaction to the troubles, his remarks were quite startling. Asked if he had read that morning's *Independent*, which had likened Sheffield to some of the more disturbed parts of Ireland, he replied: "No, I never look at your papers." When the attitude of the press was explained to him by a *Mail* reporter, the chairman suggested that the press was not competent to say what should be done.

Reporter: "But surely you have something to say on such an important subject?"

Chairman: "I never make statements to the Press. The fewer times Alfred Cattell's name appears in print, either personally or as chairman of the Watch Committee, the better!"

Reporter: "Do you not think it rather disgraceful that this sort of thing should be allowed to go on?"

Chairman: "Well, we know they are a rough lot."

Reporter: "Do you think it would be permitted in any other city in the country?"

Chairman: "I really don't know. You can say what you like about us."

Such was the concern of Alderman Alfred Cattell, leader of the City Council Conservatives and chairman of the Watch Committee, the body responsible for maintaining the forces of law and order.

Alderman A.J. Bailey, another member of that august band, was no more forthcoming: "I shall not say anything about it here," he told the *Mail*. "What I have to say will be said at the Watch Committee meeting."

In the same feature, which took up most of their front page on June

26th, the *Sheffield Mail* solicited the views of three of the city magistrates. Mr. Harry Fisher J.P., who had sat in judgement on several gang cases said: "The man in the street has been heard to say that both the Watch Committee and the City Council, and even some of the magistrates, suffer from 'blue funk'. It is beyond doubt that this local outlawry should be more drastically dealt with. Doses of soothing syrup to these delinquents are quite useless.

We have on the Bench, some few J.P.s who fearlessly grapple with the cases that come before them, but it seems to me that some of the older magistrates possess more pluck than the recent additions to the Bench."

Mr. Fisher went on to say that he had personally been threatened as he walked through the city and suggested that the vendetta had developed to such an extent that it must be crushed with a firm hand: "Until these gentry are shown—either by broken heads with a policeman's baton, or by lengthy terms of imprisonment - that they cannot terrorize peaceful citizens, very little progress will be made."

Councillor Moses Humberstone J.P., Labour leader in the city, criticised the police, saying that if it were members of the unemployed who were creating such disturbances, the police would find powers to bring an end to it. Even if they had not the powers, they would find them. "I think they should not be fined or bound over," he said, "they should be locked up until we get the whole of the gang in prison."

Alderman Wardley J.P. considered that the Mooney Gang had been allowed too much latitude, and the trouble was the result of the police not being allowed to "settle" them. Presumably referring to the Kingy Broadhead and Gutterpercha gangs, he added: "I recollect, fifty years ago, that gangs were in existence in the city that could swallow up the Mooney gang." It was not only Alderman Wardley's nostalgic reminiscence that was behind the times. He was apparently unaware that the gang which the police had not been allowed to "settle" was now two gangs, and it was the Park Brigade "settling" the Mooney Gang that had caused the recent troubles.

The next day, June 27th, the Mail suggested that Birmingham's methods of dealing with gang troubles should be an example to Sheffield. After an armed raid on a public house, when shots had been fired "right and left", the ringleaders had been sentenced at the Assizes to terms of imprisonment of up to five years.

Of the four local newspapers in existence in the mid-twenties*, the Sheffield Mail took most interest in the early developments of the gang

* *Sheffield Daily Telegraph, Yorkshire Telegraph & Star, Sheffield Independent & Sheffield Mail.*

troubles. On June 27th, in a call for drastic action, the *Mail* provided an insight for those of its readers unfamiliar with the happenings in the Park, West Bar and city centre, into the intimidatory activities of the gangmen. It is fair to comment that by this time, such activities were the sole province of the Park Bridge, George Mooney and his followers having been forced into virtual retirement from the city scene.

The *Mail* wrote:

"The leaders of these gangs of Sheffield outlaws and free booters are men who live on the fat of the land.

They are men of good appearance. They possess persuasive personalities and glib tongues. They use every possible art and device to carry on their nefarious business.

At one moment they spend money freely as though it were water....the next they are grabbing a glass of beer from a man's mouth. They are a nuisance and a danger to publicans - they break glasses, assault customers, smash windows, pull their own beer and don't pay for it. They work the confidence trick on inoffensive people, row with one another and demand drinks after closing hours. Everyone goes in fear of them and they know it.

One of their pet methods of assault is to break a glass on the counter and attack a man's face with the jagged edges."

The *Mail* went on to describe the tossing ring as the chief source of gang revenue and how anyone winning a substantial amount was obliged to hand over a share of his spoils. If he paid up, the organisers guaranteed his safety home; if he did not, they took their 'share' forcibly.

"All kinds of men are employed by the proprietors to deal with various classes of 'business'. They have glib-tongued contricksters who can lay a man out as easily as rolling over a nine-pin. One of the principals has himself been a boxer*. Others dress flashily, wear heavy gold watch-guards and display their wealth arrogantly.

These are not ignorant ruffians. They are men who have calculated quite coolly and calmly the gains to be won by their terrifying outlawry. They are prepared to put up a stiff fight for supremacy. Strong measures will be necessary to beat them down."

The following day, June 27th, the same reporter wrote that the gang feud threatened to assume proportions that would menace not only the

* Charles McKay Barlow, alias Sandy Bowler.

city, but the country generally, as the parties concerned were to settle their differences on one of the Northern racecourses: "I am reliably informed that the leader of one of the gangs has been to London to secure the services of a gang whose name is known nationally and who have been asked to travel to Northern meetings to afford their support. On the other hand, there is a suggestion that the other gang is taking steps to secure the services of a Birmingham gang."

The gang "known nationally" was the Sabini gang, whose Southern racecourse battles with the Birmingham gang - the Brummagem Boys had been regularly in the news since early 1921*. The background to the *Mail's* story was that the Sabinis would be taking Mooney's part, and the Brummagem Boys the Park Brigade's. It was a rumour that never materialised. Neither of the Southern gangs became involved and the vendetta continued where it had begun, on the streets of Sheffield.

* In the early post 1918 period, the Birmingham mob held the whip-hand and ran the rackets on all the country's racecourses. Seeing the big money to be made, the previously divided Italian and Jewish factions in London combined in 1920 and claimed the South as their own territory. When the Brummagem Boys arrived on Epsom Downs for the 1921 Derby meeting they found the area on which betting pitches were erected - which had previously been controlled by themselves - in the hands of the London mob. This led to a series of bloody battles between the two gangs and their various allies which continued until shortly before the Second World War. The Brummagem Boys were led originally by William Kimber; the London gang by Charles 'Darby' Sabini. The Sabini's 'pail and sponge' routine, in which a gangman went along the track rails, wiping the bookmakers' boards and collecting handsome 'fees' for his trouble is perhaps the best known of their numerous rackets. Born in Sicily, Charles Sabini, assisted by his two younger brothers, organised his activities from Saffron Hill. At the outbreak of war in 1939 he was interned as an enemy alien.

3. George Mooney: fugitive

Unlike more famous gangleaders, both before his time and since, George Mooney did not seek publicity. Although his name was on the lips of most of the inhabitants of Sheffield by the end of June 1923, few, other than his neighbours or members of the racing fraternity, could put a face to the name. And while his near-legendary reputation had been given weight by the newspapers, who had rarely missed an opportunity to mention that George Mooney was a gangleader, such references were usually in connection with court cases. So when, in an interview on June 27th with the *Sheffield Mail's* special correspondent, J.T. Higgins, Mooney spoke out on the recent clashes, it came as something of a surprise.

Mooney claimed there was a lot of "talking off the top" about the gang business. "They talk about two gangs, but there are a hundred of the so-called rivals and only five of us. That is my brother and me, John James Murphy, Albert Foster and Peter Winsey." It was ridiculous, he said, to talk about rival gangs with five against a hundred.

He confirmed that the root of the trouble was the Sky Edge tossing ring, with which he had been prominently associated. There were five men running the Park gang, he said, who often went about with a crowd, which, he said, explained how they kept springing up outside his house. These five organisers had got the idea that he and his friends were out to take the tossing ring off them. "They think that if they can get us to slash with razors, or kill, or whatever is going to be done - and they are trying hard to provoke trouble -we shall be out of the way, and the Park gambling ring will be left to them and their claim will not be tampered with. But we do not want to slash, and we do not want to interfere with them. There is no need to trouble to put us out. For four years we have been trying to live down the title of the Mooney Gang."

All the trouble, he claimed, was being caused by hangers-on to the ring organisers - men on relief who were prowling round terrorising publicans and others. "Everytime there is a street brawl," he said, "or these people go threatening or holding up publicans - and it is being done very often - the first thing the public say is:- 'It's the Mooney gang again', although we know nothing about it. There is Alderman Wardley for instance. He talks off the top in what he said in last night's *Mail*. Does he know who the Mooney gang are? A lot of the real gang come from where Alderman Wardley comes from but I do not blame him for that. It is absurd for him to talk about gangs fifty years ago and mix them up with us. He might be a little less loose." It was an understandable reaction to Alderman Wardley's bizarre statement that the gangs of fifty years earlier could have "swallowed up" the Mooney gang.

On the finances of the gambling ring, Mooney admitted he himself had picked up £200 out of the ring at one time, and he knew a man who had picked up £1,000. "We have no fear of drastic police action", he added, concluding the interview, "because all we want is to be left alone to live in peace."

The interview provoked a cynical reaction from both press and public. ''The spectacle of Satan rebuking sin is always entertaining," wrote 'The Passer-By' in the *Sheffield Independent*, commenting: "It is an appealing picture which George Mooney paints of the reformed outcasts trying to live down their evil past, but prevented from doing so by the unwelcome attentions of their former - and temporarily victorious - associates."

The general opinion was that Mooney had simply taken the opportunity to present his side of the story first. While there was truth in his claims regarding the Park Brigade's more recent provocations, those aware of the feud's origins could not help wondering if Mooney's laudable desire for peace would have been so evident had his initial plans not so back-fired, leaving him in the precarious position that he now found himself.

Reaction was not limited to press and public. The other members of Mooney's organisation were far from happy to see their names in the paper and the next day, June 28th, 'Spud' Murphy, Peter Winsey and Albert Foster went to the *Mail's* offices and demanded a retraction. "What we want," they said, "is for you to state that we accept no responsibility for the interview, or Mooney's statements, and that we said nothing about the gambling rings." The *Mail* duly complied. It was the spark for another sequence of clashes and attacks that would last until the end of 1923 and see the complete disintegration of the once-powerful Mooney Gang.

The same afternoon, following the visit of Murphy, Winsey and Foster to the *Sheffield Mail*, George Mooney and 'Spud' Murphy faced each other in Steelhouse Lane. A crowd quickly gathered as Mooney, taking off his coat and waistcoat, told Murphy: "This is caused by you blackmailing people." Murphy replied: "It's through you coming the cop on in the paper." At that point Mooney punched him in the mouth and a fight commenced which continued, urged on by the crowd, until the two of them were separated by detectives from nearby West Bar Police Station. On July 2nd, both appeared before the magistrates, charged with causing a breach of the peace. Mooney, who pleaded guilty, told the Bench: "I was going to settle it there and then. I said I was getting away from all my pals and this was the last finish of it." Pleading not guilty, Murphy said: "Mooney came up like a wild man, saying 'hold that', and hit me straight in the jaw." They were both bound over for twelve months in the sum of £5 each and ordered to pay costs. The fact that it was only a week since Mooney and Murphy had each been bound over in the sum of £25, for twelve months, was never mentioned in court.

Mooney and Murphy were followed into the dock by Louis Handley, of Hoyle Street. Handley, thirty-four, was summonsed for a breach of the peace in West Bar on June 28th - at the same time the Steelhouse Lane fight was in progress - and for using obscene language. Having left the *Mail* offices and parted from Murphy, Albert Foster and Peter Winsey were walking along West Bar when Handley leapt off a passing tram and set about the pair of them. Foster was knocked unconscious and Winsey received a cut ear. Handley claimed they had caused a disturbance outside his house in the early hours of the previous Sunday. The presiding magistrate, Mr. Michael Hunter, the same man who had earlier bound over Mooney and Murphy, said this sort of thing had got to be stopped and the magistrates were going to stop it. Handley was committed to prison for two months hard labour, the maximum sentence for common assault at the time.

The loyal hard-core of George Mooney's gang had begun to crumble. 'Spud' Murphy had split with him and it was not long before Albert Foster followed suit. The day after he had been knocked out by Handley, Foster appeared as a defence witness when Frank Kidnew was charged with assaulting P.C. Sapsford on May 18th. Kidnew was said to have taken a running kick at the constable during the 6 a.m. affray outside Mooney's, after the Licensed Victuallers Ball. Murphy and Winsey had already been fined for similar assaults on the same constable, at earlier courts. Kidnew said he was not present at the time of the incident. P.C. Sapsford told the court that Kidnew, who was defended by Mr. J. W. Fenoughty, had kicked him outside Mooney's house.

Councillor A.M. Jack: "Who is Mooney?"
P.C.: "George Mooney, of 23, Corporation Street."
Councillor Jack: "What has he to do with it?"
P.C.: "He is a friend of the defendant."

At this point Mr. Fenoughty asked the constable, "Are you sure of it? We don't want too much Mooney in it!" Albert Foster then went into the witness box and said Kidnew was not outside Mooney's on the night in question.

Mr. A. W. Forsdike, prosecuting: "Are you a friend of Mooney's?"
Foster: "I was."

Mr. Forsdike: "Up to yesterday?" (referring to the retraction of Mooney's interview).

Foster: "I have had a basin full."

There was loud laughter from the public gallery.

Mr. Fenoughty said Kidnew was not a friend of Mooney's and had no interest in the Mooneys. He was a Reservist, and when war broke out he joined the Colours and served right through the war until 1919. He saved money while serving in Russia and now intended to go to Blackpool to work. A widower with four children, he had only been in trouble once before - twenty one years previously for playing football in the street.

The Chairman, Councillor Jack, said the Bench had given the case very serious consideration and Kidnew would be bound over in the sum of £20, for twelve months.

So Frank Kidnew, a participant in the very first incident of the gang war - the poker attack on William Furniss - was not a friend of Mooney and had no interest in him! The first part of Fenoughty's statement was probably true; it is quite likely that after being so badly battered and slashed in retaliation for the Furniss assault, which he carried out on Mooney's behalf, Kidnew realised there was no future in association with the deposed leader. However, he certainly retained an interest in him, because, whether sea-air did not agree with him, or Blackpool was too quiet, Kidnew was soon back on the gang scene and his next court appearance was as a member of the Park Brigade - accused of breaking into Mooney's home.

After two months of persecution by the Park Brigade because of his allegiance to George Mooney, it is hardly surprising that Albert Foster considered he had "had a basin full". While, together with Kidnew, he had successfully carried out the Furniss assault back on April 29th, since then little had gone right. To begin with he had lost his revolver - confiscated in the police raid on Mooney's home after the Wheywell shooting. The day that case was heard he had been saved from the mob outside his home in Park Hill Lane only by the arrival of mounted police. Mooney had then named him in the *Mail* and on the way back from seeking the retraction he had been knocked unconscious by Louis Handley. Having publicly announced he was no longer a friend of Mooney's, Albert Foster no doubt hoped he would be left alone by the Park Brigade. Such optimism was mis-placed.

When he left the Police Court on July 2nd, following Handley's conviction for assaulting him, Foster hailed a taxi and went to the Albert Inn, Sutherland Street. He arrived at 1.30 p.m. and entered the billiard room. Minutes later another taxi arrived and William Furniss, George Wheywell, Gil Marsh and Charles Price rushed into the pub asking: "Where's Foster?"

Discovering him, Marsh picked up a billiard cue and struck Foster on the head with it, causing a wound to the bone two inches long. According to eye-witnesses, Furniss then kicked him in the eye and, as Foster attempted to escape, Price hit him with his fist. He managed to get out of the billiard room into a passage leading to the door but Wheywell hit him with a blunt instrument saying "hold that". All four attackers were arrested later the same afternoon and appeared in court the next morning.

Unusual precautions were taken at the courthouse, where a large contingent of plain clothes police were in attendance. Many gang-members who turned up to listen to the proceedings were refused admittance and continued to hang about outside until the case was over.

Mr. A. W. Forsdike, prosecuting, told the court that since the conflict between the gangs had begun, ten or twelve men had been charged with various offences. The magistrates, in their wisdom, had taken a somewhat lenient view. He suggested the time had arrived when a more serious view should be taken. Outlining the facts of the assault he described how, when the defendants had been arrested, Marsh had a razor in his possession. He urged the Bench to make an example of them.

After Foster had given evidence, with his head heavily bandaged, and denied assaulting Furniss, "so that he was laid out completely", six weeks previously, Mr. Irwin Mitchell, defending, said it seemed to be a matter of a feud, which, if his instructions were correct was now almost at an end. Each of the defendants was sentenced to two months hard labour.

Albert Foster did not wait for further trouble. As well as being hounded by the Park Brigade he was also being pursued for maintenance arrears by his former wife. Life had become uncomfortable in Sheffield, so he left and went to stay in Birmingham. It was over a year before he dared to return.

The last months of 1923 were lonely ones for George Mooney and his family. Barricaded inside 23, Corporation Street, lying low from the Park Brigade, Mooney found himself facing a second vendetta from his former friends, Peter Winsey and 'Spud' Murphy. In their reckoning Mooney bad committed a cardinal sin: he had 'named names'. Neither could forgive him for the *Mail* interview.

Just after 10 p.m. on Bank Holiday Monday, Mooney was reading in his sitting room when there was a banging on the door. Outside stood Winsey, Murphy, and an older man, William Flynn, demanding that he should go out and fight. As the door and downstairs windows were locked and barred, and Mooney refused to appear, his three would-be attackers commenced to throw bricks at the upstairs windows. Four windows and a number of ornaments inside a bedroom were broken.

On August 15th, Winsey, Murphy and Flynn were summonsed by Mooney's wife, Margaret. Mooney told the court that William Flynn was his step-father and Winsey and Murphy had been his friends, adding: "But I've got shut of them." Asked why his wife had issued the summonses he replied: "Because I'm afraid to go out. I'm under police protection. I've to be brought to the court and taken home again." The case was adjourned for a fortnight, when the charges against all three defendants were dismissed.

A month after the window-breaking incident, Murphy appeared once again at the Police Court, to answer another summons from Mrs. Mooney. It was alleged that on Saturday, September 15th at 9.50p.m., Mrs. Mooney was sitting inside the doorway of a relative's house in Trinity Street, when Murphy came up the street shouting: "Send Big Mooney out to fight." He threatened to smash up the house she was sitting in, and threw a brick which struck her over the right eye, knocking her unconscious. Mrs. Mooney, who was six months pregnant, was taken to the Royal Infirmary, where three stitches were put in the wound.

On September 22nd Murphy was sent for trial at the Quarter Sessions, the presiding magistrate, Mr. Harry Fisher, remarking: "It will be a cause of satisfaction to the peaceable citizens of Sheffield if these rowdy gang riots, leading as in this, to bloodshed, can be put a stop to. Pettifogging fines are no use." Murphy, on the dole but describing himself as a bookmakers' clerk, told the magistrates that Mooney had been wanting to fight him for six months.

At the Quarter Sessions, on October 18th, Detective Sergeant Milner told the court that when he was arrested, Murphy said: "I can produce witnesses to say that I wasn't there."

Sentencing him, the Assistant Recorder, Mr. C. Milton Barber, said: "People in the city of Sheffield, be their names Mooney or Murphy or Smith or Jones, or anything else, must know that if they come up to these courts and are convicted of crimes of violence they will be dealt with in a suitable manner. Taking into consideration all the circumstances you will be sentenced to six months hard labour."

On Christmas Eve, George Mooney's house came under attack yet again from the Park Brigade. Mooney, suffering from a cold, was lying upstairs in bed when, shortly after 6 p.m. the kitchen window was smashed, the back door broken down and four men burst in. His three children, including a ten day-old baby, were in the kitchen as one of the raiding party, Frank Kidnew, told Mooney's fifteen year old daughter: "We've come to wish your father a Merry Christmas." She managed to warn Mooney and he concealed himself in an upstairs cupboard. As the raiders rushed upstairs another of them, Sandy Barlow, urged Kidnew: "Give him some razor, Frank." Unable to find Mooney, his would-be attackers commenced to smash sacred ornaments in one of the bedrooms. The police were soon on the scene but all the men escaped.

Later on Christmas Eve, Samuel Garvin, Frank Kidnew, Sandy Bowler and Robert Crook were arrested and kept in police custody for the entire holiday. On December 27th they were all granted bail at the Police Court. Detective Inspector Naylor told the magistrates: "These men are never short of money." Crook had boasted, he said, that he could raise anything up to £1,000. After raising a laugh in court by suggesting that the four pool the £1,000 and be bailed at £250 each, the Chairman allowed them bail of £20 each. The case was adjourned.

Long before the Police Court opened on January 9th, 1924, the day of the resumed hearing, crowds had gathered outside to see George Mooney arrive under police protection. When the court adjourned for lunch he was escorted home, and brought back in the afternoon. It must have been a humiliating experience for Mooney, who, less than twelve months before, as boss of the Skyring, had been revered and respected by many of the throng who lined Castle Street that day.

Samuel Garvin, (38), Heavygate Avenue: Frank Kidnew, (40), Campo Lane; Sandy Barlow (charged under his real name - Charles McKay Bowler), (32), Stepney Street; and Robert Crook, (34), Corporation Street were charged with wilful damage at Mooney's home on Christmas Eve.

Cross-examined by Mr. Irwin Mitchell, who represented Garvin, Barlow and Kidnew, George Mooney admitted that he had fifty three convictions. "But I've never smashed anything," he added. In reply to Mr. Harold Jackson, defending Crook, he said he had been forced to remain in his house for the past nine months because he was going to be assassinated.

Mr. Jackson: "And is that a result of your terrorising the whole of
    Sheffield?"
Mooney: "No."
A witness for the defence was William Flynn, Mooney's step-father,

who, along with Winsey and Murphy had been acquitted of the Bank Holiday attack on 23, Corporation Street. Flynn said he had married George Mooney's mother some years previously and at the time of her death was living at 23, Corporation Street. Because of George Mooney's violence and threats he had been forced to give up his property consisting of twelve houses, as well as 23, Corporation Street, all of which belonged to his wife.

Mr. A. W. Forsdike (prosecuting): "Why did you leave this house?"

Flynn: "Why did the Kaiser abdicate?"

All the accused claimed they had been distributing tickets for a charity boxing match, organised by Garvin, at the time the attack took place. Mooney's elder daughter identified Kidnew and Barlow in court. Both were found guilty; Garvin and Crook were discharged. The verdict aroused considerable excitement outside the court building and several angry groups were moved on by the police. Before the magistrates passed sentence Mr. Forsdike told them: "The police wish me to say that there is only one way of stopping this class of violent behaviour, and suggest that the time has now arrived when more severe penalties should be inflicted." Sandy Barlow, who was said to have had a very good army record and to have been presented with the Military Medal on the field of battle by the Prince of Wales, was sentenced to three months hard labour. Frank Kidnew, who had been punished for his friendship with Mooney by a hundred razor slashes nine months previously, also received three months hard labour.

From being headman of the lucrative Skyring and feared leader of the once-powerful Mooney Gang, George Mooney had been reduced to little more than a fugitive: hiding day and night behind shuttered windows and locked doors, fearful that every knock might be another visit from his enemies, only daring to venture out under the watchful eye of a police escort. His lifelong friends had turned against him, even his brother John Thomas had left the scene, emigrating to America shortly after the feud began. The strain was also telling on his wife. Margaret Mooney, a respectable woman whose father was a member of the Board of Guardians, had married her husband two years earlier. After the Christmas Eve attack she spoke to a *Sheffield Mail* reporter, complaining bitterly about the treatment her husband was receiving from the Park Brigade, and about the way every assault committed was being blamed upon the Mooney Gang. "There is only my husband," she said. "He is fighting absolutely on his own and you can't call one man a gang."

The Christmas Eve attack was the last straw for George Mooney. After the resulting court case on January 9th he left Sheffield and nothing more was heard of him for twelve months.

4. Junior Gangs

Much of the lawlessness which, by 1924, had pervaded the streets of Sheffield was attributed to the activities of either the Park Brigade or the Mooney Gang. The fact that the latter had been hounded out of existence by the former meant little to the general public. Most saw every assault, robbery and street brawl merely as continuation of the rivalry which had begun at the Sky Edge tossing ring. In reality many of the incidents blamed on the Mooney and Park men were not their work at all. A new threat to law and order in the city had emerged: the junior gang.

On the evening of Saturday, August 4th, 1923, four men, on their way home from a show at the Sheffield Empire, were accosted by a gang of youths in Leopold Street. One of the men was hit on the head with a bottle. At about the same time another man was admitted to the Royal Hospital suffering from injuries to his face and mouth. He complained of a similar gang assault. The same evening, in Fitzalan Square, a young woman was standing talking to friends when she was approached by a group of youths, one of whom struck her a violent blow in the face. The young woman was severely shaken but refused to take any action, despite the police proffering their assistance. Later that evening two men, alighting from a motor coach in Barker's Pool, found themselves surrounded by a gang of youths who commenced to jostle and trip them. One of the men retaliated and a general fight ensued in which both were rough-handled. This spate of incidents, all within a quarter of a mile of each other on the same evening, heralded the presence of a new gang in the city. The members were youths in their late teens and early twenties. They frequented the city centre. By day they hustled pedestrians and shoppers in Fitzalan Square or High Street; by night they preyed on publicans and their customers.

Taxi drivers were also regular victims. Shortly after midnight on August 7th, two taximen were standing, chatting, by their cabs on Barker's Pool, when eight young men approached and demanded to be taken to Scotland Street. It was a common trick for gangmen to demand to be taken to some destination, usually a long way off, and then refuse to pay. If the driver protested he was beaten up. Scotland Street - celebrated for its twenty three pubs - lay only half a mile from Barker's Pool in the West Bar district, but the drivers refused to take the gang. Becoming menacing, one of their number pulled a cut throat razor from his pocket, opened it, and aimed a blow at the face of one of the taximen. Luckily he dodged the blow but, as the demand to be taken to Scotland Street was repeated, another of the gang produced a revolver. Somehow the other taxi driver escaped and ran up Division Street to the Fire Station where he telephoned the police. By the time they arrived the gang had dispersed. It was later stated that they were the same youths responsible for the incidents of the previous Saturday.

This gang included female members who were quite willing to take active roles in their violent practices. One September evening in Wellington Street, a girl, surrounded by youths, screamed loudly for help. One of the youths appeared to hit her in the mouth. A well-dressed man who was passing by rushed to her aid and immediately the girl and youths turned on him. Bravely the man fought back, escaped from Wellington Street, and ran down The Moor with the gang at his heels. When he dashed into the Central Picture Palace the gang remained outside but scattered on the arrival of the police. The man refused to give his name to the police. "The whole proceedings have caused considerable excitement in the city," commented the *Sheffield Mail* on September 21st, "and a new cry has been raised for the suppression of gangs." The new gang, reported the *Mail*, consisted principally of young ruffians in the guise of clerks or shop assistants. "They debauch and gamble and have one or two young girls in their train who are prepared to sacrifice themselves body and soul to the ruffianly crowd who are their masters. Their chief income is derived from picking pockets and selling dud jewellery. A new epidemic appears to have broken out," the *Mail* continued. "It will be interesting to see what measures are taken to suppress the disturbances."

The following night, September 22nd, a newcomer to the city, walking along Cambridge Street, overtook a solitary figure strolling leisurely in front of him. The man asked the newcomer if he wished to buy a ring. The newcomer replied "No thank you", at which he received a punch in the face that knocked him to the ground. He was dazed but managed to rise to his feet and as he did so five other men, who had apparently been concealed, rushed up. The man escaped and, remembering the story he had read in the previous night's paper, dashed into the Albert Hall. The police were once again called but made no arrests.

The dud jewellery trick was an operation usually carried out by gang members working in pairs. Selecting a likely looking victim, the first man approached and offered a ring for sale. While the victim was looking at it, the second gangman came up, showed great interest in the ring, and offered ten shillings for it. He then remembered, to his disgust, that he had come out without his money and appeared extremely grieved at missing out on such a 'bargain'. His regret often urged the victim to clinch the 'bargain' which he later found was valueless. Lack of interest on the part of the intended victim, as in the case of the man in Cambridge Street, meant that instead of simply rooking him, the gang assaulted him and usually robbed him of his valuables. That particular victim had been fortunate to escape.

Like their senior counterparts, the junior gang carried knives and razors at all times and, as the behaviour they demonstrated to the two taxi drivers in Barker's Pool showed, they were not averse to brandishing firearms. On one occasion the gang cavorted into the Nelson Hotel at Moorhead and began a rowdy disturbance with several of the customers. Once again a revolver was produced and this time a shot was fired into the open fireplace. Thoroughly satisfied with the effect this had on the regular customers, the gang departed.

In another incident two youths boarded a tram and one flourished a six-chambered revolver on the upper deck. The tram driver was alerted and, spotting a policeman along the route, stopped the tram whereupon both youths were arrested. In court one said the revolver was his and he had lent it to the other to have his photo taken as a cowboy! They were fined fifty shillings each.

By the end of 1924, the number of junior gangs active in the city had increased. The largest and most troublesome was the Junior Park Gang. As well as wreaking havoc in the city centre, where assaults on innocent pedestrians and parades of gang-members shouting obscenities were daily occurrences, they were also responsible for some unruly disturbances in their own district.

On one occasion they broke the tops off fifty-two cast iron railings in Granville Hill and threw them at people leaving the nearby picture palace. There were many witnesses but no one was prepared to come forward. Another evening, six of the Junior Park Gang arrived at Granville Hall where a dance was in progress. As it was 10.30 p.m. they were asked to pay half the admission charge but instead they attacked the doorman. The manager came to the doorman's assistance and together they prevented the six from entering. The gang made off but returned later and struck the manager on the head with an iron bar. He was taken to the Royal Infirmary where his wounds were stitched. A man was later charged with the assault but when the case reached court it was dismissed.

Four days after the first incident at Granville Hall, another disturbance occurred when a number of Junior Park members - including several girls - rushed in without paying. The manager immediately attempted to phone the police but found the wires had been cut. A fracas followed which culminated in the arrival of police and one of the leading aggressors being knocked out by one punch from a constable. The youth, aged nineteen, was charged with assaulting the constable. He denied it, telling the magistrates: "They must think I'm a lunatic to assault a man his size." He received three months hard labour, and a seventeen year old girl present at the disturbance was bound over for obstructing the police.

No sooner had the youth who received three months been released from prison than he was at the centre of another skirmish when two police officers, Sgt. Robinson and P.C. Lunn, following him and several companions, were met with a shower of missiles in Dixon Lane. After a chase, four men were arrested and charged with assault on the police.

In court next day, July 16th, 1925, Mr. G.H. Banwell, prosecuting, stressed the serious nature of the charge. The two officers, he said, were on duty particularly in regard to men of the type in the dock, and to prevent them gathering together in the middle of the city. It was hardly necessary, he said, in view of all that had happened in the city, to urge the necessity of having special men out to deal with those gathering in gangs. Sgt. William Robinson, giving evidence, said serious complaints had been made of people being kicked about the fairground by members of the Park Gang and there was generally a serious disturbance whenever the men banded together. "That is why we are on special duty breaking up these gangs," he said.

From the dock one of the gang held up a blood-stained handkerchief, claiming that it was he who had been assaulted by the police and not vice versa. P .C. Lunn, he said, had struck him "six or seven times." Another of the four denied any complicity in the affair whatsoever, saying: "I was waiting for a tram to have a penn'orth up to Duke Street. It is not safe to walk about up there. I suffer from my heart and I was all of a flutter when the policeman got hold of me. I was watching a chap selling a bunch of wild flowers." The recently released youth, seen by police as the ringleader of many Junior Park activities, told the court: "My life is a burden. I only came out of prison last Saturday. I had been in a chip shop when Robinson and Lunn ordered me out. Discretion is the better part of valour so I went home. I have had enough to satisfy me." Explaining the chip shop incident, Sgt. Robinson told the Bench the youth had picked up a vinegar bottle and demonstrated how people could be knocked out with it. .

The youth: "Whatever happens in Sheffield it's the Park gang that is blamed."

Sgt. Robinson: "There is another gang besides."

Alderman Benson, passing sentence, said the magistrates were not going to have the police knocked about. The ringleader was sent to prison for six months, the one who claimed to have been assaulted, for three months, and the other two were find £2 each.

The other gang mentioned by Sgt. Robinson was the Smithfields Gang who, although not as large as the Junior Park Gang, engaged in similar activities in the West Bar and Shalesmoor areas. Early in 1925 a raiding party from the Park sought out the Smithfields youths on their home ground and a fracas ensued in Scotland Street. Bricks, cellar grates and other missiles were thrown. Afterwards police found razors, a life preserver, hammer and knuckleduster which had been dropped in the battle. Two of the participants were arrested, one was bound over and the other discharged.

Stanley Street Institute, a dance hall, was a favourite haunt of the Smithfields Gang and the Junior Park were not long in seeking trouble at this venue. One Saturday night they appeared in full force and took possession of the hall for one and a half hours, forcing all the customers to leave. On another evening a brawl took place on the Institute steps which led to two Park members being injured, and their nineteen year old attacker, who told the court he always carried a cosh for self-defence, being put on probation for a year.

There were countless incidents of this nature, and also many in which gangs preyed on innocent people. In one, two youths accosted two teenage girls at 10.30 p.m. on a Saturday evening and told them: "We are the younger end of the Park Gang and frightened of nobody." One of the youths produced a razor. The girls escaped but the following week the youths, together with a dozen of their friends, visited one of the girl's homes, burst in, and threw a cellar grate at the girl's mother. In court, the mother of the youth who carried the razor said her son was not a member of any gang. "He attended Sunday School up to a few months ago," she said. He and his chief accomplice were each fined £5.

By Christmas, 1925, the junior gangs were at their worst. In a Christmas Eve affray at the Queen's Head, Pond Hill, where stool legs, coshes and razors were used, the landlord was slashed on his neck and ear. Later that night, at Blonk Street Fairground, a man was slashed so severely that when he arrived by ambulance at the Royal Infirmary, surgeons did not expect him to live more than a few minutes. This assault occurred when the victim went up to a member of the Junior Park Gang, with whom he was familiar, and wished him a Merry Christmas. The gangman replied by pulling a razor from up his sleeve and slashing his unfortunate well wisher half a dozen times, severing his jugular vein. Miraculously the victim survived, His attacker was later sent to Borstal for three years.

Shortly afterwards, a Saturday night brawl outside the Comrades Hall in Townhead Street, involving five youths, attracted such a crowd that when plain-clothes police arrived they were unable to get anywhere near the participants. It was estimated that over a hundred and fifty men and women were urging the fighters on and the police had to commandeer a corporation lorry to force a way through the crowd. When they arrested two of the youths, the other three staged a rescue attempt. The crowd, incensed at the prospect of their enjoyment being curtailed, did their best to prevent the arrests. The five instigators of the trouble eventually appeared in court charged with causing a breach of the peace, obstruction and using obscene language. Two were fined and three imprisoned for fourteen days. "You are just starting a career of tomfoolery," said the presiding magistrate, Mr. W.S. Skelton.

The junior gangs were formed by youths influenced by, and attempting to emulate, the behaviour of the Mooney Gang and the Park Brigade. With little prospect of honest work it was all too easy to band together and prowl the streets for the purpose of preying on the vulnerable. One routine which they had inherited from their elders was for three or four gangmen to enter a public house and demand drinks and cigarettes. A look-out remained outside. If the landlord refused they hurled glasses, bottles, even stools, at the big mirror behind the bar, assaulted the landlord and anyone else still around by that time, and thoroughly wrecked the place. If the landlord complained to the police they returned later and did the same again. Not surprising therefore that the city's publicans lived in fear, nor that witnesses were distinctly thin on the ground.

On the rare occasions that the police did find men or women bold enough to stand up in court, the leniency extended to the junior gangs by magistrates did little to solve the overall problem. The opinion of Mr. Harry Fisher J.P. on the "blue funk" suffered by some of his colleagues on the bench was shared by many. The vicar of St. Mathew's, Father G.C. Ommanney, believed that the gangs intimidated the bench as much as they did their victims. "They are terrorising even the magistrates and other people, and the magistrates hardly dare sentence them to punishment," he told a conference of clergymen in 1925.

The case involving the four members of the Junior Park Gang accused of assaulting Sgt. Robinson and P. C. Lunn is perhaps the most significant of the many court hearings involving the junior gangs. Not merely because two of the convicted were sent to prison by the magistrates - one for six months and one for three - but because of certain facts outlined by the prosecuting solicitor, Mr. G.H. Banwell, and confirmed by Sgt. Robinson in evidence.

Mr. Banwell told the court that the two officers were on duty particularly in regard to men of the type who stood in the dock that day, July 16th, 1925, and were detailed to prevent them gathering together in the middle of the city in gangs. "That is why we are on special duty breaking up these gangs," stated Sgt. Robinson. This was the very first occasion special police duties to combat the gang menace were publicly mentioned. Over the next few years the names of the policemen engaged in these duties - Sgt. Robinson, P. C. Lunn and a handful of others who were prepared to play the gangs at their own game and meet violence with violence - were to become known and feared as the Flying Squad.

5. Sam Garvin: deus ex machina

Sam Garvin, a native of Sheffield, first attracted the attention of the police in 1904 when he was twenty-four years old. He followed no ascertainable line of employment but frequented race meetings, generally for the purpose of gaming, although he occasionally stood as a bookmaker. His friends and associates were thieves, pickpockets, confidence tricksters and card sharpers. During the First World War, Garvin left the city and travelled the country to evade military service. In addition to five convictions for assault in Sheffield, he was convicted for illegal gaming at Ripon, loitering with intent at Doncaster, and travelling on the railway without a ticket at Leicester. He received prison sentences of twelve months for housebreaking at Cardiff, four months for stealing by a con-trick at Leek, three months for frequenting at Blackpool, and six months for larceny from the person at Douglas, Isle of Man. He also had a· number of convictions for drunkenness and disorderly conduct.

The Park Brigade was Garvin's organisation. He had been responsible for its formation in early 1923 as a splinter group of the original Mooney Gang and he was the mastermind behind most of the Brigade's activities. He found no difficulty in taking on the role of gangleader. Well-built and well-dressed he was seldom seen without a crowd at hand and it was a common practice for him to take upwards of thirty followers into a public house and stand drinks all round. When, on December 3rd, 1923, a disaster occurred at Nunnery Colliery, killing seven men, Garvin lost no time in organising a boxing tournament for the widows and dependants. With his right hand man, Sandy Barlow, as secretary and Frank Kidnew as a referee, the tournament, which took place while all three were on bail for the Christmas Eve attack on Mooney's house, was a great success and raised £130. "Congratulations have been showered upon me," wrote Garvin in a letter to the *Yorkshire Telegraph and Star* thanking those who had taken part, including many respectable members of the local boxing scene.

The Christmas Eve incident was the first time Sam Garvin's name had appeared on a court list since the gang feud erupted. When the case was heard on January 8th, 1924, he was acquitted while Kidnew and Barlow were imprisoned. On September 23rd, 1924, together with his brother Bob, Sandy Barlow and Gil Marsh, he was charged with robbing a cutlery manufacturer of £100 on a tram. The case was dismissed. The following month, again with his brother and Barlow, plus Frank Kidnew and a woman, Garvin was arrested for obstructing the police in the Yorkshire Stingo Hotel, Division Street, at 1.10 a.m. on Election Night. The gangmen maintained that they were on licensed premises as guests of the landlord, who did not contradict their story. The police, when they arrived, were jostled and told: "If you want a rough house you can have one." In court it was stated that earlier in the evening there had been disturbances among crowds awaiting the Election results outside the Town Hall and Sam Garvin had been present. Once again the case was dismissed.

It was not established whether Garvin was responsible for the Election Night disturbances, but inciting trouble at political gatherings was certainly within the scope of his organisation. The City Council, dominated by the Citizens Party (a coalition of Conservatives and Liberals), were becoming increasingly concerned at the upsurge of support for the Labour Party in Sheffield. While there is no firm evidence of collusion between politicians and gangmen, on a number of occasions Labour meetings were broken up by thugs recognisable to people present as members of the Park Brigade and when the new housing estate at Walkley was built, Sam Garvin was one of the first people to move in.*

With George Mooney out of the city, his brother John Thomas in America, and Albert Foster exiled in Birmingham, the Park Brigade embarked on a campaign in 1924 to crush once-and-for-all the remnants of the Mooney Gang. At the top of their list was 'Spud' Murphy and Peter Winsey, both of whom were having enough difficulty keeping out of trouble without provocation from the Park Brigade. In April, Murphy was arrested in Queen Street on suspicion of loitering with intent to commit a felony - break into a warehouse - and sentenced to three months imprisonment. In June, Winsey was charged with assaulting a woman in Furnace Hill. The court was told that the woman was drunk and insulted a man who was singing in the street, so Winsey knocked her down. "It's a toss up who is the better customer, me or her," Winsey told the magistrates. "We are neither of us saints." Detective Sergeant Burns stated that Winsey was on the run from the Park gang. He was sentenced to four months hard labour. As he was leaving the court Winsey said he would "do six months for Sgt. Burns" when he came out.

Col. Watson (presiding magistrate): "Did you say that?"

Winsey: "No, I have more sense than to say it in court."

Col. Watson: "I heard you myself. You are now sentenced to six

---

* To those living in the slums, a corporation house with bathroom, inside toilet and garden was almost beyond the realms of imagination. Walkley was one of the first corporation estates in Sheffield.

months hard labour."

On the evening of December 8th, 'Spud' Murphy, Tommy Rippon and their respective wives, together with Peter Winsey who was Mrs. Rippon's brother, and another couple, Mr. and Mrs. Henry Dale, were listening to the wireless in Rippon's home, 31, Furnace Hill. At 10.50 p.m. a brick through the window, followed by a revolver shot, heralded the arrival of the Park Brigade, once again on the warpath.

The gang had earlier been noticed by police, gathering in Fitzalan Square, and were followed out of the city centre towards Steelhouse Lane where Murphy lived. Finding him out they proceeded to Furnace Hill, broke in, and commenced their violent business.

The first policeman on the scene found one man smashing windows, another wrecking furniture inside the house, while two more were hitting Henry Dale with stool legs. Dale, who had been injured from flying glass, was wedged behind the sofa. Mr. and Mrs. Rippon and the rest of their guests had managed to escape upstairs. A loaded revolver was found and a spent bullet, lying beside a mangle. Five men were arrested and when asked what had started the trouble one replied: "Old broth being warmed up."

The next day Gilbert Marsh, 27ct. 1, Hoyle Street; Charles Bowler (Sandy Barlow), 29 Stepney Street; Ernest Scott, 63, Park Hill Lane; William Wareham, 6 ct. 3, Stafford Street; and William Carr, 4 ct. 7, Duke Street were all in court, charged with making an affray. Wareham, the man alleged to have broken the windows, appeared with his head and throat bandaged, injured it was said by flying glass. A loaded revolver, a razor, hammer, hatchet, iron bar, stool leg and several coshes were produced in court. All the accused were remanded in custody for a week. On December 16th they were committed to the Quarter Sessions and all were released on bail.

The night after the Furnace Hill incident, which had resulted in Henry Dale's admittance to the Royal Infirmary, another assault occurred in which a man was seriously injured. The subsequent court hearings, where George Wheywell was charged with maliciously wounding John Henry Towler, revealed something of an insight into the power Sam Garvin exerted over his subordinates in the Park Brigade.

Wheywell appeared before the magistrates on December 22nd, charged with the offence alleged to have been committed on December 9th. Mr. G.H. Banwell, prosecuting, told the court that at about 9 p.m. on the evening in question Wheywell had gone into the Nelson Hotel, Moorhead in a fighting mood, apparently determined to offend "somebody or anybody." The first thing he did was to go up to a man and knock off his hat. John Henry Towler, who was present, told him not to be silly and this seemed to have been the first sign of trouble between the two men.

Later in the evening, both went to the Barleycorn Hotel, Cambridge Street and again Wheywell's first action was to knock off a man's hat. This time he also poured a pint of beer over the unfortunate customer. Gus Platts, the licensee, an ex-professional boxer, immediately took steps to remove Wheywell from the premises, but became a little hesitant when Wheywell told him: "I'm not frightened of your reputation; I'll cut you up with a knife."

Going to the bar, Wheywell then spoke to a young woman and, getting a reply that did not appear to please him, he poured a pint of beer over her, too! Towler at this point intervened, objecting to his behaviour. Wheywell said: "Come outside. I'll teach you something, taking a bird's part." Outside, in Cambridge Street, Wheywell drew a knife and inflicted wounds on Towler's face, neck, arms, chest and over his eye. Bleeding profusely, Towler tried to escape but Wheywell continued to attack him threatening to "use a shooter" on him, and on Frank Kidnew who had come to Towler's aid.

A surprise witness for the prosecution was Sam Garvin, who described himself to the court as a commission agent. He said he was in the Nelson and saw Wheywell pull a hat over a man's eyes. He told Wheywell to "stop it." Wheywell, he said, seemed very nasty. Garvin, who admitted that he was giving evidence only because he knew he would be sub-poenaed if he refused, was hardly the most forthcoming of witnesses and Mr. Harry Morris, defending, fared no better than the prosecution, in cross examining him.

Mr. Morris: "What is your object in coming here today?"

Garvin: "To say I saw him in the Nelson."

Mr. Morris: "Is that all?"

Garvin : "That's all."

Mr. Morris: "Is Towler a friend of yours?"

Garvin: "They are all friends of mine."

Mr. Morris: "Public opinion credits you with being the leader of a gang."

Garvin: "I don't think so."

Mr. Morris: "Used Wheywell to be a friend of yours?"

Garvin: "Yes. He is up to now for all I know."

Mr. Morris: "Have you had a recent disagreement with Wheywell?"

Garvin: "I never had a wrong word with him."

Mr. Morris then made reference to the events which had led up to the attack on Thomas Rippon's house in Furnace Hill on December 8th.

Mr. Morris: "Did you meet Wheywell in Fitzalan Square the night before this affair?"

Garvin: "No."

Mr. Morris: "Were you in Fitzalan Square?"

Garvin: "I am in Fitzalan Square every night—but I didn't see Wheywell."

Mr. Morris: "Did you say to Wheywell—'We are going over to the mob on the Bar'?"

Garvin: "No. I never saw Wheywell."

Mr. Morris: "There was subsequently a disturbance there that night."

Garvin: "I don't know. It had nothing to do with me."

Mr. Morris. "Were any friends of yours connected with that?"

Garvin: "One or two friends of mine according to the papers."

Mr. Morris: "I put it to you that Wheywell refused to come with you that night. You said to him - 'All right, you are on now. We will cut you up after we have finished with this mob'?"

Garvin: "No, it's a lie."

The magistrates committed Wheywell to the Quarter Sessions.

Repercussions of the Furnace Hill incident did not end with the Wheywell-Towler fight. At 2.30 p.m. on Christmas Day, 'Ganner' Wheywell's brother, John Henry, and Henry Dale were waylaid in Fargate by about a dozen members of the Park Brigade. The police were swiftly on the scene and found John Wheywell holding the gang at bay with a revolver. P.C. Loxley disarmed him and a razor was also found on him. Wheywell was conveyed to the Central Police Offices and on December 27th appeared in court. He claimed that both gun and razor had been planted on him by the Park men after Bob Garvin had hit him on the head with a cosh. Henry Dale supported his story and the case was dismissed by the magistrates.

The matter, however, did not finish there. Three days later Bob Garvin and Gilbert Marsh appeared in court, charged with assaulting John Wheywell on Christmas Day. Marsh was already on bail to appear at the Quarter Sessions regarding the Furnace Hill affair. Defending the pair of them, Mr. W.A. Lambert said they had unenviable reputations but did not the police magnify the situation by taking up the attitude they did? (prosecuting them, presumably). And did not they endow them with false surroundings, he asked, which were worked up by members of the press? And did not Sheffield get a bad reputation throughout the country? If ever a case could be described as a storm in a teacup, said Mr. Lambert, the magistrates had it here. Announcing the verdict, Mr. J.C. Clegg said the public were entitled to be protected. Garvin and Marsh were sent to prison for one month each.

Not content with waylaying Dale and John Wheywell in the afternoon, the Park Brigade set out on Christmas Night to track down another of their enemies. George Newbould, a commission agent and acquaintance of several of the former Mooney Gang, was making his way home to Edward Street when he was set upon and assaulted in St. Philip's Road. He wound up at the Royal Hospital with a gash to his head that required several stitches. Sam Garvin, Sandy Barlow, Frank Kidnew and William Wareham were later summonsed for the assault, Barlow and Wareham being already on bail to the Quarter Sessions.

After the violent events leading up to - and during - Christmas, the New Year of 1925 dawned a little brighter for the citizens of Sheffield. On Thursday, January 1st, a headline in the *Sheffield Daily Telegraph* proclaimed: "AN ARMISTICE FOR THE NEW YEAR. FEUD TO END. PEACE CONFERENCE FOR BURYING THE HATCHET."

The two year old feud which had given the authorities so much trouble was over, said the *Telegraph*, the rival gangs opened the New Year as friends. A meeting had taken place at which all the "responsible leaders" were present or represented. "There was as much palaver," said one man who had been present, "as at the conclusion of peace between Germany and the Allies. And afterwards we had a drink all round to cement the peace."

One influential (but unnamed) leader was reported as saying: "Both the parties have found out that it is far better to be amicable to one another. We feel it is doing no good to any party to indulge in these quarrels." Another stated: "We have heard that the police have stepped in now, determined to stop this sort of thing, and we know it is the proper time to take the action we have done. We recognise that, in the public interest, the attitude of the police is the correct one."

There was a good deal of reticence regarding what had actually taken place at the meeting, but all gangmen whom the *Telegraph* interviewed were unanimous in the statement that the hatchet had been buried. One man, said the *Telegraph*, voiced the public view admirably. "People will be able to walk about now feeling that they will not be liable to interference or danger from any of these parties."

The formula for the truce was an arrangement between the Park and former Mooney men to run the Sky Edge tossing ring jointly. Six delegates from each side were to be appointed and at stated intervals the proceeds were to be divided up. Public reaction was one of caution. Why the Park Brigade, who held the undisputed control of the

Skyring, had agreed to such an arrangement was, to most people, a mystery. To the general public the meeting offered a faint glimmer of hope that peace might come at last; to the former Mooney gang it offered another bite at a cherry that had for too long been denied them. Eight days later, a year almost to the day since he had fled the city, George Mooney was reported to be back in Sheffield.

George Newbould's attackers were not slow in testing the goodwill generated by their peace agreement. On January 8th, at the Police Court, Mr. Harry Morris made a request for the summonses against Sam Garvin, Barlow, Kidnew and Wareham for the assault on Christmas Night to be withdrawn. "Apparently the festive season impregnated the men and there was a little horse-play," Mr. Morris told the magistrates, "but they have settled the differences between themselves." Agreeing to the withdrawals, Alderman S. Osborn commented: "I hope the men, and any other parties concerned, will not make any appearances in this court this year." As he was leaving the court Frank Kidnew turned to the magistrates and wished them a happy New Year.

When the Sheffield Quarter Sessions opened on January 19th, the Recorder, Mr. W.J. Waugh K.C., in his charge to the grand jury said there was a case in connection with which he was told there were two rival gangs. "They take the law into their own hands, commit assaults on each other, and create disturbances. This is a condition of things which, in a civilised city like Sheffield, is intolerable. To allow people to take the law into their own hands we might be in the backwoods of America instead of civilised England."

The following day the case - against Gilbert Marsh, Ernest Scott, Charles Bowler (Sandy Barlow), William Carr and William Wareham for inflicting grievous bodily harm on Henry Dale on December 8th - began with a sensational announcement by the prosecuting counsel, Mr. C. Paley-Scott. Dale, he said, had mysteriously disappeared on the previous morning, the date fixed for the trial. "Although a diligent search has been made, no trace of him can be found. One can only speculate as to the motives that have prevented his appearance." The case began without him.

The prosecution's submission was that, while only two of the men - Marsh and Scott - were seen actually to assault Dale, all five accused and possibly a number of others were acting in concert to pay off some private grudge, the nature of which he did not know. "Law and order may be said to have come to an end if these people are allowed to go on disturbing the peace of Sheffield in this fashion."

The first witness to enter the box was P.C. Farrily, who recounted the events of December 8th. He told how he had been on duty in Fitzalan Square where a large number of gangmen had gathered. One man was seen going from group to group and the gang then proceeded to Furnace Hill, followed by as many police officers as could be mustered from the Central Police Station. He went on to describe what happened upon their arrival at 31, Furnace Hill, Thomas Rippon's house, where Dale had been listening to the wireless with other members of the Mooney Gang. Referring to the Mooneys and the Park Gang, P.C. Farrily had reached the point where Rippon's furniture was being smashed up while Henry Dale was being hit with stool legs when he was interrupted by the Recorder.

"This is Greek to me," Mr. Waugh remarked. "What is the Mooney Gang and what is the Park Gang? Unfortunately, or rather I should say fortunately, I have not had the pleasure of their acquaintance." P.C. Farrily: "The Mooney Gang carried on this game (Pitch and Toss) for a considerable time. The Park Gang was raised in opposition. It broke up the Mooney Gang and a great many of its members had to clear out of Sheffield."

The Recorder: "Was Sheffield glad, or not?"

P .C. Farrily: "Very pleased, sir."

The Recorder: "Then the Park Gang were doing good work?"

In answer to counsel, P.C. Farrily referred by name to a number of members of the old Mooney Gang, including 'Spud' Murphy, Peter Winsey, George and John Thomas Mooney.

The Recorder: "I suppose that once a member of the Mooney Gang always a member?"

P.C. Farrily: "Some went over to the other gang."

The Recorder: "They were converted?" (Laughter in court).

Concluding his evidence P.C. Farrily said that Sam Garvin was the leader of the Park Gang and, after the affair at Furnace Hill, was seen not thirty-five yards away talking to Marsh and Bowler.

Thomas Rippon then described the raid upon his house and in reply to Mr. Willoughby Jardine, defending, said he was not a member of any gang. He had heard of them but his house was not their headquarters.

The Recorder: " If I wanted to become a member, how should l proceed?" (Laughter).

Rippon: "I don't know what constitutes a member."

Counsel: "You don't know how you join?"

Rippon: "I haven't seen a membership card." (Laughter).

Asked how he became a member of the Mooney Gang, 'Spud' Murphy said he was never elected. "The police made us the Mooney Gang." He said he had no idea where Henry Dale was.

Peter Winsey stated that he had been a member of the old Mooney Gang.

"I suppose you have taken part in many such affairs?" asked Mr. Jardine.

"Hundreds," replied Winsey, with a smile.

Mrs. Rippon gave evidence that when the raiders broke into her home and the other guests escaped upstairs, she stayed downstairs with Mrs. Dale whose husband was almost blinded by blood from a cut caused by falling glass from the windows. Marsh fired a revolver towards her and then, seeing Dale crouched behind a sofa, went over to him, saying: "I've been waiting for you a long time." Marsh fired a another shot and then he and Scott took legs from a stool and began beating Dale about the head and body. Dale's wife cried: "Don't kill my husband. I have five children and am expecting another." Marsh replied: "You get out of the way. We shan't hurt you."

Opening the rather flimsy case for the defence, Mr. Jardine called Sandy Barlow as first witness. Barlow, or Charles Mackay Bowler as he was charged, claimed that "one of Park Lads" was imprisoned at Furnace Hill. "There is nothing new in that," he added. "They have had our men shut up before." The Recorder, seizing the opportunity to once more exercise his wit, asked: "What, in gaol?" The court, obligingly, laughed. Sam Garvin had not given him this information, said Barlow, and Scott and Carr were not members of the Park Gang. In cross examination he was asked by Mr. Paley-Scott: "Where is Dale? Have you got him imprisoned?" Barlow replied that he hadn't the foggiest idea where Dale was.

After the other defendants had given evidence in which all denied taking any part in the assault, stating that those inside the house were the aggressors, the jury brought in guilty verdicts against Marsh, Scott, Bowler and Wareham and through their foreman expressed the opinion that Carr, who was found not guilty, should be reprimanded for his association with the other defendants.

A police officer, producing records against Marsh, Bowler and Wareham, referred to the gang troubles in the past. He was asked by the Recorder: "Does it not require a large force of police to look after them?" The officer replied: "We can rule them if we get assistance from the Bench. They have bound them over at times and have appeared to ridicule the matter."

In passing sentence, the Recorder described it as a disgraceful state of affairs when, in a city like Sheffield, men could assemble and conduct themselves in such a manner. Adventures of that kind, he added, must be stopped. Gilbert Marsh was sentenced to 12 months hard labour for inflicting grievous bodily harm on Henry Dale. Ernest Scott was sentenced to 6 months. For aiding and abetting the assault, Sandy Barlow received 9 months hard labour, and William Wareham 6 months in the Second Division*.

With four of the Park Brigade's leading members beginning the heaviest sentences imposed since the gang feud started, the following day, January 21st, saw George Wheywell in the dock as a result of the events of the evening after the Furnace Hill assault. Once again at the start of the case the prosecution had to announce the inexplicable absence of a witness, Ernest Broomhead. However, Henry Dale, who had failed to appear in court the previous day, turned up and sat all morning listening to the Wheywell case! The Recorder said it was a serious offence to interfere with witnesses and any such cases which were brought before him would meet with serious consequences. Towards the end of the case Broomhead eventually appeared, but when it was suggested that rather than being an independent witness he might be a gang member he was not called to give evidence. He was, in fact, a member of the Park Brigade.

George Arthur Wheywell, better known as 'Ganner', was charged with maliciously wounding John Henry Towler on December 9th outside the Barleycorn in Cambridge Street. It was alleged by his defence, Mr. G.H.B. Streatfeild, that Towler had gone to the Barleycorn with the deliberate intention of waylaying Wheywell. This, he suggested, was because Wheywell had refused to take part in the previous night's raid on Furnace Hill.

Wheywell told the court that on December 8th he was in Fitzalan Square, where the gang were congregating. Sam Garvin came up to him and said they were "going to tan a gang on West Bar" and asked him if he was going. Garvin, he said, was head of the gang and when Wheywell replied he was not going as he had three children to look after, Garvin threatened him that he would be "cut up". At the Barleycorn, the following evening, several of the gang were in and Towler had started an argument with him. When Towler appeared to be getting the worst of the fight, Frank Kidnew had helped him and took the knife from Wheywell

Kidnew appeared for the prosecution, as did Garvin who, in answer to Mr. Streatfeild, said he had not instructed Towler, Kidnew or anyone to attack George Wheywell. "No sir," he said. "He is a big friend of mine."

The Recorder said a lot of light had been thrown on the gangs during

* Three divisions of imprisonment existed at this time. The Second Division was an easier regime than hard labour.

the Sessions. Such men did not go to the police with grievances. "You have got to ask yourselves," he told the jury, "whether there was not some person behind all this, whether instructions had to be given before this case was brought. It is suggested the man called as a witness, Samuel Garvin, is the deus ex machina*. He pulls the strings and these puppets dance accordingly. After a short deliberation the jury found Wheywell not guilty. The Recorder said he quite agreed.

The comparative peace that had existed since the New Year truce came to an abrupt end on the afternoon of Thursday, January 22nd. Four of the former Mooney Gang, including a specially imported hardman from Birmingham named Tom Armstrong, had gone to Sky Edge with the intention of arranging a meeting for the share-out which they believed they were owed under the terms of the agreement. They were told that the deal was off, Sam Garvin was running the Skyring and they were to have no part. After some argument the four were returning down Park Hill Lane when a crowd of about fifty of the Park Brigade suddenly bore down on them. As they came near they ripped stones out of the roadside walls and threw them at the four, who fled to a house in Park Hill Lane, barricading themselves upstairs with chairs. When a posse of mounted and foot police arrived the crowd dispersed in all directions. One man, a Chesterfield furniture dealer whose presence on Sky Edge was purely for gaming purposes, appeared in court next day. He was said to have asked the arresting constable: "Are five shillings any good to you?" He was fined £5 for illegal gaming.

The New Year 'armistice' which, it had been suggested, offered a hope of peace for 1925, lasted just three weeks. Many people, particularly those aware of the deep and personal animosity felt by the principal gangmen towards their rivals, had not had sufficient time to overcome their initial surprise at the agreement. For the Park Brigade, who had spent most of the previous year persecuting George Mooney's former associates (and their respective associates), to not only forsake their quarries but also to agree to share the Skyring profits with them was completely out of character. But even when the truce had ended few learned the cunning motives that lay behind it.

The truth of the matter was the 'armistice' was nothing more than a well-planned con-trick, executed by the Park Brigade with the former Mooney men and the local newspapers as unwitting pawns. The New Year, 1925, had looked bleak for certain principals in the Park Brigade. Gil Marsh, Sandy Barlow and William Wareham, on bail to

* Theatrical term, literal meaning: god out of a machine

appear at the January Quarter Sessions, faced serious charges of inflicting grievous bodily harm on Henry Dale. Following the Christmas Night assault in St. Philip's Road, George Newbould had taken out summonses against Sam Garvin, Frank Kidnew, Barlow and Wareham and it was known that he had a witness to support him. Realising the likelihood of going to prison himself, and anticipating difficulties in retaining control of the Skyring with his chief henchmen similarly incapacitated, Garvin did a deal with George Newbould. If the assault charges were to be withdrawn, Newbould and his associates - mostly former Mooney men - would receive a share of the ring profits. It is hardly surprising that the gangmen were so reluctant to discuss with the *Sheffield Daily Telegraph* what had actually taken place at the New Year's Eve meeting.

The agreement also casts light on the mysterious 'disappearance' of Henry Dale. It was generally believed that Dale's failure to turn up to give evidence at the Quarter Sessions was due to his fear of the Park Brigade. At one point in the case, the prosecutor asked Sandy Barlow if Dale was afraid to come to court. Barlow replied "Certainly not." He was asked: "Will he be assaulted after this case is over?" and replied: "Why should he be?" In the circumstances Barlow's replies were truthful, for Dale, a friend of George Newbould's, was certainly involved in the New Year deal. It would appear that rather than testify against his attackers of December 8th - who he now believed to be his new partners - Dale staged the disappearing act. Fortunately, justice prevailed, the prosecution's case was unhindered, and Marsh, Barlow, Wareham and Scott were all convicted and imprisoned.

With the Quarter Sessions over, the Park Brigade had no further interest in the New Year agreement. It had fulfilled its instigator's prime purpose by saving him from prison and that was highly satisfactory to Sam Garvin. George Newbould and the former members of the Mooney Gang had fallen hook, line and sinker for the devious plot. When they pressed for their share of the bargain Garvin did a typical gangman's racecourse trick: he welshed* on the deal and turned his followers onto them. Thus the peace that had reigned so briefly ended on January 22nd. In its wake came acrimony and bitterness and a wave of violence even bloodier than that which had gone before.

---

* Before the Jockey Club set up their own detective organisation in 1925, 'welshing' was commonplace on racecourses. A punter producing a winning slip would be told the bookmaker had no record of the bet. Such bookmakers usually employed a strong arm man to deter those who pressed with their claims. An easier form of 'welshing' was to take the punter's bet and money and disappear before the result of the race was declared .

6. A Revival of Opposition

"FIRM HAND NEEDED FOR THE SHEFFIELD GANGS" ran the *Sheffield Mail* headline on Friday, January 23rd, 1925. Informing their readers that the New Year truce had come to a sudden end they went on to express once again the suggestions and criticisms they had repeatedly made since the beginning of the gang feuds in spring 1923.

Earlier in the day a representative of the *Mail* had asked the Chief Constable, Lieut. Col. J. Hall-Dalwood, why the police did not break up the gaming rings and thus destroy the cause of the trouble.

"We have broken the rings up," said the Chief Constable. "We have made numerous raids and brought the men before the magistrates, and we, as police, can do nothing more. So far as the hooliganism is concerned, it must be well known to everybody who reads the papers that we are bringing men in sometimes three or four times a week for these offences. Whenever the law is broken we bring men before the magistrates. We are handicapped by the fact that the prosecutors are sometimes "got at" and we cannot bring our witnesses, but we do everything in our power."

The *Mail* conceded that there was difficulty in raiding the Sky Edge tossing ring due to its position and the large number of sentries. They were extremely critical, however, of the lenient sentences passed on those who were caught and brought before the courts, recalling how, after "elaborate preparations", the police captured a large batch of offenders at Tinsley. The highest fine imposed by the magistrates was forty shillings: "After the cases were disposed of, a number of taxis were chartered and the men drove straight back to the ring to begin playing again. The men fined could make £40 a day out of the tossing ring."

Commenting on the Quarter Sessions held earlier in the week, the *Mail* decried the "miserably inadequate" sentences imposed by the Recorder on members of the Park Brigade. "To send these men to the Second Division is like sending them on holiday at Scarborough," they said, adding how a prominent gangman had declared prisons were becoming so comfortable that before long no one would be admitted who was not of good character!

"The present position," announced the *Mail* in conclusion, "is that no one knows precisely what will happen." The police, they said, were very discouraged at the lack of support from magistrates.

An instance of this lack of support occurred just four days after the *Sheffield Mail's* fierce leader. On January 27th George Wheywell and

Arthur Whitham, of Princess Street, appeared before the magistrates, charged with threatening to kill Thomas Bolton, steward of the Victoria Club, Sycamore Street, on January 9th.

The court was told that just after 10 p.m. both had tried to enter the club, but Bolton refused them. Wheywell said: "Do you know who I am? I am 'Ganner' Wheywell!" Whitham added that they would "get" the steward. "Your card's marked," he told him.

Mr. Irwin Mitchell (prosecuting), to Wheywell: "You know your name strikes a certain amount of terror into people's hearts." Wheywell: "I am not an angel!"

Sir William Clegg, the presiding magistrate, said Wheywell had a terrible character and explained to Whitham at length the dangers of associating with such a man. He then bound both of them over to keep the peace for twelve months, Wheywell in the sum of £25 and Whitham the sum of £10. The decision prompted a shoal of protest letters to the local papers, particularly the *Sheffield Mail*, who published a selection the following evening.

By the middle of February, Sam Garvin's witch-hunt of those he considered disloyal had resumed pre-truce momentum. On Thursday the 19th, together with his brother Bob, and George Butler of Alfred Road, he appeared once again at the Police Court, accused of assaulting Ernest Chapman in the Barleycorn Hotel on February 9th.

Chapman, of Arundel Street in the city centre, was a former member of the Park Brigade. A regular soldier for eleven years, he had worked as a tram driver until becoming a full time gangman. He had played an active part in the first storming of George Mooney's home on June 16th, 1923, and had been bound over along with William Furniss, Gil Marsh, Albert Flaherty and George Wheywell. Since that time, however, like Wheywell, Chapman had parted from the Park men and taken up association with members of the former Mooney Gang.

Chapman told the magistrates he had gone into the Barleycorn with a man known as 'Cosh' Burns and asked the landlord, Gus Platts, for two bitters. Sam Garvin, who was leaning against the bar, said: "Don't serve those two. They are traitors to me." Burns turned to Garvin and asked him how long he had been the landlord. The landlord said they had better leave as there might be trouble and both went out, Burns first. As Chapman got to the door he was swung round by Sam Garvin who struck him in the eye with an object held in his fist. "Kill 'em!" he instructed Butler, who hit Chapman on the chin. As he was laid out on the floor Bob Garvin took a running kick at him.

A witness for the defence was Wilfred Fowler, whose name, together with that of his brother, Lawrence, would a few months later be stamped indelibly in Sheffield folk history. Fowler told the court Butler had been with him all night in the singing room. The landlord, Gus Platts, said he had asked both Chapman and the Garvins to keep away from the Barleycorn.

When Chapman agreed with Mr. J.W. Fenoughty, defending, that Bob Garvin had stood surety for him two years previously but added that the Garvins were now angry because he was no longer a follower of their gang, Mr. Fenoughty objected strongly to the suggestion of a "gang case". Whenever he had to defend these men, he said, there was an atmosphere of prejudice introduced. "If a couple of schoolboys have a fight at Meersbrook it's a gang. Let us have fairness and common sense when dealing with ordinary cases of assault." The magistrates were more than fair to the Garvins and Butler - they dismissed the case against them. Once more Sam Garvin walked out of Sheffield Police Court unconvicted.

Chapman's new friends were not at all pleased with the court's decision. After the case they lined up along one side of Castle Street, with Park Brigade men facing them on the other pavement. Representatives from each side requested permission from the police to "have a go" but the police, not surprisingly, refused and the gangs were moved on their way.

It was clear by the numbers who faced the Park Brigade across Castle Street that the Mooney Gang was enjoying something of a revival. George Mooney himself had returned to the city but was lying extremely low and took no part, the nucleus of the new outfit comprising George Wheywell, Albert Foster and Tom Armstrong, three of the most violent men ever to walk the city streets. 'Ganner' Wheywell had defected from the Park Brigade, Foster returned from exile and Armstrong, who, despite being fifty years old had a fearsome reputation on the country's racecourses, had been specially 'borrowed' from the Birmingham mob, the Brummagem Boys.

Another who played an important, if less violent, role in the revival was George Newbould, the man assaulted by Garvin and his henchmen on Christmas night. Since the abortive New Year truce, Newbould had come to the fore in gang matters and, on his arrival from Birmingham, Tom Armstrong had moved into the Newbould home in Edward Street.

Any security Newbould felt with Armstrong as a house guest was dispelled in the early hours of Sunday, March 1st, when he answered a knock on his door and found John Henry Towler and two other men standing there. Towler, alleged at the January Quarter Sessions to have been instructed by Sam Garvin to assault George Wheywell, asked Newbould if Armstrong was in the house. Newbould said he was not and, after turning down an invitation to "come out and have a drink", was struck on the head with a beer bottle. Towler and his two accomplices ran off and Newbould was taken by ambulance to the Royal Infirmary with a wound on his head down to the bone.

Two days later, on March 3rd, John Henry Towler appeared before the magistrates charged with maliciously wounding George Newbould. The prosecution opposed bail, saying Towler mixed with notorious characters and witnesses might be interfered with. It was also stated that he was to have given evidence at the recent Quarter Sessions but had not turned up. The case was adjourned for three days and, much to the dismay of the police, Towler was granted bail.

When he appeared at the resumed hearing, Towler was represented by Mr. S. Grant, who, in cross-examining Newbould, endeavoured to make him admit complicity with leading gangmen.

Mr. Grant: "You are a commission agent. How many men do you employ?"
Newbould: "Five."

Mr. Grant suggested to Newbould that he had been financing gangs and said: "Is it not a fact that you have brought this man Armstrong, who is a known character - a bruiser - from Birmingham to assist you in your operation?"
Newbould: "No."

Newbould denied employing ''these gangs which are causing all this trouble in Sheffield" and denied giving them money. He was asked if it was true that after Towler had been stabbed by George Wheywell he had paid him £3 and sent Armstrong and Wheywell to take him to the station and see him out of Sheffield. Newbould denied this was true.

Mr. Grant: "Are Foster, Winsey, Wheywell and Armstrong members of a gang which has been terrorising Sheffield?"
Newbould: "I don't know."

Mr. Grant went on to suggest that Newbould had paid out a lot of money to them. Towler was committed to the Quarter Sessions.

When the case opened on April 10th, Mr. F.J.0. Coddington, prosecuting, said he was instructed to point out that the prosecutor was not Newbould, who was damaged, but the police. He outlined the facts, stating that on the night of the incident Newbould was seated in his sitting room "with the woman who for years had passed as his wife" when, at 12.30 a.m., Towler and two other - unnamed - men came to his door and asked for Tom Armstrong. Ascertaining that the Birmingham bruiser was not in the house, Towler struck Newbould with a beer bottle and the three men ran off. Mrs. Newbould, said Mr. Coddington, called the police. In evidence Newbould said he asked

Towler what he wanted Armstrong for and Towler replied: "Tha knows what we want him for."

Since the police court hearing Towler had dispensed with the services of his lawyer, choosing instead to conduct his own defence. He asked Newbould if he knew Foster and Wheywell. Newbould replied "No."

Towler: "Do you know these people terrified me for some time? Do you employ these people, finance them?"

Newbould: "No. You ought to be ashamed of yourself for asking that."

Towler: "Did you send me away at the last Quarter Sessions?"

Newbould: "Garvin sent you away."

Towler went on to say, from the witness box, that Newbould was "at the head of affairs" regarding trouble in Sheffield and he (Towler) wanted to ask him if he was going to be allowed to walk about town in peace. He said that at the last Quarter Sessions "one of these men" - Wheywell - was charged with stabbing him and Newbould had sent him (Towler) away so that he would not prosecute. He had realised this was foolish and came back. He had nothing to say about the actual offence with which he was charged and must not have been surprised when the jury found him guilty. He was sentenced to four months in the Second Division.

Less than forty-eight hours after the assault on George Newbould, the re-formed Mooney Gang struck back. Still smarting from the New Year con-trick and incensed by the acquittal of the Garvins and George Butler on the Chapman assault charge, the Newbould assault proved the last straw. Retribution was called for and George Butler, a confirmed ally of Garvin, was the man selected to suffer.

On Monday, March 2nd, Butler emerged from Edmund Road Drill Hall where he had spent the evening attending a boxing tournament promoted by Sam Garvin. As he stood outside the hall, in conversation with another man, he received a violent blow on the head. Turning, as he fell from the blow, he saw Albert Foster holding an iron bar and behind him George Wheywell with a fish mallet. Butler was taken to hospital and found to be suffering from a depressed fracture of the skull. His life was in jeopardy for ten days.

Foster, who had struck the blow, immediately disappeared from the city scene and was not apprehended until five weeks later in Birmingham. On April 11th he appeared at Sheffield Police Court charged with wounding Butler, but with the latter still in hospital the case was adjourned. On this occasion the magistrates agreed with police objections to bail and Foster was remanded in custody.

Seven weeks after he had been assaulted, Butler was released from hospital and was in court on April 23rd when the case against Foster was resumed. Mr. G.H. Banwell, prosecuting, told the court that there was great difficulty in getting witnesses. "Witnesses are undoubtedly afraid for themselves to come and give evidence against such a man," he said.

Mr. H. Morris (defending): "We cannot have that."

Mr. Banwell: "Witnesses have in this case expressed their fear of coming forward to give evidence."

Butler told the court that as he turned, on being hit, he saw Foster and George Wheywell. He heard Wheywell say to Foster: "Kill him!" "When the blow was struck," said Butler, "I shouted, 'I've been done!'." Foster was committed to the July Quarter Sessions and allowed bail. The next day, however, he was brought back before the court and sentenced to three months imprisonment for being in arrears on his wife's maintenance order.

After the optimistic hopes of peace at New Year, the first few months of 1924 had seen an escalation in violence between the gangs. Much of this had resulted from the ill-fated truce and Sam Garvin's efforts to crush the revived Mooney Gang and take over their 'interests'. Besides the traditional gangman's 'pension' - a levy of 'subscriptions' on publicans, street bookmakers, shopkeepers etc. - the new organisation had strong connections with tossing rings at Tinsley Park and Scraith Wood. Repeated police raids on the Sky Edge ring, although fruitless in terms of arrests, had seriously affected business there and these alternative pitches were now attracting many of the Skyring regulars. It was to this line of business that John Henry Towler alluded when he suggested in court that George Newbould was financing and employing gangmen. Newbould, he said, was "at the head of affairs" regarding trouble in Sheffield. That trouble now revolved to a large degree around the tossing rings which Newbould ran with the assistance of his more violent associates.

Albert Foster's retaliatory assault on George Butler outside the Drill Hall, for which, later that summer he was to be sentenced to 18 months hard labour, could quite easily have resulted in a much more serious charge than that of wounding on which he was indicted. Of the dozens of victims of gang clashes since the feuds had begun two years earlier, Butler's injuries were undoubtedly the worst. With the junior gangs by this time also indulging in increasing lawlessness, the situation was rapidly deteriorating. George Butler had, in recovering, been lucky. The next victim of gang violence would not enjoy such luck.

7. Murder in Princess Street

Detonators rang out as the train bringing home the victorious Sheffield United football team steamed into Victoria Station. It was Tuesday, April 28th, 1925, and hundreds of thousands of people were assembled in the city streets to give a rousing welcome to their heroes who, three days earlier, had beaten Cardiff City 1-0 in the F.A. Cup Final at Wembley.

Escorted by mounted police, a procession of coaches carrying the players, their wives, and officials slowly made its way through a city centre emblazoned with the United colours of red and white. On one coach a band played "See the conquering hero comes" but hardly anyone could hear for the deafening applause. Flags fluttered, scarves and hats were waved, and confetti bombarded onto the coaches all the way to the Town Hall where the team was greeted by the Lord Mayor, Alderman A.J. Bailey. Outside the Town Hall a crowd estimated at 10,000 went wild with delight when United's captain, Billy Gillespie, raised the F.A. Cup for all to see. There were special cheers for Fred Tunstall who had clinched victory with the only goal of the match. As the *Sheffield Independent* said the next morning: "It was a great occasion: it was a great reception - one befitting such an outstanding event."

Such joy was not shared by everyone in the city; some were concerned with more serious matters. At the same time that Sheffield United and their followers were celebrating, the City Coroner, Mr. J. Kenyon Parker, was opening an inquest on a man who had died in the Royal Infirmary the previous evening. The man had been admitted at 8.35 p.m. with three scalp wounds clean cut down to the bone and two wounds in the abdomen, each five inches in depth. He died eight minutes later without regaining consciousness.

From statements taken by police, said the Coroner, the man was, without the slightest provocation, violently assaulted by a gang of men. If the evidence bore out those statements, the case was one of a cowardly murder perpetrated in one of the main streets of Sheffield as early as eight o'clock in the evening, an unarmed man being attacked by a number of men, some of whom were armed.

Before adjourning the inquest, the Coroner told the empanelled jury their feelings must be of sympathy with the widow and relatives of the dead man.

"There ought to be feelings of shame and anger that such a crime should be possible in such a place in this city.

I am afraid this city is acquiring an unenviable notoriety through crimes of violence committed by gangs of men, and I know that an impression is growing among law-abiding inhabitants that even the main streets and roads are not safe at night for ordinary people to go about their business. If that is true it reflects no credit on the local government of this city or on the inhabitants, and I trust this death may have the effect of focusing public opinion and rousing that local government and the people of Sheffield generally to a determined effort to stamp out this kind of crime.

It seems to me that the safety of the lives of our people are more valuable than money, and if, as is said in some quarters, the police force is too small to carry out its duties adequately then that force must be increased, and to my mind the force should be encouraged and upheld and not discouraged as I am sometimes told it is, by misplaced leniency, either on the part of gentlemen in your position or by magistrates or by juries at the Assizes.

The police want all the help that can be given to them, they want backing up, and it is your duty and it is mine, in a proper case where the evidence is strong and clear to take the responsibility of backing them up, and in not hesitating in finding a criminal verdict merely out of sympathy or fear of taking responsibility."

The dead man was William Francis Plommer, a thirty-four year old native of Glasgow. An ex-soldier, Plommer had settled in the city after meeting his wife while stationed at Hillsborough Barracks. He had been discharged from the army in 1912 but at the outbreak of war in 1914 rejoined and served in France, achieving the rank of sergeant. He returned to civil life at the end of the war and at the time of his death was employed as a labourer by the Bessemer Company. He had four children, ranging from a son aged eleven to a three week old baby.

The incident in which Plommer received his fatal injuries was the outcome of a disturbance outside the Windsor Hotel, near to Plommer's home in Princess Street, the previous evening. A gangman had taken exception to Plommer's non-participatory role in a fight in which the gangman, Wilfred Fowler, had come off second best. The following night, Monday, April 27th, Fowler returned to Princess Street with a gang. They toured public houses in the area inquiring after Plommer and two of his friends - Arthur Whitham and Harry Rippon - and openly threatened to murder all three. As the men paraded up and down Princess Street, Plommer came out of his house,

No. 42, to meet them. What happened next was described the following day by an eye witness: "Plommer was walking down the street and when he got to Norfolk Bridge he was met by a gang of eight men. They immediately attacked him, saying 'Here is the ------Scotsman.' Plommer was a man who could defend himself and he wouldn't turn away from a bullock but they cracked him on the head with a bottle and drove him down the street. Against such odds, Plommer hadn't a dog's chance, although he fought bravely enough and practically crippled one of his eight assailants. Near the door of his house Plommer attempted to push away his attackers and, just as he was entering the door, one of the gang hit him on the head with a child's scooter. They practically knocked him into the house. As the gang went up the street they were saying: 'Now for Plommer's two pals.'"

P.C. Daniel Hogan was two hundred yards away when he noticed the gang retreating down Princess Street. He ran to the scene and found Wilfred Fowler, his brother Lawrence and another man, George Wills, sitting on the steps of a chip shop. Summoned to No. 42 he found Plommer with head injuries and two great wounds, resembling bayonet thrusts, through his stomach and side. An ambulance was called and Plommer, who had lost consciousness, was taken to the Royal Infirmary. A police search of the vicinity of the affray produced a variety of weapons, including pokers, iron chains and razors, but the weapon that had caused Plommer's fatal wounds was never found.

Shortly after the Princess Street incident, the members of the gang who had been heard threatening to murder Plommer and his friends, Whitham and Rippon, caught up with the latter outside the Bull and Oak public house on the Wicker. Rippon was slashed with a razor, hit with a life preserver and badly knocked about. He identified his attackers to the police as Sam Garvin, Bob Garvin and William Furniss. They were arrested the same evening and appeared at the Police Court the following morning charged with unlawfully and maliciously wounding Harry Rippon of 5 ct. 3 hse, Mathew Street.

Rippon said he was on his way to the Bull and Oak to sing. As he approached the pub both Garvins and Furniss were coming out. "Sam Garvin struck me with a razor and Bob struck me with what I think was a life preserver," he said. "Furniss ran towards me and they all attacked at once. I don't know what Furniss did because I was dazed by the other blows." All three accused echoed the plea of Bob Garvin whose only comment was: "I know nothing about it."

Detective Inspector Naylor, applying for a remand in custody, told the magistrates: "Possibly, in the course of further proceedings this morning, we may be able to connect this affair with something else which happened earlier in the evening." All three accused were remanded in custody for one week.

Wilfred Fowler, (23), of 12, Stevenson Road: Lawrence Fowler, (25), of the same address; Frank Kidnew, (40), of Campo Lane; George Wills, (22), of Cyclops Street and Fredrick Goddard, (18), also of 12, Stevenson Road were then put in the dock and charged with the wilful murder of William Plommer on the previous evening. Wilfred Fowler's head was swathed in bandages. Frank Kidnew leaned on the rails of the dock. "The prisoners did not appear to realise the full purport of the charge," commented the *Sheffield Mail*.

P.C. Hogan described the scene on his arrival in Princess Street and told the court Lawrence Fowler had said: "I hit him on the head." The constable had cautioned him: "Now be careful, it looks like being serious," whereupon Fowler had then said: "I did not hit him on the head." Upon being handcuffed Fowler had also said: "I did it in self defence." All the defendants attempted to make statements from the dock but were told they must keep to questions.

Wills: "What connection have I with the affair?"

P.C. Hogan: "Certain witnesses can say."

Kidnew: "Where did you see me?"

P.C.: "I did not see you there."

Detective Inspector Naylor asked for all the defendants to be remanded in custody for one week, saying that with respect to Kidnew the police would be able to bring an officer to prove that he and Robert Garvin were seen at the junction of Princess Street at about 8 p.m. The accused were remanded until the following Tuesday, May 5th.

By Tuesday four more men had been charged with the murder. Amos Stewart, (21), of March Street was identified on a parade by ten witnesses to the fatal affray and Sam Garvin, Robert Garvin and William Furniss were charged with murdering Plommer in addition to the assault on the Harry Rippon charge. All nine were brought from Leeds Prison and appeared before the magistrates handcuffed and chained together. Wilfred Fowler's head was still swathed in bandages. Mr. J. W. Fenoughty, for all the prisoners, asked for them to be kept in custody in Sheffield, as there would be difficulty in preparing the defence if they were remanded to Leeds. The Bench was advised Leeds Prison was more suitable and the prisoners returned as they had come: escorted by warders, each of whom carried a revolver. Three days later Stanley Harker, (23), a carter, of Leigh Street became the tenth man to be charged with the murder.

The situation in which an apparently unarmed man could be brutally murdered in broad daylight provoked an angry reaction from the Press and general public. On Wednesday, April 29th, the morning after the Coroner had opened the inquest on William Plommer, 'Passer By' in the *Sheffield Independent* once again issued a severe censure to those responsible for the maintenance of law and order in Sheffield:

> "Time after time the press has been accused of exaggerating the gang menace in the city, and in cases where some of these hooligans (all of them, by the way, well known to the police) have been convicted of savage assaults, the powers that be have invariably shown an amazing leniency.
>
> True it is, as the City Coroner, Mr. Kenyon Parker, observed yesterday, the city has acquired an unenviable notoriety through the prevalence of outrages by one or other of the gangs, and now that public indignation has been thoroughly aroused there must be no allowing the matter to rest until the canker has been removed, root and branch, from our midst. There is no place for cowardly ruffians in modern civilisation. There is legal machinery in existence which, if prosecuted with its utmost rigour, would soon put an end to what has become a veritable reign of terror.
>
> The Attercliffe crime has brought the government of Sheffield to the bar of public opinion, and, if necessary, those responsible for the city's good name must invoke the aid of the Home Office to secure the assistance necessary to rid it of the excrescence which has flourished for too long."

The public turned out in force for Plommer's funeral. Crowds lined the route as the cortege, followed by many ex-servicemen, made its way from Princess Street to Burngreave Cemetery. Collections were taken for the dead man's dependants. Among the crowds were many policemen and plain clothes detectives but no trouble occurred. It was estimated that 8,000 people gathered inside the cemetery.

The *Sheffield Mail* reported:

> "On many sides one heard remarks of indignation at the cruel death which had befallen Mr. Plommer, and the huge crowds which gathered at all parts strikingly demonstrates the intense sympathy which the citizens of Sheffield have accorded to the relatives of the dead man."

Shortly after Plommer's funeral a rumour began circulating that a group of ex-servicemen had banded together in a vigilante group, pledged to wage a war on the gangs. On May 7th the *Sheffield Mail* approached the Chief Constable, Lieut. Col. Hall-Dalwood, with this suggestion and found him to be horrified at the idea. "There is only one way to deal with this matter," Lieut. Col. Hall-Dalwood said, "and that is the constitutional way. It is a matter for the police alone. We can deal with it and we are dealing with it. I need only remind you once again that every time there has been an outrage we have brought someone before the magistrates. To suggest that a new body should be formed to meet the gangs with their own weapons won't do at all. It is going back to lynch law and it must not be done."

The inquest on William Plommer was resumed on May 18th with eleven defendants present, William Wild, a 28 year old steel dresser, having been added to the charge since the others' last court appearance. Forty-five witnesses gave evidence before the coroner's jury, who returned a verdict of wilful murder against Wilfred Fowler and Lawrence Fowler on May 21st. Verdicts of aiding and abetting were returned against another seven of the accused: Frank Kidnew, George Wills, Frederick Goddard, Amos Stewart, Sam Garvin, Stanley Harker and William Wild. No Verdict was found against Robert Garvin and William Furniss.

Following the verdicts, the murder charge against Furniss was withdrawn but he remained in custody on the charge of being concerned in the later wounding in the Wicker. Robert Garvin, however, who had also had no verdict brought against him by the coroner's jury was one of the ten accused who appeared at the resumed Police Court hearing on May 25th. This practice of holding inquests in murder cases and finding guilt before magisterial proceedings were completed was an issue of some controversy which was soon to be amended by Act of Parliament.

The Police Court sat for seven days in all and heard evidence from seventy-four witnesses. From the outset the defence alleged that the dead man, Plommer, had been the aggressor and had assaulted Lawrence and Wilfred Fowler with a poker and razor. It was also suggested that Plommer, along with certain principal witnesses for the prosecution, ran a tossing ring under the railway arches at Norfolk Bridge. Despite tenacious cross-examining by Mr. J.W. Fenoughty, who represented all ten defendants, not one prosecution witness said anything to substantiate either of these claims.

Many of the witnesses merely repeated what they had said at the inquest, most of the new evidence relating to the Windsor Hotel incident of Sunday, April 26th, and both witnesses' and defendants'

The slums of Sheffield. Two courtyards, photographed by the Ministry of Health in 1926.
Top – Cross Smithfields, West Bar.
Bottom – Duke Street, Park.

Sam Garvin
Leader of the Park Brigade

Robert Henry Garvin

Wilfred Fowler
Hanged for murder
3rd September, 1925

Lawrence Fowler
Hanged for murder
4th September, 1925

George Wills, top left.
Sentenced to 10 years penal
servitude for manslaughter.

Amos Stewart, top right.
Also sentenced to 10 years penal
servitude.

Stanley Harker, bottom right.
Sentenced to 7 years penal
servitude.

2 . 9 . 1925

Dear Old Skipper & Jack

Many thanks for your kind & welcome letter. Was pleased to hear from you. Would have been pleased for you & Jack to come to see me. Sorry this letter is so short But you will understand Dear Old Pals. My cup of bitterness is full. Having to go out of life innocent. It is God's will I go to meet him with a clear conscience. Surely the wrong done will find me a place in Heaven. I am hoping to meet the best pal I had years ago Billy Wood. I am leaving my Little Bab's behind me the one I Love. I hope you will do your best for her. Will close now. My best wishes to every one. Wishing you both the Best of Luck. Bidding you my last Good Bye Old Pals. My last race is run. Play up Wendesday.

With Love

Your Heartbroken

Pal Lol xx xxxxx

I have not forgot Skipper the money I owe you.

A letter, written by Lawrence Fowler two days before his execution.
Skipper and Jack were Billy and Jack Spencer, sons of Mrs. Mary Spencer, landlady of the Blucher Inn, Brightside Lane.
Lawrence and Wilfred Fowler had been customers at the pub and, for a time, Lawrence had worked for Mrs. Spencer's son-in-law, Billy Wood - referred to in the letter - who had died in 1920.
Enclosed with the letter was one penny.

Left William Francis Plommer,
     murdered on 27 April, 1925.

Below Princess Street, as it is today.
     The fatal affray took place
     on the left hand corner,
     between where the first two
     lamp standards are situated.
     Plommer's home, number
     42, was approximately
     where the car furthest from
     camera stands.

Hall-Dalwood in the uniform of Group Commandant, West Riding Volunteers Regiment.

Lieutenant-Colonel J. Hall-Dalwood, Chief Constable of Sheffield 1912-26.

Hall-Dalwood, left, at his farewell presentation, 31 March, 1926. The occasion of the "insidious influences" speech.

Captain P. J. Sillitoe.
Chief Constable of Sheffield
1926-1931.

Caricature of Sillitoe by Heap.
From *Yorkshire Telegraph and Star*,
19 October, 1928.

Sgt. William Robinson.
Leader of the 'Special Duties
Squad'.

P.C. Walter Loxley.
6 feet 2 inches tall, 19 stone.
The scourge of the gangs.

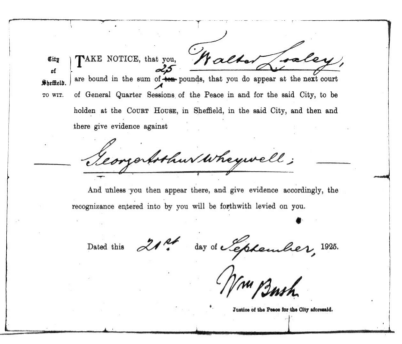

'Ganner' Wheywell's cross-summons on P.C. Loxley, following the
Red House incident, 14 September, 1925.

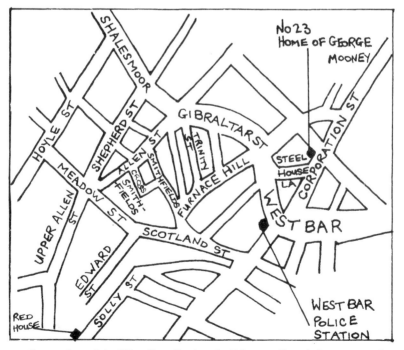

Street plan of the West Bar district, the Mooney Gang's homeground.

connections with tossing rings.

"It is part of my duty," said Mr. Fenoughty, "to say that Plommer was associated with a section of men connected with a tossing ring. The introduction of the tossing ring is not to try to associate Plommer with a set of undesirables, but to show that the section of the witnesses mentioned was animated, not by a desire to do justice to the dead man, but to do something which would react against Sam Garvin." As to why the section of witnesses should want to do this, or how Garvin was connected with them or their tossing ring, Mr. Fenoughty did not elaborate. "In any trouble regarding fighting or tossing," he told the magistrates, "Sam Garvin's name unfortunately appears to be brought into it. It is something like the hackneyed defence at the Children's Court - that they saw it at the pictures. It is a sort of stock line."

Harold Liversidge, of Upperthorpe, one of the witnesses alleged to have been involved with Plommer in the Norfolk Bridge tossing ring, told the court he had been involved in a fight with Wilfred Fowler - known as 'Spinks' Fowler - at the Windsor Hotel the night before the alleged murder. Fowler had struck him saying: "You will remember me. I am 'Spinks' Fowler." Liversidge had then gone to Plommer's house and Plommer returned with him to see a fair fight. In the course of this fight Fowler had fallen against a wall, gashing his head. Fowler had told Plommer, who helped him to his feet: "Jock, you are in for a tanning for this." Cross-examined, Liversidge said he had nothing to do with any tossing ring under the railway arches.

The evidence for the defence was opened by Lawrence Fowler on June 16th, following a two week adjournment for the Whitsuntide holidays. He said Plommer had pulled a poker from inside his trousers and hit him twice on the head with it before hitting his brother, Wilfred. In the scuffle that ensued he noticed Plommer had a razor.

Mr. Fenoughty: "Did any of the other prisoners take part in that scuffle?"

Lawrence Fowler: "There was only my brother."

The point was raised again when Mr. J.E. Wing, prosecuting, cross-examined.

Mr. Wing: "You suggest that only you and your brother were in this fight?"

Lawrence Fowler: 'There were some more of the party."

Mr. Wing: "Who were they?"

Lawrence Fowler: "I don't know."

Following his brother into the witness box, Wilfred Fowler said Plommer had started the violence. He said that neither Stewart, Wills, Goddard nor Harker took part in the Princess Street affray. He had not that day seen the two Garvins, Kidnew or Wild. He himself did not strike or kick Plommer. He had no connection with the Garvins but he had been to the tossing ring in Thompson's yard (under the railway arch). George William Thompson of Princess Street was a witness for the prosecution.

Wilfred Fowler was then cross-examined by Mr. Wing, who showed a particular interest in the witness's means.

Mr. Wing: "You say you are a bricklayer's labourer. How long is it since you worked?"

W. Fowler: "Twelve months."

Mr. Wing: "And how long did you work?"

W. Fowler: "Two hours. The police got me stopped."

Fowler said that he then went on relief and the police got his relief stopped. It was in 1919 when he worked before.

Mr. Wing: "How do you live?"

W. Fowler: "My brother, John, keeps me."

Mr. Wing: "Do you gamble?"

W. Fowler: "Yes. At Alfred Road."

Mr. Wing: "Who are the people connected with the Alfred Road Gang?"

W. Fowler: "Big Jackie and Lucky Jim."

Mr. Wing: "And who visits the tossing ring there?"

W. Fowler: "Oh, there are thousands of people every week."

Mr. Wing: "And you make money out of that?"

W. Fowler: "I was born in Alfred Road."

Mr. Wing: "Is that a qualification for becoming a member of the gang?"

W. Fowler: "It is not a gang."

Mr. Wing: "You are known as 'Spinks' Fowler?"

W. Fowler: "No. I am known as 'Pinkle' Fowler. I have never been addressed as 'Spinks'."

The question of 'Spinks' or 'Pinkle' was followed by the evidence of two of the other defendants, George Wills and Frederick Goddard, who said that on the night of the murder they were on their way to commit a burglary when they were arrested with a fish-tailed jemmy and two flash lamps in their possession. In reply to Mr. Wing, Goddard said he had only worked one week in his life. He lived by carrying parcels. All the other prisoners appeared highly amused at this. Mr. Wing commented: "You were going to carry parcels without permission that night!"

No indication of concern at the serious charges they faced was apparent from the demeanour of the accused men at any time during the Inquest or Police Court hearings. They whispered and mumbled to each other, chewed gum, and on several occasions broke into laughter as prosecution witnesses gave evidence against them. A number of times they were rebuked by the magistrates' clerk and one witness who became angry at their attitude was asked by the Coroner· not to get excited. Mrs. Rose Lemm had described seeing Lawrence Fowler jabbing Plommer in the stomach when she turned to the prisoners, saying: "Don't grin at me or I'll------." The Coroner told her: "It is not a grinning matter for them or anyone. I can quite understand your indignation, but keep it to yourself."

On the first day of the Police Court hearing there was an anxious moment when Wilfred Fowler and Robert Garvin, accompanied by a policeman, left the court for a few moments. Almost immediately they had gone there was a loud shout from below. Police officers rushed to see what was happening but it appeared that one of the prisoners, for no apparent reason, had suddenly shouted to the other.

There were several attempts to intimidate witnesses involved in the case, notably Arthur Whitham who, along with 'Jock' Plommer and Harry Rippon, was one of the men the defendants were alleged to have threatened to kill on the fatal night. The evening after Plommer was murdered and Rippon slashed, Whitham was talking to a policeman in Princess Street, only yards from the scene of the affray, when Ernest Broomhead, a member of the Park Brigade, approached and struck him a violent blow in the face. Whitham ran off up Princess Street chased by a second man, Richard Addy, and Broomhead, who was extremely drunk, was arrested. On the way to the police station a bottle was thrown at the constable, narrowly missing him. Astonishingly, in view of both parties connections with the men involved in the previous night's tragedy, Broomhead escaped with a £5 fine for the assault on Whitham. Addy, who told the court he had nothing to do with gangs as he worked for a living, was discharged.

Three weeks later, while the inquest was taking place in the Coroner's Court, Arthur Jackson of Alfred Road was fined £2 at the Police Court for threatening Whitham that he would "do him". It was stated that Whitham was a witness in the murder case but, while his name frequently cropped up throughout, and his niece and daughter gave evidence for the prosecution, Whitham himself did not appear in the witness box.

Some of the witnesses who did appear were swiftly made aware of the dangers involved. After the first day of the Police Court hearing, several of them were followed from the courthouse and onto a tram by gangmen whose threatening and intimidatory behaviour only ceased when police boarded the tram and hauled them off. On May 27th, Mr. J.E. Wing, the prosecuting solicitor, sought an assurance from the magistrates that the police would assist in preventing a re-occurrence of such a situation. "It is very material that the witnesses should have every protection," he said.

On June 17th the Police Court proceedings ended somewhat abruptly with Mr. J. W. Fenoughty stating that he did not intend to call Sam Garvin, Robert Garvin, Frank Kidnew or William Wild, but that they would reserve their defence. All ten prisoners, on whose behalf Mr. Fenoughty had entered a plea of "Not guilty", were then committed for trial at Leeds Assizes on the capital charge of wilfully murdering William Plommer on April 27th.

The next day Sam and Robert Garvin appeared again before the magistrates, charged with the unlawful wounding of Harry Rippon outside the Bull and Oak, in the Wicker, also on April 27th. The case against William Furniss was dismissed when a witness, asked to identify Furniss among the prisoners in the dock, pointed to Bob Garvin. So Furniss, who had spent five weeks in custody before being granted bail on May 30th, left the court a free man having had both murder and wounding charges against him dismissed.

Sam Garvin did not reserve his defence on the wounding charge. He told the court he had boarded a train at Norfolk Bridge, along with his brother, Kidnew and Wild, at about 7.45 p.m. and gone straight to the Ecclesall Tavern - about two miles away on the other side of the city. He met a piano tuner named 'Piano Bob' and they stayed in the Ecclesall Tavern until 9.15 p.m. "I have never been in the Bull and Oak in my life," he said. Both Sam and Robert Garvin were committed to Leeds Assizes to face trial on the charge of unlawful wounding, in addition to the murder charge.

8. The Murder Trial

The murder trial opened at the West Riding Assizes, Leeds, on Tuesday, July 28th, 1925 before Mr. Justice Finlay. The ten men accused of being concerned in the wilful murder of William Francis Plommer, of 42, Princess Street, on the night of April 27th, were:-

Wilfred Fowler, 23, of Stevenson Road;
Lawrence Fowler, 25, of Ardmore Street;
Frank Kidnew, 40, of Campo Lane;
George Wills, 22, of Cyclops Street;
Frederick Goddard, 18, of Stevenson Road;
Amos Stewart, 21, of March Street;
Samuel Garvin, 45, of Heavygate Avenue;
Robert Henry Garvin, 36, of Allen Street;
Stanley Harker, 23, of Leigh Street;
William Wild, 28, of Brightside Lane.

Eighty witnesses, together with officials, police, reporters and hopeful spectators travelled from Sheffield on the first day, special carriages being reserved on the Leeds train. As they passed through Attercliffe Road Station and over Norfolk Bridge a large crowd could be seen gathered below in Princess Street, where William Plommer had lived and where, three months earlier, he had received his fatal injuries.

At Leeds Town Hall, where the Assizes were held, the police were taking great care to prevent any trouble. Officers were posted at the door to prevent undesirables from entering and when the prisoners arrived each morning from nearby Armley Prison a cordon of burly policemen hustled them quickly into the court. The route to and from court was varied each day, as was the transport that conveyed them. Leeds police were taking no chances with the notorious Sheffield gangs.

Mr. G.F.L. Mortimer, K.C., Mr. A. Morley and Mr. L.R. Lipsett appeared for the prosecution; Mr. G.H.B. Streatfeild represented the Fowlers; Mr. J.W. Jardine appeared for the Garvins, Kidnew and Wild; Mr. A. Burnand represented Stewart, Wills and Harker; and Dr. E.C. Chappell appeared for Goddard.

Mr. Mortimer, opening the case for the Crown, said the jury would see that the great majority of the men were young; the oldest of them was Samuel Garvin, who was forty-five, and the youngest Goddard, who was only eighteen. The jury would have to distinguish between the offences as they affected the different men.

The evidence for the prosecution, he said, would endeavour to prove that the men who were actually at the assault were the two Fowlers, Goddard, Wills, Stewart and Harker, and that the other four men - the two Garvins, Kidnew and Wild - were not present at the time the killing was done. The case for the prosecution was that these men were accessories before the fact and, as such, were entitled to be treated as principals of the crime.

Describing the wounds which Plommer received, Mr. Mortimer said the ex-soldier was dead within minutes of his arrival at the Royal Infirmary, never recovering consciousness. The cause of his death was internal haemorrhage and shock. There were three scalp wounds, one inch in length, all clean cuts and down to the bone. Serious as these injuries were, they were not the cause of his death. The direct cause of his death were two blows in his stomach, both apparently deliberately delivered. Either of the wounds would have been sufficient to cause death and both had apparently been inflicted with great force.

The weapons used on that night were of a varying nature, held by various hands. There was one, probably two, pokers, several razors, and at least one short bayonet and a number of coshes. The jury might try to discover which was the hand which struck the fatal blows inflicted to the lower part of the body although it was not material. In all probability, judging from medical evidence, the weapon which inflicted the fatal blow was the short bayonet.

Mr. Mortimer then went on to describe the events which led up to the tragedy. He first mentioned the incident at the Windsor Hotel on the previous night. At eight o'clock that night, Wilfred Fowler, Wills and some others called at the hotel and, later, a man named Harold Liversidge, who was apparently a stranger to the district and to the men, came in. At ten o'clock, Liversidge went outside and stood against a wall with his hands in his pockets. Wilfred Fowler went across the road and struck Liverside a blow in the face, saying: "I will make you remember 'Spinks' Fowler."

Liversidge went off to one of the few people he knew in the district, the deceased man, Plommer, who lived in Princess Street. From that house came Plommer, followed by Mr. and Mrs. Cooper, and Plommer's child, Tommy. They went out, as Mrs. Plommer would tell the court, to see "fair play" and see that the unjustifiable assault on Liversidge was not repeated. Mr. Mortimer then went on to describe how Liversidge and Wilfred Fowler had fought and how after helping Fowler up, Plommer was told: "Jock, you have got to have a tanning for this tomorrow." He said he expected that the defence would suggest that Plommer took an active part in the affair, but even if that was the case, which was denied, that could not justify the murder committed nearly twenty-four hours afterwards. It was sometime subsequently that the story was told that Plommer had assaulted Lawrence Fowler.

Relating incidents that occurred on the night of April 27th, Mr. Mortimer said that Plommer was in his house, and up and down the street in which he lived paraded a number of men, among whom, they would be told at one time or another, were included the Fowlers, Goddard, Stewart, Harker and Wills. About 5.35 p.m. Lawrence Fowler was heard to ask at the Greystock Inn: "Where does Cooper or Liversidge live?" Visits were paid to a number of public houses at intervals during the parade. It was evident that the inhabitants were expecting trouble and the men were followed and watched by a considerable crowd.

Apparently in order to rid themselves of the crowd, some of the men who had been taking part in the parade boarded a tram and went to Brightside and returned later. About that time Samuel Garvin and the other men who were taking part in a separate parade - with the same object in view, counsel suggested - were trying to find where Plommer lived. Garvin and Kidnew were identified. They went to a public house, where Samuel Garvin said to a woman named Bedells: "I want Plommer and your brother 'Tich'." Mrs. Bedells said that she did not know where Plommer or 'Tich' were. Garvin then said: "You are a liar. We'll kill the ------s." At this point Mr. Mortimer stated that some of the language used by Garvin and the Fowlers was foul and opprobrious and he did not propose to repeat it.

About 7.45 Garvin went to the house of a man named Thompson and there asked a man named Day: "What do you know about the bother last night?" Day replied: "I know nothing about it." Garvin then said: "You soon will do." When Thompson entered the room Garvin said: "Where are 'Jock', 'Tich', and 'Spud' Murphy?" (Murphy, an active member of the re-formed Mooney Gang had been present on the Sunday evening when Wilfred Fowler fought with Liversidge). Thompson replied that he knew nothing about the affair. Garvin then said: "There has been some trouble and them what have done it will pay for it; we will cut him to pieces and 'Jock' as well."

'Jock' was killed within twenty minutes of that statement, observed Mr. Mortimer, who added Garvin then said to Thompson: "If you were working with a mob and one of your mob got 'done', what would you do?" As Garvin was leaving he said to Thompson: "You will see the streets flowing with blood." Garvin then bent down to kiss a three year old child and a razor was seen protruding from his pocket.

After that the men left the house. It was then nearly eight o'clock. At a corner quite close to where the murder took place, Samuel Garvin, in the presence of others, asked a man named Pollard: "Where are the Fowlers? We shall kill Whitham and 'Jock' and Murphy. We have a mob down here to 'do' Plommer." Kidnew then appeared and said: "Let's get on our tram and go down to the Bull and Oak." The four - both Garvins, Kidnew and Wild - then boarded a tram and disappeared from the story. The men they left behind, according to police evidence, were in an excited condition.

Just before eight o'clock, Plommer left his house and stood in the open road close to Norfolk Bridge. He had no weapon, according to witnesses, and he stood in an entirely indefensive attitude, with his thumbs in his waistcoat sleeves. He had hardly stood there when six men - who the prosecution alleged were, undoubtedly, the men in the dock - approached. A miner named Holmes, who was standing by and had seen the parade earlier in the evening, called out to Plommer: "For God's sake 'Jock', clear out."

Plommer seemed to have been a man of extraordinary coolness and courage, added Mr. Mortimer, for he said: "I shall have to stick it." All the six men then rushed at Plommer, who held up his hands and said: "If it's a fair fight I'll take you one by one." Everyone of the six men carried a weapon of some sort. Lawrence Fowler went straight up to Plommer with the remark: "You've done our kid and we are going to do you." Plommer knocked him down with his fist.

It was impossible in the story to disentangle every detail. Every witness saw his or her particular bit. Some saw one weapon, some another. After Lawrence Fowler had been knocked down he was seen to strike Plommer on the back of the neck with a poker as Plommer was engaged with Wilfred Fowler. Brave and hardy as Plommer was, the six men got him down and the evidence would show that, having got him down, they battered him in the face and everywhere else.

Wilfred Fowler was seen striking him with what Plommer's little boy described as a "truncheon", and witnesses would speak as to the collective and individual acts of the assailants while Plommer was on the ground. One witness saw Lawrence Fowler jabbing him in the stomach and, as that was being done, the mouth of the then dying man opened wide. That evidence was supported in some similar terms by other witnesses.

At that moment a motor car appeared and the occupants saw a number of men kicking a man on the ground. One of the passengers saw one man - who he thought was Wilfred Fowler - brandishing a weapon, which he described as a short bayonet. Plommer got up to his feet and tried to scramble onto the car but was unsuccessful. He then ran towards his own home, only a few yards away, and was pursued by the Fowlers. Wilfred Fowler picked up a scooter and threw it at the dying man. There came a cry: "I'll finish him." Plommer went into his house and the Fowlers sat down on the steps of a fish-and-chip shop. There would be evidence that a weapon which appeared to be one foot long and two inches wide and black in colour was seen.

Dealing with Police Constable Hogan's discovery of the Fowlers sitting on the steps, Mr. Mortimer said that P.C. Hogan would allege that Lawrence Fowler had a poker and a razor in his hand and both had fresh blood on them. Lawrence Fowler said: "Look what they have done to him (pointing at his brother); they have cut his finger nearly off. 'Jock' has done it." Counsel went on to describe the chase of Goddard and Wills with an unknown man later in the evening when Goddard was chained to some iron railings, and the discovery of various weapons which had been thrown away.

Mr. Mortimer contended that the four men who were not present at the attack - the Garvins, Kidnew and Wild - were accessories before the fact. "The case for the prosecution," he concluded, "is that the fatal blow was by the hands of Wilfred and Lawrence Fowler, or, certainly by one of them. As regards the others, the case for the prosecution is that they had joined this party; that they had a common purpose; and although the weapons they used did not lead to Plommer's death, the other four, having assisted in the attack and having played their own part in it alongside others, are equally guilty of murder, in the eyes of the law, as the two."

Mrs. Elizabeth Plommer, the widow, was the first witness called by the prosecution. Repeating the evidence she had given at the inquest and Police Court hearings, Mrs. Plommer stated that her husband had gone out of their house at about 7.45 p.m., carrying no weapon of any kind. When she went out she saw a gang of seven or eight, including the Fowlers, Wills and Stewart, going towards her husband. The one with the bandages on (Wilfred Fowler) stepped in front of the rest and the others got round her husband. Seeing her husband lying on the ground she started to run and heard Lawrence Fowler say: "Come on, let's finish him." She noticed blood running down her husband's back and he tried to get back to the house. The Fowlers followed him to the door and Wilfred threw a child's scooter at her husband. She saw Lawrence Fowler with a poker and Wilfred with a razor. The following day, at the Central Police Station, she said to Stewart: "You were with that lot last night." He did not reply. Later she identified Wilfred Fowler, Stewart, Kidnew and the Garvins as being in Princess Street on the night her husband was murdered.

Cross-examined by Mr. G.H.B. Streatfeild, counsel for the Fowlers, Mrs. Plommer said that her husband did not take any part in the fight between Harold Liversidge and Wilfred Fowler the previous night. On the night that her husband was killed he did not strike either of the Fowlers with a poker.

One of the men alleged at the Police Court hearing to have been a partner of William Plommer's in the Norfolk Bridge tossing ring, Ishmael Pollard, told the court that at ten minutes to eight on the night of the tragedy he saw Sam Garvin, Robert Garvin, Kidnew and Wild. Sam Garvin said to the witness's brother, Harry Pollard: "Where are the fighting men?" and that he would kill Whitham, Plommer and Murphy. Kidnew then exclaimed: "Let's go to the Bull and Oak and catch Murphy there." The four then boarded a tram and went away.

Cross-examined by Mr. J.W. Jardine, representing the Garvins, Kidnew and Wild, Pollard said that Sam Garvin was shouting the threats. Mr. Jardine asked Pollard: "You are really a racing man?" Pollard's reply: "I have never been to a race-meeting in my life" brought an outburst of laughter from the prisoners in the dock. "You earn your living by gambling?" persisted Mr. Jardine. Pollard replied: "No sir."

Arthur Whitham's niece told the court that she did not identify Sam Garvin at the inquest because of threats she had heard him make to her uncle, and Whitham's daughter gave evidence that on the night of the tragedy when Garvin, Kidnew and two other men told her they wanted 'Tich', Garvin said: "We have come to do him in."

George Richard Thompson then entered the witness box. Thompson, who described himself as a bookmaker and the alleged headman of the Norfolk Bridge tossing ring, told the court Sam Garvin had come to his house on the fatal night demanding to know the whereabouts of 'Tich' and 'Jock'. Thompson said Garvin referred to the Liversidge-Fowler fight of the previous evening and to 'Spink' Fowler being "done". Garvin told him: "We have been quiet long enough. It is time something was done. We are coming down here this weekend and will cut everybody to pieces. Princess Street will flow with blood." Regarding Fowler, Garvin had said: ''Those who have done him will have to pay for it."

The last witness of the day was Thompson's wife, who said that as Sam Garvin left the house he bent down to kiss her child and as he did so she saw a razor protruding from his pocket. The court then adjourned.

A convoy of taxicabs escorted by police motor-cyclists transported the defendants from Armley to the Assize Court for the second day's hearing, when the case for the Crown resumed.

Frank Griffiths, of 1, Princess Street, outside whose shop the fatal affray occurred, told the court that at eight o'clock Plommer was standing alone in front of the shop. "I was serving a child when several men rushed at Plommer," he said. "He was wrestling with a man and trying to get a poker from him. Whilst he was doing that he was struck on the head by another man with an instrument. Plommer fell down and the other four men took something from their pockets and struck him. All the men had weapons but Plommer had no weapon. A more dastardly, cowardly attack............," the witness started to say when the Judge interrupted: "No, no."

The man with whom Plommer was wrestling for possession of the poker, Griffiths said, had his head in bandages. Both fell to the ground, he said, adding that he had a clear, uninterrupted view of the fight.

Mr. Streatfeild: "You say Plommer and another man were wrestling for a poker?"

Witness: "Yes."

Mr. Streatfeild: "You don't know whether Plommer was taking the poker from the man, or the man was taking the poker from Plommer?"

Witness: "I think Plommer was taking the poker from the other man."

Re-examined, he said that Plommer lit a cigarette and was standing with his thumbs in his waistcoat. That was what made him think that he had no weapon and was trying to get the poker from the other man.

William Hazlewood, of Greystock Street, gave evidence of a gang of six or eight men parading Princess Street, Corby Street, and Sutherland Street, visiting several public houses along the way. He saw four others board a tram and five minutes later William Plommer came up and stood alone by Norfolk Bridge. The witness saw no weapon on him. The same gang who had been parading the streets approached Plommer and a man in a light suit struck him. Plommer knocked him down with his fist and a man with a bandaged head joined in. As Plommer struck him too, the gang closed in, Plommer fell to the ground, and the man in the light suit made a lunge at him as if stabbing him with something.

Mr. Mortimer: "Can you say where he appeared to be stabbing him?"

Witness: "In the left side, sir."

The witness said he afterwards saw Plommer make towards his home and heard the man in the light suit say: "Let's finish the Scotch ----." Together with the man with the bandaged head he ran after Plommer, but the man with the bandaged head collapsed on the chip shop steps. The light suited man said to the witness: "Look what the Scotch ---- has done to my poor brother." As be said this be held a razor and a poker in his hand, said the witness.

Mrs. Rose Lemm, the lady who the Coroner had asked not to get excited at the Inquest, said that Wilfred Fowler drew something down his sleeve and hit Plommer, then Lawrence Fowler struck him on the back of the neck. Plommer said: "Come fair and I'll fight you one by one." Lawrence Fowler jabbed him in the stomach while he was on the ground, but she could not see what he jabbed him with. Both Fowlers were on top of Plommer, she said.

Mr. Mortimer: "Could you see Plommer's face?"

Witness: "Yes."

Mr. Mortimer: "Could you see the effects of the jabbing?"

Witness: "I saw his mouth open wide."

Mrs. Lemm then caused a stir in the courtroom by declaring that she later saw Wilfred Fowler with a long black case, in which he was putting "a bayonet like thing". The case was the length of elbow to finger tip and two inches across, she said.

Evidence of seeing a bayonet was also given by the driver of the motor car referred to by a number of witnesses. He said he saw one of the men with "a thing like a short bayonet". His passenger in the car said that he also saw a man in the crowd with a short bayonet in his hand. He had the impression that the man was the defendant with the bandaged hand (Wilfred Fowler).

Several children were called to the witness box, including Plommer's twelve year old son. He had given evidence at the Inquest on his father and at the Police Court hearing, where he had been overcome by his ordeal and complained of feeling dazed. Now, for the third time, he told how Wilfred Fowler, whom he recognised, had hit his father with what he described as "a truncheon" and Lawrence Fowler had also hit him with a poker on the back of the neck. The remainder of the men, he said, started to fight his father, who tried to climb on a motor car but jumped off and went towards home. The boy heard Lawrence Fowler say: "Come on; let's do him in." He identified Stewart and Harker. Harker, he said, had something like a truncheon in his hand.

Another child told how 'Spink' Fowler had picked up her brother's scooter and thrown it at Plommer. A boy, aged twelve, described the assault on Plommer in similar details to the adult witnesses and said that five minutes after the fight ended he found a piece of lead on the end of a length of wire on the tram lines, about eight yards from the scene of the fight. Later in the day another witness said that he saw George Wills strike Plommer on the head with a piece of lead hanging on string from his wrist. Besides the Fowlers, Wills, Stewart, Harker and Goddard were all named by witnesses as having taken part in the attack on Plommer.

Police Constable Hogan repeated the evidence that he had given at the earlier hearings, of finding the Fowlers, after the fight, sitting on the chip shop steps. Both were dressed in light overcoats and bowler hats, he said, and Lawrence Fowler pointed to Wilfred saying: "Look at him ; they've nearly cut his finger off." When asked: "Who has done it?" Fowler replied: "'Jock'." He then repeated how Lawrence Fowler had admitted hitting Plommer but, when informed of the seriousness of the matter, changed his mind saying: "Well, I didn't hit him then." When he heard that Plommer had died, P.C. Hogan arrested Lawrence Fowler and, later, Wilfred Fowler, George Wills and Frank Kidnew.

Detective Goodwin gave evidence of taking the two Fowlers to the Royal Infirmary. On the way Wilfred Fowler pointed to Lawrence and said: "He hit him." Lawrence said at the time: "I thought he was only stunned."

The last witness for the prosecution was Dr. J.E. Schofield, resident surgical officer at the Royal Infirmary. Detailing the result of his examination of Plommer's body, he stated that the two serious wounds in the abdomen had cut right through the clothing, and part of the internal organs were protruding. There were also three scalp wounds which were clean cut down to the bone, caused by a razor or a poker. These wounds could not have caused death. The severe abdominal wounds in the stomach could not have been caused by a razor, but a weapon similar to, but smaller than, a bayonet. The cause of death was internal haemorrhage and shock.

The doctor said there was no bruising on the body, and if a man was kicked he would expect to find some. Plommer was well-clothed and that would tend to diminish bruising. Questioned by Mr. Mortimer, Dr. Schofield said that if a man died within half an hour and had lost a large quantity of blood, that would tend to diminish the bruising. Bruising did not come out after death.

Mr. Mortimer: "What force would be required to cause the wounds?"
Dr. Schofield: "Tremendous force."

The doctor inspected a bowler hat belonging to one of the Fowlers and expressed the ·opinion that a cut and a dent could have been caused by a razor and a poker respectively. The medical evidence closed the case for the Crown and the Court adjourned until the following day.

Immediately on the opening of the defence case the next morning, Mr. J. W. Jardine, on behalf of the Garvins, Kidnew and Wild, submitted that there was no evidence of wilful murder to go to the jury. The bulk of the evidence, he contended, proved conclusively that the four men were absent from the scene of the affray, having left on a tram before it occurred.

Before they could be convicted as accessories before the fact - as the prosecution had alleged they were - there must be evidence that they were persons who procured, counselled, or abetted those who were concerned in the affray. The evidence against the men, while in the main was evidence against the whole of them, was in part only evidence against Samuel Garvin.

"My submission is," added Mr. Jardine, "that the fact that these four men were going down the street emitting threats of violence against different men is quite irrelevant to the proceedings. If it was proved beyond all doubt that a body of four men were going down Princess Street to find Plommer, that does not in any way connect them with the crime committed, and does not in any way implicate them in the affair from which they were absent."

There was a conversation with a man named Pollard, he said, in which Samuel Garvin was alleged to have said: "We have got a mob down here to do Whitham in." That was not sufficient evidence to render them accessories before the fact, nor was it evidence that they instigated, counselled, or procured anybody else to perpetrate the affray.

The Judge: "I am disposed to go a long way with you in regard to the case against Robert Garvin, Kidnew and Wild, but not in regard to Samuel Garvin. There is evidence of him saying: 'We have a mob'."

Mr. Jardine: "The evidence must be that he sent the mob there that night."

The Judge: "I shall leave the case of Samuel Garvin to the jury."

Mr. Mortimer, the leading prosecuting counsel, agreed that the case against Robert Garvin, Kidnew and Wild was nothing like so strong as the case against Samuel Garvin and Mr. Justice Finlay then directed the jury to return a verdict of not guilty against the three men, who were dismissed from the case. After three months in Armley Prison, Kidnew and Wild were released, Robert Garvin being detained in custody to face the unlawful wounding of Harry Rippon charge.

The first defence witness to give evidence was Samuel Garvin. He said that he knew the Fowlers and he last saw Lawrence Fowler at Gringley-on-the-Hill races in early April. Lawrence had asked him if he knew anything and he replied: "Splash me". The horse won at three to one. Garvin said he did not know Stanley Harker, George Wills, or

Frederick Goddard.

He went on to say that he had lent his car to the prosecution witness, 'Dickie' Thompson, and on April 27th called at Thompson's house in Princess Street to see him about £17 owing in respect of the car. When he called at Thompson's, 'Dickie' had asked him about the bother on the previous night and remarked that it was something to do with the Alfred Road lads and 'Spud' Murphy. Thompson mentioned the Fowlers and said one of them had been "done".

"I said," continued Garvin, " 'has that Murphy started with his messing again.' I said, 'Four of us would beat any four amongst them'. Thompson said he had nothing to do with it and I said 'Good night' and he said 'Good night Sam.' " He went on to say that Plommer's name was mentioned as well as Whitham's. When they went to get the tramcar at Princess Street he saw a crowd of men and said to them: "I suppose you have some fighting men here. There's four of us will fight any four amongst you, 'Jock', Whitham, 'Spud' and all the lot. If Murphy comes down here he'll cause some bother." If he mentioned 'blood' it was not meant seriously, and he did not say "we have a mob down here to do Plommer." He had not seen the Fowlers for three weeks before the affray.

Cross-examined by Mr. Mortimer, Garvin admitted going to the Midland Hotel on the night of the tragedy but said he did not hear of the affair of the previous evening. He denied going to the Windsor Hotel and saying to a Mrs. Bedells, "I want 'Jock' Plommer and 'Tich' Whitham." The latter's niece was lying when she said he asked for 'Jock', 'Tich' and 'Spud' Murphy, he said. Another witness who had heard him asking for the three men was also lying. Dick Thompson was committing perjury, he claimed, and Thompson's wife had not been in the room during his visit to her husband, thus she could not have seen a razor in his pocket.

Mr. Mortimer: "You seem to be surrounded by liars trying to swear your life away?"

Garvin: "Yes, sir."

Mr. Mortimer: "I suggest to you that having laid the trail you endeavoured to save your own skin by getting away from the place."

Garvin: "I know nothing about it."

Sam Garvin was followed in the witness box by Lawrence Fowler, who said that on the day of the tragedy he had been to Uttoxeter Races, where he learned that his brother had been injured the night previously. He reached Sheffield about 6.20 p.m. and eventually went to Norfolk Bridge with Frederick Goddard. Shortly afterwards he met his brother, who was accompanied by a man he later learned was Amos Stewart, at the bottom of Thompson's yard, in Princess Street. The reason he went to Princess Street was because he had heard that 'Tich' Whitham had thrown out a challenge for £20 that Cooper, Liversidge or 'Jock' would fight his brother. (Cooper was one of the men alleged to be connected with the tossing ring at Thompson's yard). He had £8. 10s on him and "meant to fasten", he said. He went back to Norfolk Bridge and stood there for fifteen minutes with his brother, Stewart and Goddard. Goddard later left them at the Rollers' Tavern and he, Lawrence Fowler, did not see him again that night. They ran into Stanley Harker coming up Princess Street and went to the Big Gun, where Wills joined them.

Relating the incidents which led up to the tragedy, Fowler said: "'Jock' was standing at Norfolk Bridge. I was with my brother, Stewart and Harker, I said to 'Jock': 'We are going to have a straight fight tonight and no pokers to be used?' Plommer stepped back and said "I will use it on you and all." Plommer then drew a poker from his trouser pocket, or from under his belt, said Fowler, and hit him (Fowler) "backwards on top of the head." He went down, but was up immediately and saw his brother struck on the head with the poker. As Wilfred went down he, Lawrence, tried to get hold of the poker, grasping the thin end. Plommer and himself struggled with the poker, which was stuck between his legs, and it caused two severe bruises.

"I succeeded in getting it from him, but I fell on my back. I got up and saw 'Jock' strike at my brother with a razor in his left hand. I heard my brother shout out something and fall to the floor. He ran at me and I lunged forward and struck him with the poker. I hit him on the left side of the head. We stuck together, Plommer fell backwards and he fell on the tram lines." At this instant, he added, a motor car came between Plommer and himself and parted them.

Mr. Streatfeild: "Did you strike any other blow?"

Lawrence Fowler: "I did not."

Lawrence Fowler added that when Plommer was on the ground he was seven or eight yards away and had no weapons in his possession. When the motor car was passing, Plommer threatened him what he would do with a razor. He and his brother chased Plommer to make him drop the razor and when he did Wilfred picked it up. He took it from Wilfred and placed it with the poker. He denied that he said "Let's follow the Scotch ---- and do him in."

Mr. Mortimer (cross-examining): "How did Plommer get these two wounds in his stomach?"

Lawrence Fowler: "I don't know sir; I was on the floor and could only see a lot of legs. "

Mr. Mortimer: "How many were round Plommer?"

L. Fowler: "There seemed to be about ten people."

Mr. Mortimer: "Did you recognise anybody else?"

L. Fowler: "Only my brother."

Mr. Mortimer: "Did anybody assist Plommer in any way?"

L. Fowler: "Not to my knowledge."

Mr. Mortimer: "Then the whole of the ten persons were going for Plommer?"

L. Fowler: "They were all around him."

Mr. Mortimer: "Did anybody kick him?"

L. Fowler: "No, sir."

Mr. Mortimer: "Did you see any coshes?"

L. Fowler: "No, sir."

Mr. Mortimer: "Did you see any razor other than the one you say Plommer had?"

L. Fowler: "No, sir."

Mr. Mortimer: "How do you suggest Plommer's clothes were cut about?"

L. Fowler: "I have no idea."

Mr. Mortimer: "Did he do it himself?"

L. Fowler: "He could not very well."

Mr. Mortimer: "Who did it then?"

L. Fowler: '' 'That is what we are here for."

In further cross-examination Fowler said the evidence of two witnesses who said they saw him jabbing at Plommer was pure imagination. The police officer who took him to the Royal Infirmary had told a deliberate lie, he said and, although he could give no explanation of the wounds in Plommer's stomach, he admitted that "it happened down at the bridge."

Replying to Mr. Jardine, Fowler said he did not see Sam Garvin on the Sunday or Monday. He last saw him at Gringley-on-the-Hill races in early April. Garvin, he said, was "his own gaffer" and was not a member of any gang.

Wilfred Fowler began his evidence with the trouble of the night preceeding the tragedy. Harold Liversidge and he had a straight fight, he said, with Plommer and Cooper looking on. He (Fowler) was getting the better of the fight when the other men interfered. Plommer seized him by the throat with one hand and hit him on the head with a poker which he carried in the other. He remembered nothing more. He had four stitches put in the wound. On the following morning he heard that Plommer, Liversidge and Cooper were prepared to lay a wager for £20 for a fight with him. His object in being in Princess Street on the Monday evening was to see about the bet, but he had no intention of fighting that night.

When he saw Plommer at Norfolk Bridge he said: "It's going to be a fair fight tonight and no pokers are going to be used." Plommer replied: "I will hit you with a poker" and, drawing one from his trousers, "smacked" Lawrence on top of the head with it.

"My brother fell down," Fowler said, "and I went for Plommer and he knocked me down. When I got up I saw Plommer and my brother struggling, each holding one end of the poker. Plommer was kicking at my brother. My brother got the poker and fell over on his back. Plommer fetched a razor out of his pocket, either the coat pocket or waistcoat, with his left hand. I went over to grab it and he slashed down and caught my thumb. I sat down and wrapped my hand up and then I saw my brother smack at him with a poker. Plommer struck at the same time."

He continued that Plommer slipped down but was quickly on his feet and he (Fowler) saw somebody "go for" him. At that moment a motor car came between them. Fowler denied that he struck a blow. "I never had a chance," he declared. He also denied that he threw a scooter and he corroborated his brother's statement about Plommer dropping the razor. Plommer was the aggressor, he asserted.

Cross-examined by Mr. Mortimer with reference to the fight with Liversidge, Fowler contended that Liversidge was the aggressor because he was jealous about some women. When Liversidge returned with Plommer the latter hit him on the head with a poker.

Mr. Mortimer: "Were you very angry?"

Wilfred Fowler: "No, I always learned to keep my patience."

He admitted that he was followed by a lot of children on the Monday in Princess Street because of his involvement in the previous night's fight.

Mr. Mortimer: "They were admiring the hero of the fight?"

W. Fowler: "It looks like it."

Mr. Mortimer: "I put it to you that they knew you were out for trouble?"

W. Fowler: "No."

Mr. Mortimer: "When you went up to Plommer were there a number of people about?"

W. Fowler: "About sixteen."

Mr. Mortimer: "Was Plommer standing in the roadway alone?"

W. Fowler: "Yes."

Mr. Mortimer: "So the sixteen people could see what was going on?"

W. Fowler: "Yes."

Mr. Mortimer: "And you heard some of them in the box yesterday?"

W. Fowler: "Yes."

Mr. Mortimer: "How did Plommer get the injuries from which he died?"

W. Fowler: "'I don't know. He only went down once."

Mr. Mortimer: "And when he was down he was killed?"

Wilfred Fowler did not reply.

In the course of further replies, Fowler was seen to smile. Mr. Mortimer asked him: "Do you think it is a laughing matter?" Fowler: "No."

Mr. Mortimer: "Well don't laugh then."

Asked if his case was that somebody stabbed Plommer while he was out of the crowd, Fowler replied: "Somebody must have." Mr. Mortimer then asked why, on being charged with the offence, he replied: "I reserve my defence." Fowler answered: "I always do; I always have a lawyer."

In further replies Fowler said that he could not explain the cuts on Plommer's head, but anyone who said coshes were used was telling lies. He concluded his evidence by denying that he saw anybody brandishing an instrument shaped like a bayonet.

George Wills, in his evidence, said that on the night of the tragedy he was visiting his girl, who was sick, at her home in Princess Street. While he was there he saw the Fowlers going by the window followed by the others, so he put his cap on and went after them. Plommer was standing in the roadway with his fingers in his waistcoat sleeves when Lawrence Fowler spoke to him.

Wills then corroborated the story of the Fowlers with regard to the poker and razor incidents. He denied that he took part in the attack, saying he had no weapon and never possessed one. There were fourteen or fifteen men around Plommer, he said. Wills declared that he never spoke to the Garvins, Kidnew, or Wild prior to being in custody with them, but he knew the Fowlers; in fact he had been brought up with them. He had been at the Windsor Hotel the previous evening, but had not seen the fight between Wilfred Fowler and Liversidge. The next day Fowler said he was going to have a "straight fight" with Plommer.

Cross-examined by Mr. A. Morley, he was asked did he think the Fowlers stood much chance against Plommer unarmed. Wills replied: "I think so." Mr. Morley then asked why he did not go to the rescue of his two friends, "who were being attacked by a strong man armed with a razor and a poker." Wills replied that he had nothing to do with the matter. The people who had said he took part in the fight were not telling the truth.

Amos Stewart also corroborated the Fowlers' story relating to the poker and razor incidents. He also denied that he took any part in the affair, but said he saw other people with weapons. "It seemed like a mutiny," he added. "They all seemed to be shoving each other about." After the affray, Wills and Harker accompanied him on the way home and the following day he heard that Plommer had died. He went to Attercliffe Police Station, voluntarily, to give evidence and was sent for subsequently. While he was talking to some of the witnesses a police officer said: "Come on my lad, we want you," and arrested him.

Cross-examined by Mr. L.R. Lipsett, Stewart said Wilfred Fowler told him: "They did me last night and I'm going down." He himself went "because of the boxing match." It was pointed out that his evidence varied considerably with the statement he had made to the police when he initially visited Attercliffe police station the day after the tragedy.

Stanley Harker said that he had known the Fowlers all his life. He met them on the Monday night and Lawrence asked him to go for a walk. After visiting the Big Gun Hotel and catching a tram they returned to Norfolk Bridge. He described in detail what happened there, corroborating the story given by the other prisoners. Harker also said he was merely a spectator of the tragedy and had no idea anything was going to be done to Plommer when he took the tram ride with the other men. Harker had been charged after stepping out of an identification parade, stating the he knew a certain witness would pick him so he thought he would save him the trouble!

Frederick Goddard was the last of the prisoners to be called to the witness box. He said he was not near Princess Street when the disturbance took place, but heard of it from Wills when they met by appointment at about 9.15. He and Wills were going to do a breaking-in job, he said, but it was too light at the time. They decided to have a walk down Princess Street to see if there was anything still going off, but when he saw the police he ran because he knew Wills had a fish-tailed jemmy on him and he himself had two flash lamps. He did not wish to be caught with these in his possession. Goddard's girlfriend and her mother both gave evidence that he had been visiting them on the night of the tragedy. He had arrived at 7.45 p.m., they stated, and stayed until 9 o'clock.

On the fourth and final day of the murder trial an elaborate ruse was employed by Leeds Police to get the prisoners from Armley Prison to the Town Hall as secretly as possible. Travelling in horse-drawn cabs and followed by a motor car, the prisoners arrived from a different direction to that anticipated by the large crowd gathered outside the Town Hall entrance. The few members of the public who were present when the procession arrived were kept well away from the prisoners by a large cordon of police who stood shoulder to shoulder around the vehicles.

The opening submission by defence counsel was on behalf of eighteen year old Frederick Goddard. Addressing the jury, Dr. E.C. Chappell referred to him: "This unfortunate boy who finds himself here on what must be to him one of the most terrible crimes. By this time, I am sure you will have formed the conclusion that if Wilfred Fowler had not taken him in as a lodger he would not now be in this position. He had to confess in the box as to what his plans were on that night." Referring to the evidence of Mrs. Hannah Beever, the only witness who had stated that Goddard was one of Plommer's attackers, Dr. Chappell added that she was the type of person who thought it was her specific duty to support the police. She was, however, speaking the truth when she said that she saw Goddard go up and down Princess Street on that fatal night. He had lived in the district all his life.

The jury knew how people lived in Princess Street, Dr. Chappell said. They would be sitting on their door steps, yet only one witness had come forward to say that Goddard was present at the time of the affray. Goddard's story, said Dr. Chappell, was that of Stewart, who related his version before he was charged.

Mr. Mortimer, replying for the Crown, said that if after hearing the whole of the evidence the case was not proved against Goddard, the jury would find him not guilty. He still stood in the dock and still awaited their verdict because the prosecution considered there was evidence for the jury's consideration on the matter.

Addressing the jury with regard to the case against the other prisoners, Mr. Mortimer said the affair outside the public house of the evening before was only important as it appeared to supply Wilfred Fowler and the rest with the object for the outrage committed on the following day. Whether it was Plommer or not who struck Wilfred Fowler on that night they had heard nothing which suggested that Plommer was the sort of man to do "such an unworthy, unfair and un-English thing." It was obvious that Wilfred Fowler, from that moment, had felt that a wrong which had been done had to be avenged. The jury had seen Wilfred Fowler's Christian patience in the dock. They had heard that he felt no grievance at all, and what was the good of being angry when the act had been done? The jury would judge whether that would be the attitude Wilfred Fowler would adopt to those whom he believed to have done him an atrocious wrong. It was no defence to say that Plommer had a razor and a poker because they knew Plommer received these terrible wounds when lying helpless on the ground.

The jury had to decide two opposite cases. On the side of the prosecution they had a large body of evidence with regard to what happened from the moment that Wilfred Fowler and his brother stepped across the road towards Plommer. It was odd that if, as the prisoners said, there were quite a large number of spectators of the tragedy, that no single person had been called to support the story put forward by any of the prisoners as to what happened.

On the one side the large weight of evidence; on the other the prisoners alone. The prisoners evidence, added Mr. Mortimer, left the crucial point unsolved: "How did poor Plommer meet his death?" The prisoners suggested it was one of the crowd quite apart from them who had inflicted the fatal blow. This statement was entirely contrary to evidence of witness after witness of the assault on the defenceless and unarmed man.

Mr. Mortimer went on to suggest that the cut on the web of Wilfred Fowler's thumb was consistent with the whole story told on behalf of the prosecution - that the cut was caused by Wilfred Fowler himself, in the course of the scrimmage, with his own weapon. He suggested that the story of Plommer bringing a poker was not credible and, on the contrary, that the poker was brought by Wilfred Fowler.

"It might occur to you," said Mr. Mortimer, "that a lurid light is thrown upon what happened at Norfolk Bridge by the parading up and down Princess Street. Was this a mere innocent Monday evening walk; was it purely an innocent walk taken for the purpose of finding somebody with whom money for a bet could be placed."

Mr. Mortimer added: "From nobody but the prisoners have we heard any story about a wager by 'Tich' Whitham who is said to have offered a wager for £20. Were not the words used by Lawrence Fowler in the beginning of the fight fatal to the story that they were out to fix a bet? The words he used were: "We will have a fair fight!" Later Lawrence Fowler said: "If only I had said what I meant to say."

Mr. Mortimer said that he did not propose to deal in detail with the evidence as it stood against Wills, Harker and Stewart except to point out that there was this in favour of the witnesses for the prosecution - they selected three men who were there on the night, who were in and about Norfolk Bridge at the time of the tragedy. They took part in the parade up and down Princess Street. It was not a country walk; it was, he suggested, an indication to Plommer that the clans were out and an indication to Plommer, a known brave man, to come out and face them. Then those men went away on the tram, but only to the next stop, leaving reports to reach Plommer that the men had gone away, that he could come safely out, that the danger had passed. But in a short time they returned, and found Plommer at Norfolk Bridge.

Dealing with the case as it affected Sam Garvin, Mr. Mortimer said that the prosecution did not suggest that Garvin was one of the assailants. If he were to be found guilty he must be found guilty as an accessory before the fact.

What was a man who lived three and a half miles away doing there that night? He lived in the district eighteen years ago. He had given some story of explanation as to what brought him to Princess Street - visiting Thompson regarding the money he was owed - but there was scarcely one thing that Garvin would admit that any witness had said about the matter, said Mr. Mortimer.

"If you come to the conclusion that in that box yesterday Samuel Garvin lied," he told the jury, "you can ask yourselves: 'why should an innocent man lie if he had never heard of the assault against Wilfred Fowler?' Why should he say he had not been to the Windsor Hotel?" He added that Garvin denied going to the Windsor but two witnesses . had stated that he did, and that he asked for 'Jock' and Whitham. What did Garvin want with these men, asked Mr. Mortimer. The reason, he suggested, was that Garvin regarded the alleged attack by Plommer on Wilfred Fowler as an attack upon him in some sense.

"'King' Garvin had been annoyed," declared Mr. Mortimer. "There had been treason against 'King' Garvin. 'Jock' Plommer had struck his friend, Wilfred Fowler, and, for some reason unknown to the prosecution, 'Tich' Whitham had been dragged into the matter and had to be slaughtered too.

You will have to decide, then, who is telling the truth. Are Thompson, Mrs. Philips, Mrs. Thompson and Day (all had been present in Thompson's house when Garvin visited), or is Samuel Garvin? If you accept the evidence of the four people I have named, how can this have been a chance visit to the Attercliffe district on another matter by a man who had never heard of the trouble on April 26th until he was told by Dick Thompson?"

Referring to the threats alleged to have been uttered to other witnesses by Samuel Garvin at Norfolk Bridge, Mr. Mortimer asked: "What is all this talk of a man 'Tich' Whitham and Murphy? I suggest to you that it means that Samuel Garvin regarded himself in some sense a protector of the Fowlers and those working with them and, finding that a wrong, as he thought, had been done to Wilfred Fowler, he - the great man - had come down to the district to see about it, to see the wrong was righted, if there was a wrong; to right a wrong - right it by death.

Whether by chance or design, and knowing that there were those to do this work, Samuel Garvin, with his three friends, gets on a tram and passes out of sight and leaves only ten minutes at the outside before the moment that the Fowlers appear at Princess Street, rush across the road, and commence an assault on Plommer which ended in a very few minutes in Plommer's death."

Following Mr. Mortimer's lengthy submission to the jury, Mr. Streatfeild addressed them on behalf of the Fowlers. He pointed out that the parading of the men in Princess Street was for the purpose of fixing up a challenge for a fight. What evidence had the jury that the Fowlers were out on the night of the tragedy to seek their revenge and that they were armed to do so? It was alleged that one or other of the Fowlers had something in the nature of a short bayonet, dagger or knife. He suggested that the little evidence there was was so shaken that it was extremely unsafe for a jury in a case of such gravity to act upon it.

Out of fifty witnesses only five people had spoken of that dagger or knife or bayonet, said Mr. Streatfeild. He suggested most strongly that there was no evidence that the two Fowlers had any weapon of that description upon them. The facts corroborated the prisoners' story of Plommer having a razor and a poker, went on Mr. Streatfeild. He could not however, he said, overlook the fact that, perhaps, the jury might not accept the whole of the prisoners' story. In that case, he suggested that they took the middle course - that the prisoners were guilty of manslaughter. Mr. Streatfeild submitted that the ingredients of the crime of manslaughter were present in the case. If the men were guilty of anything they were guilty of manslaughter.

Mr. A. Burnand, for George Wills, Amos Stewart and Stanley Harker, contended that they took no part in the death of Plommer. He suggested to the jury that the story of Sheffield gangs had "got about" and that Sheffield was in such a state that if a few men were seen together, people immediately jumped to the conclusion that it was a gang. That was the state in which witnesses appeared to give evidence, he said. Their statements were full of exaggerations and imaginations had run wild.

"Shut all ideas of gangs out of your minds altogether," urged Mr. Burnand, arguing that there was no evidence of association between the men. The jury would never have clear consciences again if they returned a verdict against the three men, he maintained. If either of those men had joined in a fight which resulted in a man's death, then the jury might return a verdict of manslaughter. The weight of evidence was against such a verdict. Many of the witnesses had imagined things and made exaggerations. He concluded that it was done quite honestly and was particularly liable in street affrays.

Mr. J.W. Jardine, making the final defence submission, on behalf of

Samuel Garvin, contended that no evidence had been produced to show that he commanded the Fowlers or anybody else to commit the crime. Though Garvin might have uttered threats as to what he would do to certain men, that was not sufficient to convict him of being an accessory before the fact. There was no evidence of association between those men.

The Judge, in his summing-up, pointed out that all the prisoners were charged with murder and the case as to six of them was that they were all actually present and actually took part in the assault which resulted in the death of the unfortunate Plommer; therefore they were all responsible and guilty of murder.

The case as to Samuel Garvin, which his Lordship said he would deal with at the end of his summing-up, was that he was not actually present at the assault, but counselled or procured or instigated and was, therefore, responsible for what took place. Mere malevolence on Garvin's part was not sufficient to convict him. The jury had to be satisfied that he was the directing mind in the actual assault which took place on that night.

There were many aspects of the case, said his Lordship, that, no doubt, would receive the serious consideration of the police authorities in Sheffield, but the jury was only concerned with the case before them. The great Duke of Wellington once said that a battle was like a ballroom from the spectators' point of view. That, of course, applied to a street fracas where a number of people saw incidents in different circumstances and might tell the story somewhat differently. He asked the jury to consider the case of each prisoner separately and dispassionately.

Concluding his summing-up, his Lordship said that whatever suspicion the jury might have in regard to Samuel Garvin they might think it stopped short at suspicion, and that direct evidence to connect him with what actually took place was lacking: that was to say, that there was not enough evidence to say that Samuel Garvin procured or directed what actually took place. The fact that Garvin went round the district breathing fire and thunder was not sufficient to convict him.

The jury retired at six o'clock, Mr. Justice Finlay having occupied three and a half hours in summing-up.

At ten minutes to seven, after an absence of only three quarters of an hour, the jury returned. There was a great hustle and bustle as barristers and solicitors who had taken advantage of the interval by enjoying a stroll of the corridors, together with the large number of reporters, made a rush for the Court.

The public gallery, reserved for women, contained several wives and female relatives of the accused men. The elderly mother of Lawrence and Wilfred Fowler sat amongst them, a picture of tense anxiety.

With the prisoners placed in the dock, surrounded by warders, a complete silence fell over the Court as the Judge took his seat. The Clerk of Assize asked the jury Foreman to stand up and put to him the question:

"Gentlemen of the jury, are you agreed upon your verdict?"

"We are," replied the Foreman.

"How say you, do you find Lawrence Fowler guilty of murder or not guilty?"

"Guilty," replied the Foreman

"Do you find Wilfred Fowler guilty of murder or not guilty?"

"Guilty."

And so the questions were asked and answered. Amos Stewart, George Wills and Stanley Harker were found guilty of manslaughter, Samuel Garvin and Frederick Goddard not guilty of murder or manslaughter.

When the sensation had died down the Clerk of Assize gave instructions that Garvin should be taken below and kept in custody on the Harry Rippon wounding indictment, that Frederick Goddard should be released, and that Stewart, Wills and Harker be placed below.

Wilfred and Lawrence Fowler were left in the dock. Surrounded by warders, they advanced to the rails as the black cap was placed over the Judge's wig. As Mr. Justice Finlay pronounced the death sentence on each of them they stood calmly, only Lawrence making any comment. A short, sallow man, his black hair brushed back from his forehead, he retained the cool, detached attitude he had shown throughout the four day trial. He said: "I spoke the truth. I only struck one blow with the poker. I am innocent. If his wife would only speak up. It is an impossible decision."

His brother appeared momentarily stunned. Wilfred Fowler had nothing to say; he stood in the dock, his expression blank, until a warder touched him on the arm and he disappeared below. Before Lawrence was taken down he asked the Judge if he might see his wife before he left the Court. The request was refused.

George Wills, Amos Stewart and Stanley Harker were then returned to the dock. Asked if they had anything to say, all replied in the negative. Wills was smiling, while Harker's face bore the same impassive look that he had shown throughout. A Sheffield police officer gave evidence of the records of the three men. Wills and Stewart had previous convictions but nothing was known against Harker.

Addressing the men, the Judge said that, having been found guilty of manslaughter, each of them must feel fortunate. That it was an extremely serious case of manslaughter nobody who heard the evidence could doubt for a moment. While the sentence must be adequate to the gravity of the offence he drew some distinction between them in view of the fact that Harker was of previous good character. Amos Stewart and George Wills were each sentenced to ten years penal servitude, Stanley Harker was sentenced to seven years. Stewart smiled, bowed to the Judge and said "Thank you, sir." The three men were taken below and the Court rose.

Fifteen minutes after the jury had returned, the Court was empty. In that quarter of an hour two men had taken the first steps towards a condemned cell; three more had been sentenced to long terms of penal servitude; an eighteen year old boy had stepped from the dock to freedom; a seventh man, freed on the murder charge, was in custody on another count and a tired jury had been released from service for seven years.

9. Strenuous Appeals

Languishing in the condemned cell, with the hangman's noose an imminent reality, Lawrence and Wilfred Fowler were made harshly aware of their predicament. The lighthearted, diffident and arrogant bravado that had characterised their numerous court appearances during the three months they had spent on remand vanished when Mr. Justice Finlay pronounced sentence. As the Judge uttered those grim words: "And the sentence of the Court upon you is that you and each of you shall be taken.......to the place of lawful execution, and there you shall be hanged by the neck until you are dead," his chaplain offering an "Amen" to his Lordship's "May the Lord have mercy on your soul," Wilfred Fowler, at least, appeared deeply shocked. An observer from the *Sheffield Mail* commented: "It seemed as if his mind had ceased to work for the moment and he stood, a silent automaton..." His reaction, coupled with Lawrence's words to the Judge, suggested that, despite the prosecution evidence that they had heard, neither brother had seriously contemplated such an eventuality.

In a letter to their parents shortly after being sentenced they confirmed this shock. The letter read:

Dear Mother and Dad and All,

Don't take it too much to heart. We never expected this, but Fenoughty is making an appeal on our behalf. While there is life there is hope.

Bear up. There is still time for things to straighten out. We are happy and well considering the blow, and keeping in the best of spirits. If any of you want to come and visit us you must send us word. You will write to us both, as we don't go out together.

From your ever loving sons,
Lol and Wilf.

The brothers signed the appeal papers on August 7th. Mr. J. W. Fenoughty, who had instructed all four defence counsel involved in the trial, stated that there were eight grounds of appeal. The principal ones were:

That the verdict was against the weight of evidence brought forward.

That there could not be any distinction between the men sentenced to manslaughter and the Fowlers.

That one of the Fowlers might have been found guilty of manslaughter yet there was no direction on that point.

Three days after he was sentenced to death, on August 3rd, his own twenty-fourth birthday, Wilfred Fowler's wife gave birth to a baby daughter. On Saturday, August 15th she visited her husband in the condemned cell at Armley, taking the baby and their other small daughter. Afterwards Mrs. Fowler said she had found Wilfred much more cheerful than she had expected. The warder allowed him to take the baby in his arms for a few minutes but, said Mrs. Fowler, "he broke down when he handed the child back to me." Lawrence Fowler's wife had visited her husband the previous Saturday.

On Tuesday, April 18th the brothers' appeal was heard in the Court of Criminal Appeal in London. They were present at the hearing, travelling from Leeds by train, handcuffed to prison warders.

Mr. G .H.B. Streatfeild, who appeared for both brothers, stated that the grounds of appeal were mis-direction and non-direction of the jury, and a contention that the verdict was against the weight of evidence in the case. He said that after careful consideration he could not ask the court to quash the conviction in toto. He could only ask them to quash the conviction of murder and substitute one of manslaughter.

The chief ground of the appellants' complaint, said Mr. Streatfeild, was that whereas the Judge differentiated between the three other prisoners - Stewart, Harker and Wills - in dealing with the question of common intent, throughout his summing-up he coupled the two Fowlers together in one group. He made no differentiation between the two Fowlers.

That, he said, had a very serious effect on the minds of the jury. Mr. Justice Finlay should have directed them on the question of intent as between the two Fowlers. Had he done so, the question as to which of the two Fowlers, if either, had struck the fatal blow, would have been a matter of vital importance.

Mr. Streatfeild maintained that if the Judge had given a double direction, the jury could not possibly have come to the conclusion that both the Fowlers were guilty of murder. They would then have concluded that one of the Fowlers, if not both, was in the same position as the three men found guilty of manslaughter. The only course open to the jury then would have been to find both Fowlers guilty of manslaughter.

Dealing with the Judge's summing-up, Mr. Streatfeild contended that Mr. Justice Finlay had made a most unfortunate remark by telling the jury that whereas all five of the prisoners might have been guilty of the murder, the two Fowlers certainly were guilty of the murder. In connection with manslaughter, the two brothers were not mentioned from first to last.

Upon the evidence of the attack on Plommer, the part taken by the two Fowlers was certainly not worse than that taken by the three other prisoners. Countless witnesses had said the other men gathered round Plommer, beating him and cutting him with razors. The only differentiation between the Fowlers and the other three men was the suggestion that one of the Fowlers had a short bayonet.

The evidence, Mr. Streatfeild said, was so confusing and conflicting that it would be quite impossible for any jury to make up their minds with reasonable certainty as to which of the Fowlers had the bayonet. He added that there was rather less evidence against Lawrence Fowler than against the other three men.

After considering the appeals, Lord Chief Justice Swift stated that the jury could hardly have done otherwise than find the Fowlers ringleaders in the murderous affray. They were inspired from first to last with the intent to kill Plommer he added, the blow administered by one of them undoubtedly did kill him and they were both equally guilty.

Possibly the jury might have found some of the other men guilty of murder, but there was not a shadow of material upon which it could reasonably be said either that they ought not to have found these two men guilty or that the extremely careful summing-up of the Judge was in any way deficient. The summing-up was as favourable as it could be to the appellants.

Dismissing the appeals, the Lord Chief Justice said it was obvious that the jury, upon overwhelming evidence, had picked out the two men mainly responsible for this brutal murder. He emphasised the word "mainly". Whether they should have also convicted others was no concern of his court. As the Fowlers left the dock one of them shouted: "Others are guilty as well."

On the strength of the evidence, the Lord Chief Justice had little alternative but to dismiss the appeals and, in presenting them, Mr. Streatfeild could not have reasonably expected any other result.

Two main factors contributed towards the differentiation between the Fowlers and the other accused: (i) witnesses' statements that they saw one or other of the brothers with a bayonet and Lawrence actually jabbing Plommer with it, and (ii) the Fowlers' own evidence at both Police Court and Assizes that only themselves and none of the other prisoners were involved. Many of those following the case felt that by saying this the Fowlers virtually invited the jury to find only themselves guilty of murder.

Mr. Streatfeild's contention that, in dealing with common intent, the Judge differentiated between Wills, Stewart and Harker, whereas he had not between the Fowlers, was inaccurate. Mr. Justice Finlay had indeed coupled the two brothers together but there was some evidence of them acting together - with the common intent of avenging Wilfred's injuries of the previous night by finding Plommer and "doing him in." They approached him together at Norfolk Bridge and both chased him as he retreated towards his home, Lawrence shouting: "Let's finish the Scotch ----."

With regard to the other three men, the Judge did not in fact make any differentiation between them on the question of intent. He stated quite clearly that the distinction he drew between their sentences was in view of Harker's previous good character.

Surprisingly, Mr. Streatfeild does not appear to have raised the matter of the missing murder weapon, allegedly the bayonet stated by witnesses to have been in the Fowlers' possession. Despite an intensive search of the Attercliffe district, including the Fire Brigade using an electro-magnet to scan the River Don from a rowing boat, the weapon which killed William Plommer was never found.

It is surprising that a greater importance was not attached to this by the defence at the trial for if, between the incident with Plommer and their confrontation with P. C. Hogan on the chip shop steps, the Fowlers had the opportunity to dispose of a bayonet, a question that must be asked is why had they not also disposed of the poker and razor found on them by the police officer?

Evidently, another person present at the scene of the affray removed the weapon, as it is extremely doubtful that either of the Fowlers could have disposed of it in such a way that it would never be found, between Norfolk Bridge and the chip shop steps in Princess Street - a distance of barely fifty yards - with all eyes on them. None of the witnesses who identified Lawrence and Wilfred Fowler as being in possession of the bayonet claimed to have seen them dispose of it, so, what became of it? The defence seem to have been content to allow its disappearance to remain a mystery. Had the question been explored, however, perhaps the Fowlers' explanation for the poker and razor - that they took them from Plommer - might have been given greater credibility.

As most of the evidence in the case was based on identification by witnesses, and both the Fowlers, Wills, Stewart, and Harker were convicted on the strength of this, it is interesting to note details of the various identification parades held by the police, as given in evidence at the Police Court hearing.

In Wilfred Fowler's case 10 people failed to identify him; 12 failed to identify Lawrence; 18 failed in regard to George Wills and only 4 succeeded; 20 failed to identify Frederick Goddard and only one succeeded. Nine people identified Sam Garvin while eight failed. In the case of Robert Garvin 11 people failed to identify him; 10 failed over Amos Stewart, and 27 over William Wild who, like Frederick Goddard, was acquitted of the charge. As may be gleaned from this information, the standards relating to the acceptability of identification evidence in the courts were not so high as they are today.

The day after the Fowlers' appeals were dismissed, the murdered man's widow received an anonymous threatening letter at her home in Princess Street. The letter said that Mrs. Plommer had "sworn the Fowlers lives away," as she knew her husband had a poker. It asked was she "ready to meet her doom" as she was to be "done in." The authors threatened that when they had "done T. and D. in" they would "swing like Kings" for them. The letter, which arrived in the post, was immediately handed to the police. "T. and D." were presumed to be Thompson and Day, both of whom were alleged to have been friends of William Plommer and who had given prosecution evidence against Sam Garvin. Three days later, on August 22nd, Mrs. Plommer received a second anonymous letter, the author claiming that he knew the identity of the first writer. By this time Mrs. Plommer and her children were receiving police protection.

However, anonymous letters were not confined to the victim's family. On August 24th, Mrs. Wilfred Fowler also received an illiterate note through the post. Scrawled in pencil on cheap paper the letter was abusive and finished by saying "might write later I here anything."

With their appeals dismissed, Lawrence and Wilfed Fowler knew that time was running out. On Thursday, August 20th they were visited by their parents and two of their sisters. The brothers were part of a family of nine children, five sons and four daughters. One of their sisters said after visiting them that both were feeling their position keenly and had very little to say. They were, she said, still hopeful of a reprieve.

On August 23rd, after taking statements from several people in the Attercliffe district, Mr. J. W. Fenoughty sent a letter to the Home Office enclosing new evidence on behalf of Lawrence Fowler. Two days later he wrote again, urging the Home Secretary to advise His Majesty, King George V to grant a reprieve. On Saturday, August 29th Wilfred's wife, daughter and baby visited him in Armley. Nothing had been heard regarding Mr. Fenoughty's pleas but Mrs. Fowler said, after leaving the prison, that her husband was hopeful that his comparatively young age and the fact that he had two young children might tell in his favour.

On September 1st came the reply from the Home Office that Lawrence and Wilfred Fowler had been dreading. Addressed to Mr. J. W. Fenoughty and dated 31st August 1925 it read:

Sir,

With reference to your letters of the 23rd and 25th inst. on behalf of Lawrence Fowler, now under sentence of death, I am directed by the Secretary of State to inform you that he has given careful consideration to all the circumstances of the case, and I am to express to you his regret that he has failed to discover any grounds which would justify him in advising his Majesty to interfere with the due course of the Law.

The letter was signed by the Under Secretary of State for Home Affairs.

No new evidence was offered to the Home Secretary on behalf of Wilfred Fowler.

On Wednesday, September 2nd a notice of forthcoming executions was posted up outside Armley Prison stating that Wilfred Fowler would be executed the following day and Lawrence the day after. Shortly after the notice was posted Mrs. Wilfred Fowler visited her husband for the last time. She found him very weak and told the *Sheffield Mail*: "My little daughter climbed on his back but he was unable to bear her weight for very long. He told me to be brave and to try to forget." Despite this Mrs. Fowler still refused to give up hope. "The eleventh hour has not yet come," she told the newspaper reporter. Wilfred was lodged with three warders and spent a great deal of time playing cards. It was reported he was allowed to smoke and to have anything he asked for in the way of food and drink.

Mrs. Fowler's desperate optimism proved to no avail. At 9 a.m. on Thursday, September 3rd her husband, Wilfred, took the twenty-five yard walk from the condemned cell to the scaffold. Hanged alongside him in a shed normally used to garage the prison van was a Rotherham iron worker, convicted of murdering a picture palace attendant.

The crowd, which had begun to gather outside the prison an hour earlier, numbered around three hundred by nine o'clock. Several Sheffield men were present and a man from Horncastle who claimed to have stood in exactly the same spot when the notorious burglar and murderer, Charlie Peace, was executed on Shrove Tuesday, 1879. A number of uniformed and plain-clothes police were in the vicinity but the crowd was undemonstrative, content to speculate as to why the brothers should be hanged on different days.

About the time it was supposed the executions were taking place a hush fell over the crowd. No bell was tolled and the prison clock was not allowed to strike, presumably in consideration for Lawrence Fowler. The official notice of execution, which was carried out by Pierrpoint, the public hangman, was posted outside the prison at 9.15 a.m.

From the moment he was sentenced, Lawrence Fowler repeatedly protested his innocence and visitors noticed that he was becoming haggard and weak as the strain increasingly told on him. At nine o'clock on Thursday, when his brother was hanged, he collapsed in his cell and remained in a state of acute distress. Later in the day it was reported that Wilfred had made a last minute statement before his execution, confessing to the murder of Plommer and exonerating Lawrence from all blame. Immediately, Mr. J.W. Fenoughty addressed a lengthy communication to the Home Secretary, asking him to reconsider his decision with regard to Lawrence Fowler, but Sir William Joynson-Hicks refused to accept Wilfred's confession. "I know of no such statement," he said, adding: "There has been nothing to justify interference with the carrying out of the sentence."

The same afternoon, Lawrence's parents, wife, and several other relatives paid their final visit. Earlier, interviewed by the *Sheffield Daily Telegraph*, his wife said: "It is not fair. His brother Wilfred has confessed that he did it ." In a very sad and emotional letter to his eight year old daughter, Lawrence wrote: "You must always remember your daddy was innocent. Never let it worry you at any time as your mother will tell you when you begin to understand more fully."

Twenty four hours after his brother, on Friday, September 4th, Lawrence Fowler walked, unaided, to the Armley scaffold. When the passing bell was heard outside the prison all heads were bared and a number of woman wept. Many friends of the doomed man had travelled from Sheffield to be present. Once again the police were much in evidence but there was no sign of trouble. At 9.10 a.m. the official notice was posted and the crowd melted away.

So the Fowler brothers were executed in the name of justice. But was it justice? Were they responsible for William Plommer's fatal wounds? While such questions will never be answered, it was, and still is among the few old enough to remember, a widely held belief that Lawrence and Wilfred Fowler were hanged for a crime they did not commit.

As to who did kill Plommer, rumours abound to this day. The facts concerning Sam Garvin's timely departure from Norfolk Bridge have been suitably blurred by time and the theory that, after killing Plommer himself, he hopped on a tram and went to the Wicker, where, to establish an alibi, he jumped off the tram and assaulted the first man he saw, is now a popular, if utterly apocryphal, piece of local folklore.

At the time of the trial, the demeanour of George Wills and Amos Stewart when they came up for sentence was regarded in some quarters as being significant. What had Wills got to smile about as he entered the dock and why did Stewart, having been sentenced to ten years penal servitude, bow and thank the Judge? Both had maintained that they took no part in the incident with Plommer, yet their reactions were far removed from what one might expect of innocent parties wrongly convicted of manslaughter. It is possible that they were simply intent on continuing their air of nonchalant bravado to the very last.

On the other hand there is the question of Wilfred Fowler's last minute confession. Was it genuine, or was it the gesture of a man who knew he himself was doomed trying to save his brother's life? After the fact that he had made the statement was reported in the local papers of the evening that he was hanged, nothing further was heard of Wilfred Fowler's confession and, as mentioned earlier, the Home Secretary, Sir William Joynson-Hicks, publicly stated that he did not know of its existence.

Sir William's resolute refusal to consider the strenuous appeals on behalf of the Fowler brothers was consistent with his avowed intention of stamping out gang terrorism. There had been a summer of trouble on the northern racecourses with disturbances at Newcastle, Haydock, Carlisle, Catterick, Ripon and Thirsk, as rival gangs fought for control of the various rackets associated with the Turf. On August 25th, a week before the Fowlers went to the scaffold, the Home Secretary announced that he intended to deal vigorously with the problem. He said that he was considering the possibility of a short Act of Parliament empowering magistrates to inflict heavier punishments, on police evidence alone, in cases of gang hooliganism. Sir William added that he had contacted the Sheffield authorities.

There was little sympathy for the Fowlers from the national press. On August 20th in a leading article, the *Daily Mail* commented: "We may hope that the dismissal by the Court of Criminal Appeal of the application for leave to appeal made by the brothers Fowler, found guilty of the murder of a man in Sheffield in brutal circumstances, will have the effect of striking fear into these gangs and of breaking them up."

One of the cruellest aspects of the Fowlers' case was that they were not allowed to die together. It was reported that, on learning that his brother was to be executed the day before him, Lawrence asked to be hanged alongside him. Since another man was hanged alongside Wilfred Fowler there would appear to be no practical reasons why Lawrence's wish could not be granted. No doubt Sir William Joynson-Hicks considered even such small mercy inexpedient to his anti-gang campaign.

10. Head Men Fall

On Saturday, August 1st, 1925, the day after he was acquitted of being concerned in the Plommer murder, Sam Garvin once again stood in the dock at Leeds Assizes before Mr. Justice Finlay.

Garvin, who described himself as an agent, was charged with wounding Harry Rippon on April 27th. His brother, Robert Henry Garvin, faced a similar charge. Both men pleaded not guilty.

Mr. L.R. Lipsett appeared for the prosecution and Mr. J.W. Jardine once again represented the Garvins.

Opening the case, Mr. Lipsett explained that the charge was in reference to an attack on Rippon at the Bull and Oak public house, Sheffield. At about 7.45 p.m. on April 27th, he said, Samuel Garvin went into the house of Charlotte Thompson in Princess Street, stooped down to kiss Mrs. Thompson's little child, and as he did so she noticed a razor in his pocket. While he was there Bob Garvin entered and said: "Come along Sam." Both then left the house.

A few minutes later they were seen with two men, Wild and Kidnew, by Harry Pollard. To Pollard someone said: "Let's get on a car. We'll go to the Bull and Oak and do Murphy in." The four men then got on the tram. At the Bull and Oak they looked around the concert room and then left. Within a very short space of time after their departure, a scream was heard outside the public house. Some of those present rushed out and Rippon was found in a dazed condition. He was taken to the Bull and Oak and ultimately to the Royal Infirmary, where he was found to be suffering from severe injuries to the head.

Rippon's story, said Mr. Lipsett, was that he was in the Wicker, walking towards the Bull and Oak to fulfil a singing engagement, when the prisoners approached him. Rippon saw Samuel Garvin with a razor in his hand. Garvin went up to him and slashed at him with it, but Rippon dodged aside and put up his hand, escaping serious injury but receiving a cut on his hand. Bob Garvin then joined in the assault and attacked Rippon with something like a life-preserver. He struck Rippon on the back of the head.

Rippon, stated counsel, had no doubt whatever as to who the two men who attacked him were. At the Infirmary he was found to be suffering from a lot of bruises and a jagged scalp wound 1½ inches in length. Both prisoners were arrested and both said: "I know nothing about it."

The first witness for the prosecution was Mrs. Charlotte Thompson of 11-8, Princess Street who gave evidence regarding Samuel Garvin's conversation with her husband. She stated that she saw Garvin stoop down to kiss her little boy and noticed that his hand was bandaged in a khaki handkerchief. In his pocket she saw the steel top of a razor. Cross-examined by Mr. Jardine, she described how Sam Garvin was dressed and denied that his handkerchief was a red one.

Harry Pollard related how, standing in Attercliffe Road at about 8p.m., he was approached by four men, one of whom was Sam Garvin. They affirmed their intention of "doing in" Plommer, 'Spud' Murphy and two others.

After two more witnesses had described being in the Bull and Oak, seeing four men enter and then leave, and hearing screams shortly afterwards, Harry Rippon gave evidence. He said he was approaching the Bull and Oak just after 8p.m. when he saw the prisoners emerging from the hotel about ten yards ahead. They came towards him and Sam Garvin, whom he had known for fifteen years, slashed at him with a razor. He saw the razor quite distinctly. Bob Garvin then struck him on the head with what appeared to be a life preserver. He received a number of blows afterwards. Cross-examined, Rippon denied that he had ever had any quarrel with Sam Garvin or that he was connected with Plommer or Whitham.

Following evidence from several more witnesses, including a man who was standing opposite the Bull and Oak and said he actually saw the Garvins assault Rippon, Mr. Jardine addressed the jury. He said that he did not want to disguise the fact that the two defendants had been before the court charged with murder and acquitted. He invited their serious consideration on behalf of each of the men separately. His case was that the two men had separated and both were in different places at the time of the alleged occurrence. Both men would say that they did not go to the Bull and Oak.

In evidence, that was exactly what both men did say. Sam Garvin gave his customary performance in the witness box, denying any knowledge of Rippon's injuries and replying to all Mr. Lipsett's questions in cross-examination with "I don't know" or "I have no idea." He strongly denied being in the Bull and Oak.

William Wild said that he was with the Garvins and Kidnew in Princess Street. He got on the car to Millhouses with them at Norfolk Bridge at ten minutes to eight. He did not hear Kidnew say: "Let's go to the Bull and Oak and 'do' Murphy." In reply to questions by Mr. Lipsett, Wild admitted convictions for assault, being drunk and disorderly, and street betting.

Frank Kidnew, like Wild, giving evidence on behalf of the Garvins, recounted a similar story regarding their movements on the night in question. He denied "looking for some fighting men" but admitted convictions for assaulting a policeman and assaulting two women.

Robert Garvin said that he alighted from the tram in the city centre and went directly to the Prince of Wales Hotel, St. Philips Road, arriving at 8.10 p.m. He denied the evidence of the hotel's licensee who had placed the time of Garvin's arrival at 8.30 p.m. The licensee, Charles Wall, had described Garvin as being in an excitable condition. He had said Garvin told him he had "had a row" with someone called Rippon in the Wicker and that he had struck him. Cross-examined, Bob Garvin described the licensee's evidence as "pure invention." Counsel: "Why should the licensee say this if it is untrue?" Garvin: "I don't know. All I can say is Wall is a very frightened man." Counsel: "Is there any reason why Rippon should be mistaken?" Garvin: "There have been a lot of things in Sheffield lately. There have been summonses for nothing. There are a few of them in Sheffield who are delighted to get us summoned."

The Judge: "To get you summoned?"

Garvin: "Yes. They would put any tale out to do us."

In his summing-up, Mr. Justice Finlay said he would be very brief as the case was a very simple one, and the evidence lay within a small compass. The jury, who did not retire, were only one minute considering their verdict. Both Samuel and Robert Henry Garvin were found guilty of wounding Harry Rippon.

After the verdict, Detective Sergeant Flint was called to make a statement regarding Sam Garvin, whom he said he had known personally for thirteen years. Describing Garvin's activities on the race tracks, and the type of company he kept, Det. Sgt. Flint said that for some time Garvin had been strongly suspected of being a receiver of stolen property. He confirmed that since the gang feud started, in early 1923, he had been the leader and mastermind of the gang known as the 'Garvin Gang'. This title had become more common as the Park Brigade extended their horizons beyond their home district. Det. Sgt. Flint added that, although Garvin had not been convicted of any assault committed by his gang, it was well known that he had sometimes been in the near vicinity when such assaults occurred. Garvin, he said, was a very dangerous man and he considered him to be one of the cleverest criminals in Sheffield.

"You are as bad as they are," exclaimed a woman from the public gallery. She was immediately removed from the court.

In respect of Robert Garvin, Det. Sgt. Flint said that he was employed for twelve years at Hadfields, a steel firm, prior to the war, and bore a good character. Since the war he had associated with his brother. "And his downfall," continued the detective, "is purely the result of the bad influence of his brother, Sam." Robert Garvin had two previous convictions, for street betting and assault.

Passing sentence, the Judge told Sam Garvin: "You have been found guilty of unlawful wounding, and on evidence which must carry conviction with everyone. Sam Garvin, you have a bad record. I would almost say a very bad record, and little or rather nothing that is good can be said of you. I take a serious view of this crime. It is a most dangerous and most intolerable thing that men like you should be going about a town like Sheffield with razors and other weapons. It is a thing which cannot be tolerated for one minute and I think it is my duty to pass a very substantial sentence." He then sentenced Garvin to twenty-one months hard labour.

To Robert Garvin, his Lordship said: "I am willing to believe you have been led away by your brother and therefore I can take a more lenient view of your case." He sentenced him to nine months hard labour.

So 'King' Garvin, indeed a very dangerous man, was at last convicted. But in the circumstances, his sentence, far from being the very substantial one promised by Mr. Justice Finlay, was surprisingly light. On such a serious charge, with his record, which the Judge rightly described as very bad, Garvin might well have considered himself fortunate to receive only twenty-one months. Perhaps the Sheffield police tempered any disappointment they might have felt at the lightness of the sentence with the consolation that Garvin was at least convicted. During the previous two years he had been charged on five separate occasions. Each time he had been acquitted.

While September 1st, 1925, was a momentous day for Sam Garvin, it was not uneventful for his erstwhile arch-rival, George Mooney. Since being hounded out of Sheffield by Garvin's mob in early 1924, Mooney had stayed out of trouble and remained at a safe distance from the gang scene. Although he was back in the city by the beginning of 1925, when opposition to Garvin was undergoing a revival through a number of his old associates, Mooney took no part. Ironically, the re-formed organisation was still referred to by both police and public as the Mooney Gang.

At the same time that Garvin was facing his second trial of the week in Leeds, Mooney was attending pony races at Worksop, Notts. Returning in the early evening, he climbed into a railway carriage at Worksop station to be greeted by the very man from whom he had taken control of the Sky Edge tossing ring six years earlier, William Cowan. Cowan, who had been pursuing his business as a bookmaker at the pony races, was accompanied by two assistants. Mooney had with him another man. William Cowan and George Mooney subsequently told differing versions regarding what happened next, but before they had been travelling many minutes a fierce fight broke out between them, the train was forced to halt, and Cowan found himself with three fractured ribs and minus part of an ear.

The first indication the train guard had of the trouble was the sound of a window being smashed and then the communication cord was pulled. Whoever pulled it evidently wished to remain anonymous for he or she did so from the privacy of the lavatory. As passengers piled onto the track the guard and driver entered the carriage and found Cowan lying bleeding on the floor. A window opposite him was broken.

When the train arrived at Sheffield Victoria an ambulance was waiting. Questioned by railway police as to what had happened, Cowan refused to say. His face was covered in blood and he appeared in considerable agony, groaning "Oh my back, oh my back." However, when one of the men accompanying him named Mooney as the assailant, Cowan became very angry and exclaimed: "What did you tell him that for?" At the Royal Infirmary, where he was detained for several days, he adamantly refused to make a statement.

Nearly four weeks after the incident, at 8 a.m. on Wednesday, August 26th, George Mooney was arrested in Leeds and taken to Rotherham Borough Court. Charged with inflicting grievous bodily harm on William Cowan by biting his ear and fracturing three of his ribs, Mooney replied: "I never bit his ear." Said by Supt. Horton of Sheffield police to be a man who never worked and not a safe subject to be on bail, Mooney said he could prove he had work to go to and he had a wife and six children to support. He was remanded in custody.

On September 8th, when the case was resumed, Mooney was committed for trial at West Riding Quarter Sessions. Pleading not guilty, he said Cowan had said "You are getting very independent, Mooney," and struck him. He considered himself a lucky man because if he had not struggled he would have been pushed through the train window.

Replying to Supt. Horton, regarding his friends who accompanied him to race meetings, Mooney said: "I have no friends."

Mr. Harry Morris, applying for bail, said it was unfortunate that the accused's name was George Mooney. If that had not been his name, he would not be standing in the dock, Mr. Morris added rather pointlessly. Mooney had not been in prison since the war and it was a case of "give a dog a bad name." They could not get away from the fact that the prisoner's name was George Mooney, a name known to every man, woman and child in the district, and a name that conjured up all sorts of visions. Mr. Morris pleaded successfully; Mooney was bailed in the sum of £50 plus two sureties of £25.

At the West Riding Quarter Sessions, Wakefield, on October 21st, the conflicting accounts of what happened on the Worksop - Sheffield train were heard. Mr. G.H. B. Streatfeild who, two months earlier had defended the Fowler brothers, opened the case for the prosecution by stating that the victim was an unwilling witness and came under sub-poena. He alleged that Cowan, who was fifty-five years old, twenty years Mooney's senior, was sitting in the railway carriage with two men, Kennan and Woodhouse, when Mooney entered. Cowan said: "How do you do, George. Are you coming to sit down here?" Mooney replied: "I'm going to sit where I like." Cowan said: "What is the matter George?" and received a blow in the face which knocked him out of his seat, onto the floor. There was a scuffle between them and a window was broken. Witnesses said Mooney climbed onto a table and jumped on Cowan's back, kicking him in the side several times. The heads of the two men were seen close together on the floor and someone shouted "Stop him, he's biting off his ear." Cowan's ear was bleeding and when the two men separated, as the train ground to a halt, both their faces were covered in blood.

Mooney's version of the incident was quite different. He said that when he got into the carriage he did not want anything to do with anyone. Cowan said to him: "You are very independent, aren't you?" adding, "Garvin hasn't been topped yet." Mooney asked him what he meant by that and Cowan said "You ---- big Mooney" and struck him in the face. Woodhouse joined in the fight against him saying: "Throw him through the window," and Mooney said he had to fight for his life. "I fought like a tiger, the best way I could," he said. He emphatically denied biting Cowan's ear and said he could not have kicked him as it was impossible in the restricted space of the compartment.

Regarding Woodhouse's alleged suggestion to throw Mooney through the window, Cowan said Woodhouse would not dare say such a thing to George Mooney.

After the jury had found Mooney guilty, Det. Insp. Shaw gave evidence of his record. He said that Mooney had forty-three previous convictions - a lot of them for assault, also for unlawful wounding, loitering, breach of the peace, drunkenness and other offences. He was a notorious bad character and, until it was broken up, was head of the Mooney Gang. The Inspector appears to have omitted ten of Mooney's convictions for, on January 9th 1924, Mooney admitted in cross-examination by Mr. Irwin Mitchell to fifty-three convictions. Whatever his previous record, he was sentenced to nine months hard labour for inflicting grievous bodily harm on William Cowan.

Garvin and Mooney, probably the two most familiar names in Sheffield at the time, were not the only prominent gangmen to begin lengthy spells of incarceration during the latter half of 1925.

On July 11th, Albert Foster, a principal in the revival of Mooney's old gang, appeared at Sheffield Quarter Sessions charged with the wounding of George Butler. The assault, in retaliation for an attack on George Newbould on March 1st., occurred on March 2nd outside the Drill Hall, where Sam Garvin was promoting a boxing show. Butler, a close friend of Wilfred Fowler and a member of the Garvin Gang, received a fractured skull, caused, it was alleged, by an iron bar. Foster denied the charge, saying he had intended to go to the boxing show but heard there was a disturbance and went instead to the Truro Tavern, where Peter Winsey, George Wheywell and Tom Armstrong were present.

The Recorder: "How do you become a member of these gangs?" Foster: "Well sir, I have known these men for years, from being a boy. As a matter of fact we have been boys together."

He went on to say that he did not know there were any gangs, as the Mooney Gang had broken up. He added: "We all meet together and go to theatres and fights." Despite Foster's three cronies going into the witness box and stating on oath that he did not go to the Drill Hall on the said night and did not attack Butler, the jury found him guilty. Sentencing him, the Recorder, Mr. W.J. Waugh, K.C., issued a stern warning. "I give notice to these gangs," he said, "that if they won't stop it, it will be penal servitude next tune. It is intolerable, in my opinion, that we should have Sheffield disturbed by these two rival gangs." Albert Foster was sentenced to 18 months hard labour.

In the course of the Foster trial, the Recorder commented on a Sunday newspaper article he had read in which it was suggested that everyone in Sheffield lived in fear of the gangs and even the magistrates were afraid to commit them. The Recorder said he hoped that was not the case. Later the same day, Peter Winsey went into the Italian Club, Scotland Street, with a man known as 'Cosh' Burns. In the club, playing bagatelle, was sixty year old Patrick Mooney, uncle to George, and a man who Winsey- brought up by Mooney's family after his own mother died - knew well. For no apparent reason, except that as he did so he exclaimed: "You are as bad as big Mooney," Winsey went up to the older man and struck him on the head with a heavy instrument. Two days later Patrick Mooney woke up in the Royal Infirmary with a suspected fractured skull and a jagged wound on his head. A week after the assault Winsey appeared before magistrates in the police court on a charge reduced from unlawful wounding to assault and was sentenced to two months hard labour. He had thirty previous convictions.

11. The Flying Squad

The Special Duties Squad, as it was officially titled, came into being on May 1st, 1925. It was formed four days after the Plommer murder, following Home Office instructions to the Sheffield authorities that urgent measures must be taken to suppress the gangs. There were four men in the initial squad, each selected because of a proven ability to hold his own in a dangerous situation and because of previous single-handed encounters with the gangs.

Detective Sergeant William Robinson, fifteen years a police officer and an ex-Coldstream Guardsman, led the squad. P.C. Walter Loxley, a 6ft.2in., 19 stone 8lbs. giant, whose experience in Central Division had brought him into many skirmishes with the gangmen, was an automatic choice. During the war P.C. Loxley had served in France with the Royal Garrison Artillery, where his enormous strength earned him the reputation of champion shell-carrier of his battalion. Slightly shorter than Loxley, but no less effective, was ex-heavyweight boxer, P.C. Herbert Lunn. Jerry Lunn, as he was always known, joined the police force in 1912, a year earlier than Loxley, and also served in the R.G.A. in France. At Bullecourt in 1917 Sgt. Lunn was awarded the Military Medal for keeping communications intact and rescuing wounded under heavy shell fire. The fourth member of the squad was P.C. Jack Farrily, another hardman well versed in the techniques of rough-house and back-alley brawling.

The squad's instructions were simple. Transferred to plain-clothes duty they were given a free hand to go where they liked in the city. Their task was solely to suppress the gangs and they were not restricted by any hard-and-fast rules as to how they did it. Carrying the war into the enemy's camp, they would go to any public house where they knew gangmen had collected. Calling over the licensee and pointing out the undesirables, they would suggest that he asked them to leave. Either the gangmen would do so, or they would show fight. If they elected to fight, the squad were only too happy to accommodate them. The razors and life-preservers much favoured by the gangs were countered by fists, boots and regulation truncheons. The squad's habit of suddenly materialising wherever trouble was expected soon earned them the popular title of the Flying Squad and in a very short time their arrival in any tap room or saloon heralded the swift departure of gangmen.

The strong arm tactics of the Flying Squad aroused considerable controversy and came in for some heavy criticism by defence solicitors. One incident that received national, as well as local, publicity occurred at the Red House, Solly Street on September 14th, 1925. After a lunchtime melee involving members of the revived Mooney Gang and P.C.s Loxley, Lunn and Farrily, George Wheywell was later charged with assaulting P.C. Lunn in the execution of his duty. Wheywell cross-summonsed all three constables for assault.

On Monday, September 21st, P.C.s Loxley, Lunn and Farrily sat in the second row of the dock at Sheffield Police Court. In front of them sat twenty-seven year old Wheywell. The two cases were heard simultaneously.

Mr. G.H. Banwell, prosecuting Wheywell, said the incidents occurred about 1.30 p.m. after Wheywell and several associates, popularly referred to as the Mooney Gang, entered the Red House. The landlord, Horace Clark, telephoned the police and the three constables arrived to find ten men, eight of whom they knew. Five went quietly when ordered out, but the other five - Wheywell, Harry Rippon, Peter Winsey, Herbert 'Cosh' Burns and another man objected. Wheywell, alleged Mr. Banwell, said: "Let's all have a go together." As he said it, he struck P.C. Lunn and it was seen that there was something glittering in his hand. P.C. Lunn drew his truncheon and hit Wheywell with his fist. P.C. Loxley also hit him. Wheywell's friends, said the solicitor, were apparently not prepared to go to such lengths, and left quietly. Mr. Banwell described the cross summons as "an attempt to throw dust in the eyes of the court."

Mr. Harry Morris, representing Wheywell, asked P.C. Lunn: "What Wheywell has done to you, you paid back at 4,000 per cent interest?" P.C. Lunn replied: "I did not look at it like that. I only did my duty, knowing the man as I do." Further questioned, he said: "These men have been ganging together. No licensees in Sheffield want them. They will only serve them through fear. We have had enough of gangs."

Mr. Banwell asked P.C. Loxley: "Did you use a cosher?"

P.C. Loxley: "No. I never use anything like that."

Mr. Banwell: "Are you one of the Flying Squad?"

P.C. Loxley: "Yes."

Mr. Banwell: "And your main duty is that of a sort of gang disturbance queller?"

P.C. Loxley: "Yes, principally."

Mr. Banwell: "Who refers to you as the Flying Squad?"

P.C. Loxley: "Different classes of people. I have not heard Wheywell use the expression. It is used by his mob."

Mr. Morris said the police were suggesting that the summonses against the three officers were in retaliation but, in fact, it was the reverse - Wheywell got his summons in first. "This case is in the nature of a test case," he said. "There is a system of assaults on these men." He suggested that coshers were used by the police, the beauty of the weapon being that it could do a lot of damage without leaving much of a mark. The public might applaud that sort of thing. "But that would be the substitution of an alleged gang terrorism for terrorism by the police." He called the doctor who treated Wheywell at the Royal Infirmary. He said that when Wheywell was admitted he had four fairly severe bruises, was dazed, and looked as if he had had a fair knocking about.

In evidence, George Wheywell denied striking P. C. Lunn and claimed that, rather than saying "Let's all have a go together," he said: "Let us all go together," but was prevented from leaving the Red House by the officers. Cross-examined by Mr. Banwell, he described what the officers did as "a cowardly assault." Lunn struck him with something heavy - he could not say what - and Loxley "laced me on the back of the head for three solid minutes." He claimed that Loxley hit him "about a thousand times" and the landlady fainted. On another occasion the police had thrown a man through the panel of a door, he said. Wheywell said the whole incident took ten minutes and he never struck a blow.

Witnesses for the defence included Harry Rippon, Peter Winsey, Henry Dale and Herbert Burns. They each alleged that P.C. Loxley was standing by the door and hit them with a rubber cosh as they went out one by one. One witness said it was like a scene at the pictures. Peter Winsey said as he attempted to leave the pub P.C. Loxley kicked him in the ribs and coshed him. Several said they had been treated in a similar manner before.

Surprisingly, the licensee, Horace Clark, gave evidence for Wheywell, saying he had no objection to the men going in his house. He denied the prosecution's statement that he called the police and said: "The Sheffield Police have told me I must not serve these men. It is not through a complaint of mine." He added that the police did not give him names, they just told him not to serve any gangmen.

All three police officers and George Wheywell pleaded not guilty and were committed for trial at the Quarter Sessions.

At the opening of the Sessions, on October 22nd., the Recorder, Mr. W.J. Waugh, said, in his charge to the grand jury:
"If there is a prima facie case against the officers of having, not in the execution of their duty, assaulted this man - because it may be necessary for constables to use violence where people are disturbing the law and ought to be taken into custody - you ought to find a true bill.

On the other hand, if you are satisfied that at the time when this man Wheywell was assaulted, that he had begun by striking the officer, as, I believe, the evidence shows, and that what the officer did was after that, believing he was going to offer further violence, then you must find a true bill against Wheywell."

A true bill was returned against Wheywell, and no bill against the police officers, Loxley, Lunn and Farrily.

Wheywell, who told the court that he was not a member of any gang, was found guilty of assaulting P. C. Lunn in the execution of his duty. Det. Sgt. Burns, giving evidence of Wheywell's record and background, said Wheywell joined the Park Brigade when they decided to "out" the Mooney Gang. Referring to one of the earliest incidents in the gang feuds, he said that Wheywell took "an active part" in the slashing of Frank Kidnew at Sky Edge. He was a man who was "constantly in rows," said Sgt. Burns. The Recorder said the police must be protected from acts of violence and sentenced Wheywell to three months hard labour.

On November 25th, Mr. Harry Morris launched another strong attack on the Flying Squad when he defended two men charged with assaulting Sgt. Robinson in the Commercial Hotel, Button Lane, the previous evening.

The accused, George Sawdon and Thomas Carr, both appeared at the Police Court in a battered condition, having spent the previous night in police custody. Mr. Morris claimed the police had used a rubber cosh on them. Carr, who had his nose covered in sticking plaster, was alleged by his co-defendant to have been knocked unconscious by P.C. Loxley. Sgt. Robinson said the men's injuries "might have been caused by falling down the pub steps."

In evidence, Sawdon said he tried to run away when he saw Sgt Robinson with P. C. Farrily and Loxley, as he knew they were the Flying Squad and "knew what to expect." He was friendly, he said, with members of the Park gang, though not a member himself. He had been warned to stay away from licensed premises.

For the defence, Mr. Morris said: "I used to look upon this court as a court of law, but now it is more like a theatre for the staging of comic opera, and the police have a cheek to bring these men into this court today.

Look at that man's face. These men are charged here today because if they had got away last night the first thing they would have done would have been to issue a summons against the police.

Complaints have been made against this Flying Squad. It is all very well for Robinson to go into the box and pretend that he does not know why these men ran away. Robinson is as cute as a wagon load of monkeys.

The police have no right to tell anyone not to go into public houses. These men had disobeyed that warning and the police executed summary vengeance."

Mr. Morris's statement made little impression on the magistrates: Sawdon and Carr were each sentenced to two months hard labour.

On Christmas Eve, 1925, Thomas Windle, aged twenty six, was released from prison having served nine months hard labour for slashing a man with a razor on Easter Monday. His victim, Jack Fisher, who was reputed to eat only horse-meat, admitted at Windle's trial that he was known in the Park district as 'Iron Man' because he possessed "a bit of a punch." His punch, however, had little effect against Windle's razor. Assisted by two fellow members of the Junior Park Gang, after he had been thrashed by Fisher in a fair fight, Windle accosted the 'Iron Man' outside the Industry Inn, Park, dragged him to a street grate, and literally cut his throat over it. Fisher sustained a wound six inches long which required twelve stitches.

The Flying Squad, formed during Windle's absence, lost no time in letting him know of their existence upon his return. On Christmas Day, Windle was drinking in the Norfolk Arms, South Street, in the heart of the Park, when Sgt. Robinson approached him and said he wanted to speak to him outside. Outside the pub Windle found PCs Loxley, Lunn and Farrily, all in plain clothes, waiting for him. According to the police, Windle began to shout obscenities and, without provocation, struck P.C. Loxley in the eye with his fist. There was a violent struggle and Loxley fell on Windle before the four officers managed to handcuff him and take him to the police station. On the way he fell down twice.

Three days later, on December 28th, Windle appeared before the magistrates charged with assaulting P.C. Loxley. His head was completely swathed in bandages and he was wearing a blood-stained muffler.

Mr. Harry Morris, by this time making a name for himself as a leading opponent of the Flying Squad, addressed the bench: "Just look at the defendant. It is a case of the Flying Squad on the warpath again. It ought to be a charge of attempted suicide!"

Supt. Denton, prosecuting for the police, said to P.C. Loxley in examination: "It may be suggested that he received his injuries from the police."

P.C. Loxley: "No. It was through falling."

Mr. Morris: "It always is."

He added that it was a cock-and-bull story to suggest Windle had received his injuries through falling.

After a three day adjournment, during which Windle was remanded in custody, the case resumed with Sgt. Robinson being cross-examined by Mr. Morris. Robinson told the court that Windle was not creating a disturbance inside the pub and the reason he asked him outside was to warn him. He had heard that Windle had been to the police station to complain about not being served with drink.

Mr. Morris: "How did he get his black eyes?"

Sgt. Robinson: "I expect with falling down."

The magistrate then asked P.C. Loxley: "Have you done anything to make him rage like a mad bull in the street?"

P.C. Loxley: "No sir. That is his general conduct."

Mr. Morris: "That may be said of policemen, too. You have not got
    two black eyes."

Mr. Morris asked the magistrate if it was likely that, having left the pub voluntarily when requested, his client would go suddenly mad and strike one of the officers. Windle, he pointed out, had two black eyes and had had to be taken to hospital, but Loxley had not a scratch. It was extraordinary, he said, that in all the Flying Squad cases the defendants came in battered.

The presiding magistrate asked Mr. Morris: "Can you suggest any reason why the officers should assault this man?"

Mr. Morris: "Certainly. It is part of their duty to give these men a good
    tanning."

The Magistrates Clerk: "You are alleging that the police are instructed
    to assault these men. You ought not to say that unless you intend
    to prove it."

Mr. Morris: "How can I prove it against the evidence of these four
    officers?"

Thomas Windle, giving evidence, said he came out of the pub quietly. When he got out, Loxley struck him and Lunn bustled up shouting: "Handcuff him." On the way to the police station he was knocked down three times and struck with something like a whip from behind.

Alderman Knowles, chairman of the bench, told him: "We consider this is a very serious assault. The police must be protected in their onerous duties. You will be committed to prison for four months with hard labour."

As Thomas Windle had painfully discovered, the Flying Squad were a law unto themselves. Not waiting to quell trouble when it occurred, they combed the city looking for it, making the lives of 'undesirables' increasingly uncomfortable. They assumed the prerogative of judging who was 'undesirable' and thus who could or could not be served on licensed premises. They also introduced a rule which forbade gangmen to go about in groups of more than three. Transgressors knew what to expect.

Many years later, recalling the part he had played in smashing the gangs, Sgt. Robinson said:

"I remember best out of all the memories of those troubled years, the night we as good as challenged one of the mobs. I heard they were planning to get us because we had turned them out of a pub the night before.

I decided not to wait for them to come to us and I took Loxley and Lunn to a pub in West Bar.

Sure enough they were there, about a dozen of them. I knew we would have trouble so I told them I was going to search them. We found razors and coshes on them, but they knew we were out to settle it once and for all.

Then the fun started. It was quite a set-to and I shall never forget it. It was the only way to settle it and we three showed the twelve of them what for.

That's how we stopped it. We kept after them all the time. We harried them until we wore them down."

Unconstitutional such measures may have been, but it must be remembered that the Flying Squad had been created because normal methods of suppressing the prevalent lawlessness had failed. Home Office instructions were that the gangs must be crushed and certainly, in the few months since its inception, the squad had achieved great progress in that direction. Frequent bursts of violence resulting from long-standing grudges, intimidation of publicans and their customers, harassment of respectable citizens on the city streets - all these hitherto daily occurrences began to decline in the second half of 1925. The gangmen of Sheffield began to realise that tangling with the ubiquitous Flying Squad was an experience from which they could not hope to benefit.

12. Insidious Influences

By the autumn of 1925, the position of the Chief Constable, Lieut. Col. John Hall-Dalwood, was giving rise to much speculation in the city. Despite the spectacular success of the Flying Squad in the war against the gangs, there were strong rumours circulating that all was not well within the Sheffield Police Force. On October 15th, Colonel Hall-Dalwood's position was discussed at a meeting of the Watch Committee and two days later it was officially announced that he had been granted one month's leave of absence.

Alderman Cattell, chairman of the Watch Committee, would neither confirm nor deny that Hall-Dalwood was about to resign. "I can only say that the Chief Constable has not resigned. He has one month's leave of absence on account of ill-health," was all he would say. It was stated that the discussions which had taken place at the Watch Committee meeting would be made public at the next meeting of the City Council on November 9th.

On October 21st, four days after the Chief Constable began his month's leave, the *Sheffield Mail* in a leading article informed its readers: "The Sheffield Watch Committee is not yet at the end of its difficult problems affecting the discipline and good conduct of the City Police force. Whether the chairman, Alderman Cattell, will be in a position to make an adequate statement at the next City Council meeting on 9th November remains to be seen."

The article went on to say that several subordinate officers would be concerned in charges of withholding from the Chief Constable information which should have been known to him and to the Watch Committee. "These charges raise questions of loyalty as well as more personal issues of cliquism and favouritism," said the *Mail*. "The confidence of the rank and file in the impartiality of certain of their superior officers has been shaken. It can be regained only by changes affecting these officers."

The article continued: "Most of the responsible officers in the city police force are entirely immune from any association with the trouble. In fairness to them and to the general efficiency of the rank and file (which is unquestioned), the people of Sheffield will do well to discount heavily much irresponsible talk that is being circulated and to await the official statement, which will be made, no doubt, at the earliest possible moment."

An official statement regarding the internal problems of the police force was never made. Nor were the Watch Committee discussions regarding the position of the Chief Constable made public at the City Council meeting of November 9th. There is no mention of either issue in the minutes of Council meetings for the period.

On October 29th, Colonel Hall-Dalwood's leave was extended for a further three months. A certificate issued by the Senior Police Surgeon stated that the Chief Constable had not been in good health for some time and that he needed a complete rest and release from his official duties for a period.

Before his leave of absence expired, Colonel Hall-Dalwood resigned. His resignation, on health grounds, was accepted by the Watch Committee on January 7th, 1926. The previous evening, the local papers had released the news, which came as no surprise to anyone. As early as November 6th, only a week after speculation had been given added momentum by the extension of leave, *Police Review* and *Parade Gossip* commented:

"The responsibility of making a new appointment if Lieut. Col. Hall-Dalwood's early retirement is confirmed, as is now anticipated, will rest on the Watch Committee to be appointed this month. It is a duty not to be lightly regarded. The city of Sheffield needs a strong and alert man at the head of its Police Force, and there are reasons why the man appointed should not only possess first-rate police experience but should be free from all local ties."

Lieut. Col. Hall-Dalwood had been Chief Constable of Sheffield since 1912, succeeding Commander Charles Scott. A barrister-at-law, he had served in the Connaught Rangers for fifteen years and retained his military connections as Commander of the No. 6 Group West Riding Volunteers Regiment. Following service in the Royal Ulster Constabulary, he was for five years Deputy Chief Constable of Kent, and for five years before moving to Sheffield was Chief Constable of Leicester.

On March 31st, officers and men gathered at the Court House to do honour to their former Chief. Presenting him with a three valve wireless set, Chief Supt. Hollis said it was a spontaneous and free gift from members of the Force. When he rose to reply Colonel Hall-Dalwood was warmly received. He said his official career had terminated a little earlier than he had anticipated and he was extremely sorry to leave the service of the force:

"It has been my misfortune to become the victim of some insidious influence from outside, which for years has been working against me. At times during the war, and since, my anxieties have been seriously increased by this disquieting and horrible element which rendered one's position almost intolerable. Perhaps, after twenty-four years experience, my impression of what a chief officer of police should be may be wrong, but at any rate I knew what I wanted. I got it in efficiency. I am particularly satisfied with the results in spite of the evil attempts to undermine my authority.

The force is much under strength, as I have urged for the past thirteen years, but in spite of all this and other difficulties, the results that have been achieved, thanks to your willing co-operation and good feeling, are wonderful in a city so large, and in the part bristling with serious problems, greater perhaps than any other in the country.

I saw in a police paper a very mild suggestion that there was a recrudescence of drinking among the rank-and-file. I desire to publicly state that this is not a statement of fact. There is not a cleaner force in this respect today. Any case which has come to my notice has been adequately, but not vindictively, dealt with. No doubt statements of this kind were engineered for a purpose, but of proof there is none."

At this, Colonel Hall-Dalwood received loud applause. He ended by wishing his successor well and added that if the force extended the same support that they had given to him, the new Chief Constable would be in the proud position of commanding one of the most efficient forces in the country. At the conclusion of the presentation the company gave three cheers for Colonel and Mrs. Hall-Dalwood and sang "For he's a jolly good fellow."

The references Colonel Hall-Dalwood made in the early part of his farewell speech were received by the press and public with great astonishment. What was the insidious influence from outside which for years had worked against him? Who or what were the disquieting and horrible elements? Who was behind the evil attempts to undermine his authority? Later the same evening a *Sheffield Mail* reporter sought answers to these questions but the former Chief Constable refused to elaborate. "I don't think it wise to say anymore," he told the reporter. The following night in their 'Under Vulcan's Eye' column, the *Mail* opined that Hall-Dalwood would have been wiser if he had said very much less. By not qualifying his observations, said 'Vulcan', he had placed members of the Watch Committee in an invidious position.

If the Watch Committee had been placed in an invidious position, their chairman, Alderman Cattell was not going to admit it. When asked if he had anything to say on the matter he replied, predictably, "No, I have not."

However, Sir William Clegg, leader of the ruling Citizen's Party in the City Council, did express an opinion. "I read the statements of Colonel Hall-Dalwood with a considerable amount of surprise," he said, "and undoubtedly, things would have been decidedly better had the words never been uttered. If there is any truth in them, it was his duty to communicate the facts to those in authority, so that they might have been properly investigated at the time. It is rather late now to make any suggestion that he was being adversely and unfairly criticised."

The *Sheffield Daily Telegraph* publicly demanded an explanation from the former Chief Constable. Their 'Current Topics' column of April 3rd read:

"We may perhaps venture to suggest that Colonel Hall-Dalwood should go a little more into detail regarding the 'insidious influence from outside' which he claims has for years been working against him. It seems to us a public duty he owes to Sheffield and its citizens.

Especially should we like to know whether the disquieting and horrible element still exists, and whether it is likely to continue to interfere with the work of the police.

It is the future that interests us more than the past, and if Colonel Hall-Dalwood would be a little more explicit he might perhaps enable us to safeguard the police force against influences which he declares seriously increased his own anxieties and rendered his position almost intolerable."

In spite of all the calls upon him, Colonel Hall-Dalwood never made a further statement. His reluctance - when coupled with his extended leave on health grounds - was seen by his critics as an opportunity to dismiss the retiring Chief Constable's farewell speech as the bitter outburst of a sick man. While this theory might have been convenient to some, there is little doubt that Hall-Dalwood's attack was aimed at those same people - the City Councillors and Watch Committee members who for years had refused his appeals for extra manpower, and the local magistrates whose failure to support the police had led to the situation which, three years earlier, Hall-Dalwood had prophecied to the *Sheffield Daily Telegraph*. That warning had been ignored, as had an opinion he expressed in an interview with the *Yorkshire Post* in April 1925 when he stressed yet again that the punishments meted out by both judges and magistrates in cases of gang violence were too lenient to act as a deterrent. Hall-Dalwood stated that he believed the power to use the 'cat' should be extended to cases of wounding such as those emanating from the gang troubles.

The full reasons for Lieut. Col. Hall-Dalwood's resignation will never be known but, ironically, the circumstances surrounding his departure bore great similarity to those preceding his appointment in 1912. Like Hall-Dalwood, his predecessor, Commander Charles

Scott, had been Chief Constable of Sheffield for thirteen years and, like Hall-Dalwood, he too had fallen foul of the Watch Committee. Scott was obliged to resign following an inquiry into the discipline of the City Force, when it was alleged that certain officers had been found in the Police Club on a Sunday, in contravention of regulations. At the same inquiry a charge of drunkenness in the street was made against a chief inspector. Drinking was a serious problem within the force at this time, which might explain Hall-Dalwood's anxiety to dispel rumours that there had been a resurgence. When Commander Scott died, a month after Hall-Dalwood retired in 1926, the *Sheffield Mail* commented:

"The internal troubles of the Sheffield Police Force weighed on him heavily during his last days here." The same epitaph might well have befitted Lieut. Col. John Hall-Dalwood.

13. Captain Sillitoe

Captain P.J. Sillitoe took up his duties as Chief Constable of Sheffield on May 1st, 1926, the first day of the General Strike. It was estimated that 75,000 men were out in the city, mostly from the coal and steel industries and transport services. There was no interference with the Post Office, gas or electric supplies, but no trams or buses ran. While a large crowd gathered at the Town Hall to volunteer for emergency services, another was occupied outside a public house in King Street, preventing beer from being delivered by a non-unionist driver. The police, fully engaged in controlling the rallies and strike meetings, were assisted by special constables, hastily enrolled under the Government Volunteer Scheme. The *Sheffield Daily Telegraph*, published in abbreviated form, reported that there was very little disorder in the city but the city authorities were taking no chances. By May 10th they had enrolled 7,200 special constables, over ten times the regular force.

Capt. Sillitoe was selected out of fifty-three applicants for the post, which carried a salary of £1,000 per year, rising to £1,250. Thirty-eight years old and with only three years police service in England, many doubted whether Sillitoe had either the maturity or experience to handle the problems of a city so large as Sheffield, problems which had already despatched one Chief Constable to an early retirement. Sillitoe himself had no such qualms. Arriving from Beverley in the East Riding of Yorkshire, where the main function of the Chief Constable was to accompany the landed gentry on hunting and shooting expeditions, Sillitoe relished the challenge that a hotspot with Sheffield's reputation presented. Experience of the big city he might have lacked, but Percy Joseph Sillitoe had a thirst for work and adventure second to none.

Born in Tulse Hill, London, in 1888, as a boy he sang solo treble in St. Paul's Cathedral Choir. At nineteen, after a brief job with the Anglo-American Oil Company, he signed on as a trooper in the British South African Police and set sail for Salisbury in Southern Rhodesia. Commissioned as a sub-lieutenant in 1911, he achieved the rank of captain by the outbreak of war in 1914 and spent the first two years fighting the enemy in German East Africa. Fluent in Chinyanja, the native language, and in Swahili, Sillitoe was promoted to Assistant Political Officer and for the rest of the war was employed establishing British prestige among native tribes, many of whom had never seen a white man before. In 1920 he resigned from the British South African

Police and returned to England in order to marry before taking up an appointment with the Colonial Service in Tanganyika.

In 1922, at the age of thirty-four, Sillitoe left Africa for good and applied for the position of Chief Constable at Hull. Unsuccessful, he decided to read for the Bar and enrolled as a student at Gray's Inn, but the following year, urged by a friend, he applied for the post of Chief Constable of Chesterfield and, much to his surprise, was accepted. In 1925 he moved on to the East Riding where he was to spend an unhappy year and make himself unpopular with the gentry by prosecuting one of their number, alleging abusive language to a police constable. Frustrated by the lack of lawbreakers, apart from the occasional exception of a drunk or poacher, when Sillitoe saw the Sheffield post advertised he applied at once. "I felt sure that whatever else I might find in Sheffield, there would at least be plenty of hard work," he later wrote. Capt. Sillitoe was not disappointed.

The story of how Sillitoe broke up the Sheffield gangs has, over the years, been recounted many times in newspapers and magazines. To the popular press he was 'Britain's Ace Gang Buster', the man who, having smashed the Mooney and Garvin mobs, went north to Glasgow and did the same with the Billy Boys and Norman Conks and who, in 1933, was invited to Chicago to discuss the gang problems of that city with J. Edgar Hoover. Such is the extent of the Sillitoe legend, which began in Sheffield and continued until after he retired as Director General of MI5 in 1953, that he alone has been widely credited with the suppression of the gangs - while Hall-Dalwood's part has been ignored. Perhaps the greatest misconception is that it was Sillitoe and not Hall-Dalwood who was responsible for the formation of the Flying Squad, an impression Sillitoe did nothing to rectify in his autobiography, *Cloak Without Dagger*, published in 1955:

"I called my senior officers together and asked them to select very carefully for me some of the strongest, hardest-hitting men under their commands. I had 700 policemen, each with a minimum chest measurement of thirty-six inches and height of five feet ten inches, all fit and healthy men, and none of them was disinclined to play the gangsters at their own game and meet violence with the strong arm of the law.

It was not difficult to pick a dozen of the best of these to form a 'Flying Squad' specially to deal with the gangster problem."

The Flying Squad for which Sillitoe claimed, and received, full credit had been formed twelve months to the day when he took over in Sheffield on May 1st, 1926. It had reached the notice of the general public on July 16th the previous year in a court case involving four members of the Junior Park Gang, although on this occasion it was referred to by its official title - the Special Duties Squad. On September 21st, in the case resulting from the Red House incident a week earlier, Mr. G.H. Banwell, prosecuting, asked P.C. Loxley: "Are you one of the Flying Squad?" Loxley replied: "Yes." This was the first mention of the Flying Squad as such and it occurred during Lieut. Col. Hall-Dalwood's time as Chief Constable, while Capt. Sillitoe was still in the East Riding of Yorkshire.

But although the Flying Squad was his inheritance rather than invention, there is no doubt that Sillitoe was determined to continue where Hall-Dalwood left off, and that he did his utmost to maintain the progress against the gangs that had been made during the previous year. He introduced the European Ju-Jitsu Champion, Harry Hunter, to train the force in self-defence. Each man received seven weeks tuition after which he was said to be competent to deal with any one of sixty methods of attack. This, said the *Sheffield Mail*, presented "a new terror for the Sheffield gangsters." The original terror, the Flying Squad, still led by Sgt. Robinson was strengthened in numbers by such men as P. C. Pat Geraghty who stood 6ft. 5in. and could hold seven tennis balls in one hand, and Sillitoe let it be known - not only to the members of that elite unit, but to the entire force - that in any dealings with known gangmen he would stand by them whatever happened. In a newspaper interview, long after his retirement, Sgt. Robinson recalled his first meeting with the new Chief Constable:

> "The Captain had been here two weeks when he called me into his office. He said to me, 'I have not met you before, but I've read a lot about you and what you have done. I want to congratulate you on the work you and your men are doing....' He told me to carry on the good work and he would always be there to back me and my men up. He always appeared in court to stick up for his men."

Capt. Sillitoe's first court appearance, on September 28th, created quite a stir. The previous Saturday night, at pub closing-time, police officers had arrested a husband and wife who were fighting each other in Meadow Street, West Bar. The police had been greatly harassed by a crowd which had tried to release the couple, but eventually they were removed to the police station along with one member of the crowd. In court, after all three had been found guilty of assaulting the police, but before they had been sentenced, the prosecuting solicitor

asked permission for the Chief Constable to enter the witness box.
Capt. Sillitoe took the oath and appealed to the magistrates to support him in his attempt to stop such disturbances:

"It is perhaps rather unusual to come in a case like this, but there have been so many cases of this kind recently that I wish to ask that in this case exemplary punishment be given to these people. There has been a series of outbreaks of hooliganism in this district and I feel that the police must be protected.

The only way is by exemplary sentences so that other people cannot think they can do this sort of thing. I am determined to stop this kind of thing so long as it rests in my power to do so, but it rests with the Bench whether I shall be supported or not. There is an unruly element in this district who use filthy language and, when the police remonstrate with them, attempt to take the law into their own hands."

The husband was given six months hard labour, his wife fined £2 and the obstructor one month hard labour. When the presiding magistrate announced sentence on the husband, a woman at the rear of the court shouted: "Oh never! You bad man! Give him a chance!" She had to be carried out.

As Capt. Sillitoe had told the magistrates, there had been a series of incidents that autumn in the West Bar and Shalesmoor districts, mostly involving members of the local Smithfields Gang and their rivals, the Junior Park Gang. The worst of these incidents had been assault on a police constable, John Dawson, and might very easily have resulted in another murder charge. On August 13th, six weeks before the Chief Constable appeared in court, P.C. Dawson had warned a gang of youths, congregated at the same spot in Meadow Street where the later domestic affray occurred, about their language. Seeing the constable was alone, the gang turned on him. P.C. Dawson, kicked, punched and slashed with a razor, was saved only by the arrival of another policeman and amazingly the two officers managed to arrest two of the gang. A vast crowd gathered as people spilled out of public houses to watch the affair and the officers had to work their way down the length of the street with their backs to the wall, still holding their prisoners, until they reached a public house where P.C. Dawson collapsed owing to loss of blood. On December 10th, Isaac Bernard, aged 21 and Richard Lawman, 23, were sentenced to seven years penal servitude for the attempted murder of P.C.s Dawson and McPherson. A nineteen year old youth was also sentenced to five years.

It was in the wake of this vicious assault on two of his officers that Capt. Sillitoe appealed to the magistrates. He certainly achieved his objective of attracting attention to his campaign: the local press, accustomed to a traditional reticence on the part of Chief Constables when it came to making statements, seized upon Sillitoe's remarks with great enthusiasm. In an article headed "CLEAR OUT THE HOOLIGANS", the *Sheffield Mail* commented:

"Every citizen of Sheffield will echo the determination of Captain Sillitoe, the Chief Constable, to put an end to the hooligan outbreaks, a recrudescence of which in the Shalesmoor quarter has been productive of several ugly affrays of late. We are pleased that the Chief Constable did not plead in vain to the magistrates to support him in his task by taking a serious view of a typical hooligan assault on a police officer. A sentence of six months hard labour will, no doubt, tend to cool the ardour of the amateur Apaches with a penchant for interfering with policemen......

We think we may promise in the name of the citizens that the Chief Constable will have the support of all good citizens, the Bench of magistrates, and the civic authorities in every effort to teach the volatile elements of the underworld that violence pays dividends only in the form of hard labour.

Sheffield is not Chicago. Human life and limb are not exposed to American crime risks or a percentage of those risks. Way back in Michigan our Sheffield gang affrays would seem small affairs to the gunmen and machine-gun bandits. But let us take a step away from the Chicago complex. We would trim the nails of our comparatively mild hooligans without any municipal hysterics. Decent working folk have no time to tolerate an attempt at rule by street corner bullies."

A week after his first appeal, Capt. Sillitoe once again addressed the magistrates in another case of assault upon the police. A crowd of two hundred had gathered outside West Bar Police Station following the arrest of a man involved in a street fight. The police had gone out and dispersed the crowd, one of whom was alleged to have struck two officers. "Something must be done to let people realise that this hooliganism will not be permitted," said Capt. Sillitoe, "and that if an arrest has to be made they must not interfere." Mr. J. Hunter, chairman, said the magistrates were determined to protect the police and, as on the previous occasion, the defendant was sentenced to six months hard labour.

The Sheffield gang phenomenon has, in the past, often been judged purely on the strength of what happened during Sillitoe's time as Chief Constable. His own recollections, in his autobiography, make no concession to what had gone before he took over in 1926, the over-riding impression being that the gang feuds were at that time only just beginning.

After briefly describing the problems of breaking up the Sky Edge tossing rings, where, he says, five halfcrowns were used for the toss*, Sillitoe states:

> "The gang leader who controlled the tossing ring at this time was George Mooney, chief of the Mooney Gang; but, because it was a very enviable source of income, the members of the Garvin Gang coveted it, and were already beginning to skirmish and fight for its possession."
>
> He adds that: "Each gang had hundreds of members."

By the time Capt. Sillitoe took up his appointment in May 1926, the skirmishes and fights over the Skyring had been going on for three years and for most of that time George Mooney had been in enforced retirement. Although his former associates had enjoyed a brief revival and continued to be known as the Mooney Gang, their former leader had taken no part and that group had disintegrated before the end of 1925.

One might excuse Sillitoe's claims and exaggerations by the fact that a quarter of a century elapsed between him leaving Sheffield and writing his memoirs. The pressures and responsibilities upon him during those years - at the very top of his profession in Glasgow, Kent and finally MI5 - could well have caused certain aspects of the Sheffield situation to become slightly blurred by time. Another possibility is that even Percy Sillitoe possessed a little vanity and after being dubbed "The Gang Buster' for so long he felt he had to go along with that public image in his book. If so, perhaps this explains such curious anecdotes as the following:

> "There was a typical case for instance, of a gangster named Foster. He was a 'razor king' and carried a razor blade stuck into a bit of wood hidden up his sleeve and fixed to a piece of elastic. On the least pretext he would pluck the razor blade down from his sleeve and use it mercilessly. He had several convictions for assaulting and slashing people,

* There is no evidence that anything other than three halfpennies were ever used at Sky Edge.

and had been merely fined each time. The more convictions he got the greater he was held in fear, and the quicker his fine was paid for him. He had developed a contempt for authority that was hardly surprising.

One night there was trouble at a licensed house in West Bar. Loxley and Lunn strode in. One of the men there was Foster and as soon as he saw Loxley he jumped at him with the razor flashing.

He was promptly seized with 'reasonable force' and removed from West Bar to the police charge office, a distance of 200 yards. The desk-sergeant refused to accept the charge until Foster had been treated at the Infirmary. He was charged with being drunk and disorderly and assaulting P. C. Loxley.

Next day I was in court. The public gallery was crowded with Mooney gangsters. As soon as the proceedings began, Foster's solicitor stood up and said he objected to the charge. He cast a significant glance at huge P.C. Loxley and then at the figure of his bandaged and cowed client in the dock and said solemnly: 'I wish to have the charge amended your worship, from 'assaulting the police' to one of 'attempted suicide'.'

There was a howl of laughter in which all the gangsters in the public gallery heartily joined, and I remember that even the magistrates permitted themselves to smile."

This amusing story has been quoted as fact many times by those responsible for perpetuating the Sillitoe legend. It is, however, pure invention. Albert Foster - the only person of that surname concerned in the gang troubles - was not a 'razor king', an expression common in Glasgow gang-lore but virtually unknown in Sheffield. Since the gang feud began Foster had never been fined and indeed, if he had, it is unlikely that his fines would have been paid for him, as on April 24th 1925 he was imprisoned for three months when he could not pay £44.10 shillings he owed his wife for maintenance. The 'attempted suicide' plea was made by Mr. Harry Morris, defending Thomas Windle on December 28th, 1925. Neither Foster nor Sillitoe were present; the former was in prison serving an 18 month sentence, the latter in the East Riding where he remained as Chief Constable for the next four months.

Putting a perspective on Capt. Sillitoe's achievement in the suppression of the Sheffield gangs is not easy. To some extent it is natural that he should receive the lion's share of the credit, for certainly within twelve months of his appointment the gangs had disappeared, never to return, and ordinary law-abiding citizens could at last walk the city streets unmolested. Public memory is short and with Hall-Dalwood's contribution to the eventual success being conveniently overlooked by a press only too willing to champion a Chief Constable who appreciated publicity, Capt. Sillitoe soon became a folk hero. His fame was not long in spreading. The *Pictorial Weekly*, applauding Sillitoe's impact during his first year in Sheffield, commented:

> "Without doubt Captain Sillitoe of Sheffield is the doyen of England's higher police officers. One has only to see his work and to notice the results he has achieved during the comparatively short period he has been Chief Constable of Sheffield to realise the concentrated energy and resourcefulness of the man who has thrown down the gauntlet to the criminals of this city, who no one will deny are among some of the most vicious in the country."

On the other hand, how serious was the situation when Sillitoe took over? Public outrage at the Plommer murder, the deterrent factor of the Fowlers' executions, and the Flying Squad's purges had all contributed significantly to a decline in gang power. More and more witnesses were becoming prepared to give evidence and in the four months preceding the new Chief's arrival in May 1926 there were only two gang incidents reported, both involving junior groups.

The principal gangs were leaderless: Sam Garvin, George Mooney and Albert Foster were all in prison, as was Tom Armstrong - the 'Bruiser from Brum' brought in to add muscle to the revived Mooney Gang. He had been arrested following an affray in Brighton between the Brummagem Boys and a London mob.

Two men with excellent qualifications for assessing Sillitoe's role in the suppression of the gangs were Sgt. William Robinson and P.C. Walter Loxley. In retirement, both founder members of the Flying Squad expressed opinions on their former Chief. Their opposite views serve only to add to the enigma.

In Walter Loxley's words the gangs were "bent if not broken" by the time Lieut. Col. Hall-Dalwood retired in March 1926. He considered Sillitoe something of a showman and always believed the wrong man got the credit for breaking up the gangs.

According to William Robinson, the police under Hall-Dalwood took a tolerant attitude towards the gangs. He was not at all surprised when Sillitoe received the credit, for he recalled how, when the new Chief called him into his office in May 1926, he told him: "I want you to understand that although, when we clear up these gangs - as we surely will - I shall get all the credit and praise, I shall be relying on you to keep at it." Ex-Detective Sergeant Robinson told the *Sheffield Telegraph* in 1962: "He was a damn fine chief was the Captain and there is no doubt about that."

14. Latter Days

Rumours that George Mooney and Sam Garvin were planning to face each other in a stand-up fight began to circulate after both returned to the city on completion of their prison sentences in 1926. A local boxing promoter, Harvey Flood, was reputed to have offered a £100 purse for the fight which would settle once-and-for-all the feud between the two men. It was said in Sheffield that Mooney v Garvin would attract a larger crowd than United v Wednesday in the F.A. Cup. Certainly a confrontation between two men whose bitter hatred of each other was well known would have aroused considerable interest, but if Flood's purse offer was genuine he soon lost interest in the promotion following a tap-room incident at his public house, the Raven Tavern in Fitzwilliam Street.

On February 28th, 1927, Sam Garvin was sitting in the tap-room, playing a quiet game of draughts with his brother Bob when at 7.45p.m. George Mooney, 'Ganner' Wheywell and 'Spud' Murphy arrived on the scene. Murphy had only recently been reconciled with Mooney after a three and a half year rift. When the three men saw the Garvins there were cries of "Let's cut their heads off" and a threat by Wheywell that he would shoot both brothers. The licensee, Flood, immediately sent for the police and endeavoured to push Mooney, Murphy and Wheywell out of the pub, but it was not until police officers arrived that they consented to leave. As they went, Wheywell, who had been arguing vehemently about the Plommer murder with Sam Garvin, shouted: "You have got two men hung but we will get you yet."

At the Police Court on March 10th, Mooney and Murphy were each fined £1 for disorderly behaviour. Wheywell failed to appear and a warrant was issued for his arrest. Cross-examined, the licensee, Flood, denied that the trouble had been caused by Sam Garvin ordering him not to serve the defendants. He also denied ever having offered a purse for Mooney and Garvin to fight. "I have never entertained such a suggestion," he said.

In addition to the Raven charge, Mooney and Murphy were also accused of assaulting Sgt. Robinson on the same evening. Following their departure from the Raven, the two men had parted from Wheywell and made their way to the Royal Hotel, Hoyle Street, in West Bar. They had only been in the Royal a few minutes when the Flying Squad arrived in the shape of Sgt. Robinson, P.C. Loxley and P.C. Lunn, and Mooney and Murphy were ordered to leave. Loxley and Lunn picked up Murphy and threw him out of the pub, whereupon

Sgt. Robinson hit him, knocking him to the ground. Mooney followed quietly but nevertheless received the same treatment. Both men were then arrested and charged with assaulting the police.

Mr. G.H. Banwell, prosecuting, told the court that the landlord had called the police and requested that they eject Mooney and Murphy. In the witness-box, however, the landlord denied this, saying he had not called the police and did not know why they had come. Sgt. Robinson, giving evidence, said that both men were violent, Murphy behaving "like a madman" on the way to the police station. He denied using a cosher or hitting Mooney - who said he had been " belted all the way to the police station" - on the back of the neck with his truncheon.

Mr. L. H. Brittain, defending: "I put it to you that in Sheffield it is a case of give a dog a bad name and hang, draw and quarter him, and that you are hounding these men from place to place and out of Sheffield if need be."

Sergeant Robinson: "That is not for me to say."

Alleging that Mooney and Murphy had been molested by the Flying Squad, Mr. Brittain said: "At one time Sheffield was noted for its gangs, but now it is more notorious because of its organised gangs of police, who chase these men from one licensed house to another, and will not let them behave themselves when they want to."

Despite their solicitor's pleas, both Mooney and Murphy were found guilty of assaulting Sgt. Robinson and sentenced to two months imprisonment each.

With Mooney back behind bars, nothing more was heard of the proposed fight rumours. In retrospect it is doubtful if either thirty-seven year old Mooney or Garvin - ten years his senior - ever seriously contemplated such an event, for, as sceptics pointed out when the rumour first surfaced, neither was the type to become involved in an equal man-to-man situation - both were more accustomed to others fighting on their behalf.

While there were sporadic clashes between the Junior Park and Smithfields Gangs for the remainder of 1927, until they too became weary of the Flying Squad's attentions, the February 28th affair at the Raven Tavern and Mooney's subsequent experiences in Hoyle Street, marked the final incident in the four year old feud with Garvin. When Mooney had served his sentence he returned to his home in Rose Street, where he had moved two years earlier, and retired for good from gang matters.

For the rest of their lives Mooney and Garvin remained familiar figures on the northern racecourses. Using pseudonyms, both stood as bookmakers: Garvin as 'Captain Mee' in white hat and ice-cream man's smock and Mooney as 'George Barratt'. George Mooney, at least became a law-abiding citizen of Sheffield. He was a familiar sight in the betting ring at Owlerton Greyhound Stadium, where he had a regular pitch until long after the Second World War. Sam Garvin was a different proposition. He continued to keep the company of thieves and pickpockets, adding to a criminal record which had started in 1904, until his death in the early 1950s. George Mooney died in 1961.

During his five and a half years in Sheffield, Chief Constable Sillitoe was responsible for a number of pioneering developments in police methods. A forensic laboratory - anticipating by years the police laboratory at Hendon - was set up in 1929 under the supervision of Dr. J.M. Webster. Sillitoe persuaded the Watch Committee to give every assistance in the way of equipment for Dr. Webster, who was one of the first people in Britain to realise the value of scientific evidence. Shortly after the laboratory was set up, photographic and fingerprint sections were added. The police box system was another innovation of Sillitoe's. He had first seen police boxes in Newcastle-upon-Tyne and introduced them to Sheffield soon afterwards. It was after studying the Sheffield system that the Metropolitan Police introduced them to London.

The morale and welfare of his men concerned Sillitoe throughout his career and in Sheffield he did much to improve conditions. He persuaded the Watch Committee to find £4,000 for the purchase of a ten acre site which became the Niagara Sports Ground, the first police recreation ground in Britain. At the section house for unmarried officers he installed a matron and chef and again persuaded the Watch Committee to spend money on making the quarters a model establishment. The welfare of older officers received no less consideration; any man nearing the end of his service who showed signs of strain was transferred to light duties. Thus, certain long-serving officers were spared having to retire prematurely on health grounds and lose considerable pension rights.

But the darker elements that had preyed upon his predecessors did not escape Sillitoe completely. Early in 1930 the city was rocked by disclosures of bribery of policemen by bookmakers in Sheffield's East End. At Leeds Assizes fines of up to £250 were imposed upon the bookmakers by Mr. Justice Humphries, who made some pointed remarks about Brightside Division. At the subsequent Watch Committee inquiry fifteen police officers were dismissed from the force and seven others fined. It was no secret that Capt. Sillitoe was dismayed and disgusted by the corruption which had been revealed amongst a section of his force.

In 1931 Capt. Sillitoe was appointed Chief Constable of Glasgow, taking over a force second in strength only to the Metropolitan. He remained there for eleven years during which time he received the C.B.E. and later a Knighthood. It was as Sir Percy Sillitoe that he moved to Kent County Police as Chief Constable in 1942 and, four years later, to MI5 as Director-General, responsible only to the Prime Minister. Sir Percy Sillitoe died at his home in Eastbourne in 1962.

The Flying Squad continued its activities until 1928 when there was no longer need for its specialised work. The purge had been completed. In 1936 Sgt. Robinson retired from the police force to be followed in successive years by P.C.s Lunn and Loxley. At his farewell presentation in December 1937, Jerry Lunn referred to the suppression of the city's gangs and said he would like to place on record the assistance given by the then Chief Constable, Lieut Col. Hall-Dalwood and Supt. Denton of Central Division. Twelve months later when Walter Loxley retired, after spending his last three years in the Charge Office, he gave an interview to the *Sheffield Telegraph and Independent* describing some of the many skirmishes he had been involved in as a member of the Flying Squad. "We had some very interesting times, one way and another," he said. On how the gang members had settled down, P.C. Loxley commented: "Eighty per cent of those boys are now going about their business in a proper way."

Gang warfare in Sheffield began as a result of violent competition for the exclusive and lucrative rights to the Sky Edge tossing ring. The chief protagonists were men long renowned for their criminal behaviour and disinclination towards honest toil, men whose company the law-abiding citizens eschewed - mainly out of fear. When violence erupted, it was this fear of becoming involved that led to a situation where prosecution witnesses in gang cases were almost as unique as guilty pleas on the part of defendants. An undermanned police force, lenient and out-of-touch magistrates, and a city council whose members concerned themselves with little that occurred outside their own chamber, resulted in a reign of terror that existed in Sheffield for several years.

The Princess Street murder was a turning-point in gang power. Home Office intervention and widespread press coverage of the events leading up to Jock Plommer's death finally brought home to the city authorities the seriousness of the situation. Ironically, when the police did begin to receive support from the courts by way of realistic sentences, the Chief Constable, who had repeatedly appealed in that direction, resigned.

Whatever the actual nature of the "insidious influences" that

Hall-Dalwood claimed had worked against him, the problem did not extend to his successor. Perhaps the members of the Watch Committee - to whom Hall-Dalwood was obviously referring in his farewell speech - learned by the mistakes of the past. Publicly at least, Sillitoe spoke only of the Watch Committee's co-operation and support during his time as Chief Constable.

The defeat of the Sheffield gangs was achieved by hard line measures that would never be permitted today. Whether or not they were justified, without those measures the gangs might well have flourished indefinitely. Sir Percy Sillitoe, in *Cloak Without Dagger* wrote:

> "I believe that there is only one way to deal with the gangster mentality. You must show that you are not afraid. If you stand up to them and they realise that you mean business, they will soon knuckle under. The element of beast in a man, whether it comes from an unhappy and impoverished background, or from his own undisciplined, lustful appetites, will respond exactly as a wild beast of the jungle responds - to nothing but greater force and greater firmness of purpose."

The gangs indeed realised that Sillitoe meant business and that the Flying Squad epitomised "greater force and greater firmness of purpose." Sillitoe's inheritance from Hall-Dalwood was not squandered; on his arrival he strengthened the squad; until he left he supported its members' every action. As George Mooney was known to remark in later years, when recalling the gangs and Sillitoe's handling of them: "He was rough, but we couldn't have gone on like that forever." Perhaps, as Sillitoe maintained, the end justified the means.

Index

OXF[ORD]

TEACHING GUIDES

HOW TO

Teach For Progress

Classroom Approaches For Improving Practice

ANDREW CHANDLER-GREVATT

OXFORD

UNIVERSITY PRESS

Great Clarendon Street, Oxford, OX2 6DP, United Kingdom

Oxford University Press is a department of the University of Oxford.
It furthers the University's objective of excellence in research, scholarship, and
education by publishing worldwide. Oxford is a registered trade mark of Oxford
University Press in the UK and in certain other countries

British Library Cataloguing in Publication Data
Data available

978-0-19-842328-7

Kindle edition

978-0-19-842329-4

10 9 8 7 6 5 4 3 2 1

Paper used in the production of this book is a natural, recyclable product made
from wood grown in sustainable forests. The manufacturing process conforms
to the environmental regulations of the country of origin.

Printed in Great Britain by CPI Group (UK) Ltd., Croydon CR0 4YY

Links to third party websites are provided by Oxford in good faith and for
information only. Oxford disclaims any responsibility for the materials
contained in any third party website referenced in this work.

The Publisher would like to thank Doug Forbes, of Newgen Publishing UK for
his help in the production of this book.

Dedicated to Geoff, for believing in me

About the author

Dr Andy Chandler-Grevatt has a doctorate in classroom assessment and a passion for assessment, teaching and learning. Having worked as a Science teacher for ten years, of which five were spent as an Advanced Skills Teacher, Andy has a deep understanding of the pressures and joys of teaching in the classroom. Beyond the classroom, Andy has worked with primary and secondary teachers in a variety of contexts around the UK and in Canada, Kazakhstan and China. Alongside his national and international research in school assessment, Andy is a teaching fellow on the initial teacher education course at the University of Sussex, UK, and is a successful published assessment author and editor.

Contents

Contents

Contents

Contents

Acknowledgements

Thanks to the OUP support team, particularly Doug Forbes, Jane Anson, Sarah Flynn, Amie Hewish, Sarah James and Lamorna Newcombe. It's great to feel part of a nurturing team. Thank you.

The peer reviewers, for their insightful and constructive comments on each part of the book: Dr Christine Harrison (Professor in Education, King's College London), Rachel Ind (Lead Practitioner in Art and Design, The Warwick School), Gabriella Rowles (History teacher and educational consultant), and Steve Illingworth (Senior Lecturer in History Education at Edge Hill University). Their input really helped shape this book. Any mistakes and omissions remain my responsibility and decisions.

Colleagues who have challenged my thinking beyond the science teacher mindset include Dr Ally Daubney, Richard McFahn, Matthew Westgarth, and Mike Lambert. A whole range of teachers and headteachers from the UK, Kazakhstan, Canada, Barcelona, and Beijing have influenced my thinking and practice. Here, I want to thank you all and include particular mention to acknowledge the teachers who have helped me. Primary-school teachers include Gillian Emerson, Amelia Mackness, and Danielle Mussellwhite. The secondary-school teachers include Rebecca Leong (History), Becky Prior (Science), Aletia Hagedon (Psychology), Anastasia Papanastasiou (History), Michelle Rea (Modern Foreign Languages), Ruth Ashenden (English), Arif Said (Science), Dennis Chikobvu (Science), and Gavin Terry (Biology).

Thank you to my patient and understanding family, particularly Geoff for patience, belief, and gin, and Rosabella and Zentu for cuddles.

Thinking about progress in school

A personal introduction

This is the book that I have wanted to write for about ten years now. Since I started teaching, how learners learn and develop at school has fascinated me, particularly how we 'capture' that learning and development as teachers.

I have now been training teachers for the same length of time as I was teaching in the classroom. As a classroom teacher, I started with a focused view on my classes, in my lessons, in my school. As I developed and took on more responsibility, that focus widened. I was fortunate enough to work with other learners and teachers within my school, in other subjects and also with other teachers and learners in other schools. My frame of reference expanded from what I was doing with my own classes to how this compared to other teachers, other subjects, and other schools within England. This experience was invaluable in understanding differences between teachers, subjects, phases, and schools.

My interest in assessment and learning across the school system developed and my understanding deepened, to a point where I wanted to take it further and do a doctorate[1] in classroom assessment, with a focus on a type of rubric, the 'Level Ladder'.[2] This single sentence makes it sound a simple task, but over five years I read, researched, and thought deeply about classroom assessment and how learners make progress. This widened my perspective into the research base of education as an academic discipline, the challenges of actually doing education research in schools, and the very nature of what knowledge and evidence are in terms of education.

None of this was purely intentional; I was just following my interests and opportunities as they arose. Then, quite unexpectedly, I had three opportunities arise overseas: first to work with Cambridge Examinations in developing a school-based assessment system in Kazakhstan; second in

[1] **A. Chandler-Grevatt** (2010). *The use of levelled assessment tasks and their impact on teaching and learning in science education*, Doctoral dissertation, University of Sussex.
[2] **A. Grevatt** (2005). *Badger Key Stage 3 Science Year 7 Levelled-Assessment Tasks*, Stevenage: Badger Publishing.

Waterloo, Canada, to develop a school for the future; and more recently to work with teachers in Beijing, China. These experiences increased my world view of teaching, learning, and education exponentially. Alongside this, I am involved in initial teacher education at the University of Sussex, where I work closely with 10–15 trainee teachers each year; visiting them on placement, mentoring, coaching, teaching, and assessing. To a further 300, I deliver lectures on assessment and progress across primary and secondary phases.

Over my career so far, my perspectives have become wider nationally, and deeper and broader internationally, and on a daily basis I am able to keep an overview of the developments, challenges, and experiences of teachers and schools in England. I have studied teaching, learning and the curriculum in depth, including the challenges we have in carrying out assessment, particularly of progress.

In this book, I draw on all these experiences. Based on the foundations of critically reviewed educational research, I offer my perspective on classroom progress and challenge you to consider yours. I will present you with condensed research, educational theories, practical examples, and case studies that you may wish to apply to your classroom. Let's see how we progress.

The progression obsession

At times, when researching this book, I was forced to consider whether progress and learning were the same thing. Why not just call this book, 'How to help your students learn'? There are very good reasons why the term 'progress' is an important focus for this book. It is a debated term and can be used for good and for bad, as you will see.

The 2011 Teachers' Standards for England one-page document mentions the word 'progress' five times[3] as follows:

2 Promote good **progress** and outcomes by pupils

- be accountable for pupils' attainment, **progress** and outcomes [...]

- guide pupils to reflect on the **progress** they have made and their emerging needs [...]

---

[3] **Department for Education** (2011). Guidance: Teachers' standards. Available at: <https://www.gov.uk/government/publications/teachers-standards> accessed 3 April 2019

- make use of formative and summative assessment to secure pupils' **progress**
- use relevant data to monitor **progress**, set targets, and plan subsequent lessons'

2011 Teachers' Standards for England

From this, progress is clearly considered an important concept in teaching, according to the Department for Education in England. On the back of this, the word 'progress' has become entrenched in the language and concerns of teachers, classrooms, and schools. In fact, it could be seen as a 'progression obsession'. It appears to have become an obsession with senior management in schools, which has manifested in regular data collection, a plethora of progress-tracking approaches, and a proliferation of commercial tracking platforms. Schools have moved their focus from learners to data. Data is everything.

Now don't get me wrong, it is important that teachers and schools support, enhance, and facilitate all learners' progress through their compulsory education. However, I, along with many other educators, think that this progression obsession has morphed to focus on often meaningless numbers, become distant from the purpose of education, and narrowed the attention of what is important in childhood development.

In this book, I want to challenge the rather unfocused understanding of the term 'progress' and attempt to redress the balance towards a more meaningful approach to facilitating, promoting, and enhancing progress for each learner through their school days.

Through discussion of theory, policy, and practice from around the world, I hope that this book will give teachers food for thought, develop their understanding of the term, and most importantly offer practical ideas to support their learners in making progress at school in a holistic way.

The quest for a unified theory of education

It's been an ambitious quest of mine to find a unified theory of education, or at least a unified theory of assessment. So far, I have failed. Although natural scientists are on the same quest for the unified theory of everything (and they might find it), I have come to doubt that their unified theory will include education. We may well come to understand how the universe is held together, but to be able to develop a predictive and effective model for teaching every learner seems unlikely to me.

I'm a natural scientist by training; I have a bachelor's degree and masters in biological sciences and taught secondary-school (high school) level sciences. It wasn't until my doctorate that I became more of a social scientist and started to understand education as a social endeavour. Natural science and social science are very different disciplines; they have different assumptions, different methods, and different contributions to make to human knowledge.

The thing I find most exciting about researching education is that it is a human endeavour and really isn't a discipline in its own right. Instead, we can understand education through multiple disciplines, drawing on philosophy, psychology, neuroscience, cognitive science, sociology, and cultural studies, to name but a few. Education can also be understood through a range of perspectives including social class, gender, racial, sexuality, religious, political, social, and cultural. This richness is both a curse and a challenge.

Education is not a natural science, and natural science methods alone will not give us a full understanding of it as a human experience. Learning, however, may be understood using natural scientific methods, particularly in light of the neuroscience and cognitive disciplines. Although in isolation from the context of education and schooling these insights might be useful to inform some pedagogical practices, understanding the impact of the social environment on these is also essential to make them effective.

The neuroscientific and cognitive theories are seductive in their apparent simplicity. The promise of 'teach like this and your students will succeed' offered by many books these days is alluring, but we are yet to reach this panacea. I contend that this is because formal learning in education is so complex: learners are not coming to a laboratory classroom as blank slates, responding to a single stimulus and giving a single outcome. Instead, they are a product of their past experiences before they even set foot in a classroom, surrounded by social pressures within and beyond the classroom, with different motivations, wants, and needs.

The importance of culture

At this point in my career, I find sociocultural theories very useful to understand and inform classroom practice. My previous book, *How To Assess Your Students*, mostly used sociocultural theory to help understand classroom culture and the practices associated with assessment. Practices are informed by beliefs, values, and behaviours, and these beliefs, values, and behaviours are changeable depending on current education policy, cultural understanding of what schools and education are about, and the experience of the teacher.

Cognitive theory, neuroscience, and quantitative methods dominate the discussions of teachers, particularly on social media, often ignoring that the cultural and the social are important factors in understanding the classroom, schools, and education. In some cases, some of the most influential educational theories are being rejected completely on rather unsophisticated criticisms. My view of classroom research is that a critical understanding of the disciplines used within education and their appropriate application is a measured and productive approach to understanding education and classroom practice.

Sociocultural perspective accounts for motivation, interest, identity, and context beyond just the biological, cognitive, and psychological processes of learning. Learning is rarely an individual experience: all school learning takes place within a social situation. There are cultural power relationships between teachers and learners, there are parents' expectations (often based upon their own experience of schooling), and there are peer relationships in classrooms between the learners that will determine the motivations and behaviour of those learners.

How learners progress in school is a complex process, influenced by many factors. Although schools on the surface appear similar, there are different management cultures: cultures emerge from the types of teachers and their range of experience. I visit many schools and the atmosphere differs in each one: some are friendly and open, others are more defensive and closed. These behaviours of the staff are indicators of the type of culture in the school and this will feed down to impact the learners.

In this book, I will encourage you to evaluate your assumptions, beliefs, attitudes, and practices associated with progress in school and to compare them to the culture of your school and the learners you teach. These evaluations should help you to make decisions about what to do next to improve the progress culture in your classroom.

The focus of this book

I have written this as if I am talking to a colleague who is a teacher or who is learning to become a teacher. It is a teacher handbook that I hope will inform, challenge, and support teaching and learning.

The first part of the book seeks to inform and challenge thinking about what progress is in schools and what it perhaps should or could be. My focus is on the culture of education, and the exercises and analyses attempt to take culture into consideration when considering what is best to apply to your own practice and classroom. However, I introduce a range of educational theories that can be applied to practice and give practical applications of pedagogical approaches that support learners' progress.

The focus of the book is on teachers and classroom practice, so I give little attention to whole-school management and cultural change. Although I will hint at it where appropriate, it would really need another book.

How to use this book

You are welcome to read this book from cover to cover, but equally, dipping in a section at a time will be useful for your classroom practice and pedagogical thinking. In my view, it is essential that all teachers are critical thinkers about education, schooling, the curriculum, and their own practice. Being able to evaluate current practices and interrogate them can only make us better teachers and give our learners the best chance of success in school (whatever that looks like). Part 1 will help to give a range of perspectives on these issues and hopefully equip you to understand the context of your own practice.

Part 2 is full of practical approaches to try, with the caveat of understanding the culture you are working in and what you might have to do to adapt to that culture or how you might change the culture yourself. It is not a list of things that I think every teacher must be doing in their classroom, more a menu of ideas that you can decide to use or adapt to your context.

Finally, Part 3 is a guide for developing your assessment literacy, a professional toolkit through which to reflect upon and improve your skills at supporting learners to progress through effective assessment, planning, and teaching.

Throughout the book, you will find boxes that contain supporting information (*Evidence*, *Research* and *Case studies*), promoting critical reflection and professional change (*Discuss* and *Reflection*) and signposting connections and further reading (*Further reading* and *Also see*).

I have tried to draw on peer-reviewed papers for my citations where appropriate. Currently, I know that not all teachers have access to these journals, but those doing a university-based training course or a Masters in Education will have. In the Further reading sections, you will find a list of books and articles that are open access and that you should be able to source from libraries or bookshops.

Part 1
What is progress?

> 'Educational experiences do not leave people as they were. People become, in an important sense, different *persons*.'[4]
>
> **R. Pring** (2004). *Philosophy of Educational Research.*

I can recall a particular Year 10 (aged 14–15) class that I taught in the early part of my career. I was teaching them Science (Biology, Chemistry, and Physics), and they were a small group who were all classed as 'low attaining'. My task was to help them achieve at least the lowest grade in their GCSEs (terminal examinations). As a class, they were a real mix of learners who were dealing with a lot of external issues: some were from abusive families, others from lower socioeconomic groups, some with specific learning difficulties. I saw them for three hours a week, every week, and it took a long time to build a trusting relationship and a constructive learning environment. Although I was teaching them Science, often in a very creative way to engage them, I was also teaching them about appropriate behaviour, dealing with conflict, and self-confidence. I took them on up until their final exams and all passed; two even got an unexpected C grade[5]. They had made academic progress, but they had also made personal progress in life skills.

This part of the book is to help you challenge and sharpen your understanding of the term 'progress', to help you conceptualise it into a more meaningful and useful idea that can be applied to your professional situation, and to offer my own proposal of a framework within which to promote, assess, and communicate progress in your classroom and school.

---

[4] **R. Pring** (2004). *Philosophy of Educational Research*. 2nd edition. London: Continuum International Publishing, p.15.

[5] Grades A–G (with A high and G low) are common across most school and examination systems. Note that in England, a new system of 1–9 (with 1 low and 9 high) has been implemented between 2017 and 2019. https://ofqual.blog.gov. uk/2019/02/01/gcse-and-a-level-reform-is-nearly-complete/

Reflection

Before you read ahead, consider the following questions:

- What does the word 'progress' mean to you in your educational context?

- To what extent do you and your colleagues have a shared understanding of the word 'progress'?

- What does 'progress' look like in your educational context?

1.1 What do we mean by 'progress'?

This fundamental question to start with may, on the face of it, seem relatively straightforward. However, once I start to unpick the term 'progress', it becomes complex and multifaceted. In simple terms, if I consider just one learner in my class, I will want them to make progress during the next term and definitely during the next year that I am teaching them. This sense of 'progress' is related to learning new ideas and skills. We want individual learners to make advancements in their knowledge, understanding, and skills. We want them to be 'better' at what they do after a year of our teaching.

'Being better', 'improved', and 'progressing' are all terms that teachers use to express this. These qualitative terms are, of course, sometimes expressed in more quantitative ways, for example, 'they reached their target grade', 'they got grade A in their exam', or 'achieved a merit for their coursework'. This indicates we have some kind of measure, usually in the form of exam results from external (to the school) standardised tests.

Now, if we compare what a primary teacher may say about a child in their class, to what a secondary Science teacher may say, to what a secondary Music teacher may say, and to what a secondary Languages teacher might say, things start to unravel. The specifics of what learners should do to get better in their phase and within their subjects are different. This depends on the phase. I recently did just this in a workshop on progress and assessment literacy, and here are some of the perspectives.

A holistic approach was offered by Danielle, a junior-school teacher:

'Learners progress in lots of different ways. They mature and are able to be more empathetic and understanding. They are more patient and can focus for longer... Learners can make progress emotionally as well as they acclimatise to a new class and teacher.'

Becky, an experienced secondary Science teacher, identified the tension between what progress seems to be in her school and what she thinks it should be:

> 'At work, "progress" is a term used to track how well our students are doing, sort of as a success indicator. I think it is more about how we can plan for interventions to improve [the progress] of the students "underperforming" and how to secure those making good progress... Every student makes progress, but at different rates.'

A secondary English teacher, Ruth, offered a practical example:

> 'Are pupils getting any better? For example, a Year 11 pupil at beginning of term would only write two lines for an assessment, by the end of the year he could write two pages of well-structured response.'

Progress can be considered as making progress through time or making progress through knowledge, understanding, and skills. The former is based on the idea that a learner progresses as they learn more and more about a subject over time. The latter concerns acquiring new knowledge, understanding, and skills, applying them to new situations or consolidating them.

The reality is that in school, when the word 'progress' is used, we are usually talking about 'progress through the curriculum'. The curriculum is that statutory document against which learners, teachers, and schools are measured. Although, for many schools in England, the National Curriculum is no longer statutory[6], the content of any external standardised test ensures that most schools include specific topics and subjects. We have to accept that the National Curriculum, and later in the school, the exam board specification, is the driver of all learning in schools.

So, to start out, I am offering you a tentative definition of progress as:

> 'The learning and application, over time, of curriculum knowledge, understanding, and skills within school.'

However, this is a very pragmatic definition, highly contextualised, and arguably ignores some important factors. There are multiple perspectives of what progress is and how it can be used within education. I discuss these in the next section.

---

[6] **Department for Education** (2013). The national curriculum. Available at: <https://www.gov.uk/national-curriculum> accessed 2 December 2018

Reflection

Reflect on these statements after reading this section.

- What are your thoughts on my definition of progress?

- To what extent does it fit with your professional context?

- Would you adapt my definition? If so, how?

 Further reading

It is easy to get wrapped up in your own country's curriculum. These books offer perspectives on the theory and types of curriculum available:

A.V. Kelly (2009). *The Curriculum: Theory and Practice*. 6th edition. London: Sage.

A. Moore (2015). *Understanding the School Curriculum: Theory, Politics and Principles*. Abingdon and New York: Routledge.

M. Myatt (2018). *The Curriculum: Gallimaufry to Coherence*. Woodbridge: John Catt Educational Ltd.

1.2 Types of progress

'Is our progress more towards human doings or human beings?'[7]

W. Ord (2017). Chapter 7: What is progress? In I. Wallace & L. Kirkman (eds) (2017). *Progress (Best of the Best)*.

Progress in education is a complex idea, and having had a good read of educational research papers, books, blogs, and discussions on social media, it is clear there is a diverse understanding of the term.

We are all born with a great urge to learn; as babies we use our senses to explore our surroundings, make connections between cause and effect, and start to recognise and read faces. We then start to explore the world further,

---

[7] **W. Ord** (2017). Chapter 7: What is progress? In I. Wallace & L. Kirkman (eds) (2017). *Progress (Best of the Best)*. Carmarthen: Crown House Publishing, pp. 65–71. Reproduced with permission.

our overwhelming curiosity driving us to discover what things feel like and do; we listen to sounds, try to repeat them and, in our innate desperation to communicate with others, we develop language, which we use to understand and shape the world around us. Our hunger to learn, when the basics are learned, is handed over to school, where gradually, for many, this motivation is slowly drained away. Some learners excel in school and others flounder. The rest just do okay.

The progress of development of the child compared with progress of the learner in school reveals the difference between informal and formal learning. Some teenagers will spend hours learning to play the guitar, succeed at a video game, or draw their favourite cartoons, but will be apathetic about the opportunities to learn about our collective human knowledge at school through subjects. The magic of numbers becomes a monotony of practice questions, the excitement of the Bunsen burner becomes the abstract use of balanced symbol equations, the joy of story writing becomes a quagmire of grammatical conventions. Many teenagers reach a point in education of 'What's the point?' All learners progress while at school; this can be within school or outside in their own hobbies. They all are developing as people, as friends, as citizens, but not necessarily in what the curriculum demands and what schools use to measure progress.

I would love to say that there is just one definition of progress, but behind the term lies a multitude of assumptions, beliefs, and attitudes about the purpose of schooling and education. Educationalists have a lot to say about progress in school, whether it is the social injustice of education systems, the structure of the curriculum, or the nature of learning. So, to interrogate my definition above, I offer some perspectives on progress for you to consider that will hopefully reflect and sharpen your definition and understanding of the concept of progress.

Having read widely in preparation for this book, I have been able to come up with seven key types of progress from some of the dominant thinkers and practitioners in the field. Many of these types overlap, but I feel the following seven categories provide a good starting point for discussion:

1. progress as a human endeavour

2. progress as a social mobiliser

3. progress through education

4. progress through learning

5. progress through pedagogy

6. progress through assessment

7. progress as a management tool.

1 Progress as a human endeavour

Let's start with the big one. We often think of human civilisation progressing, beyond the randomness of evolution, through the human quest for improvement: progress in knowledge, technology, and medicine; a striving to make a better life for ourselves, for humanity; a mission to reduce suffering, increase longevity, and improve the quality of life. We strive for self-improvement. Individuals, local communities, politicians, countries, and cultures all pursue improvement.

Part of this human endeavour is education, to build on our past, to protect our cultures, and to prepare our young for the future. However, education can be used as a form of control to reproduce cultures and histories, and create citizens with identical knowledge. Education has a political purpose; education is political. At the other extreme, education is emancipatory, freeing an individual to think independently, to be democratic, creative, and socially mobile.

Different cultures value different forms of progress. Although I am cautious to make sweeping generalisations, when I have worked in China and Kazakhstan and read about their cultures compared to my own culture in England, there are some cultural differences between the East and the West. Western values focus on the progress through individuals, whereas it can be argued that Eastern values focus on progress through the state. The Chinese cultural approach to education historically has been a monoculture[8], whereas the Western approach is more diverse.

Progress is a human endeavour; we are striving for a better world, but agreement on what that world looks like varies. Is it individualistic or is it more collective, for the state or country? Is it to reduce poverty or reduce the gap between rich and poor? Is it just a blind adaptation to circumstance or strategically planned?

What does this have to do with the school and classroom teaching? I think the story we tell and show to learners can shape how they feel about their own progress. In primary schools, it is often apparent that personal development is as important as academic development. However, as the

---

[8] **Y. Zhao** (2014). *Who's Afraid of the Big Bad Dragon? Why China Has the Best (and Worst) Education System in the World.* San Francisco: Jossey-Bass.

experience in secondary school commences, it is easy to see the balance tip in favour of academic development and success in final examinations. The story that plays out is that if you work hard, you will get good grades. Good grades increase life chances; going to university means you will get a higher than average paid job and therefore will be more successful. It can often feel in the English system that every child has to achieve top grades in every subject they take, which makes the vast majority feel they have failed.

Summary: Progress as a human endeavour

- Humanity wants to progress as a collective through making the world a better place.

- What we teach, particularly the values we share with our learners, has an influence on that progress.

 Reflection

- How do you perceive progress in your education and career?

- Which types of progress are valued in your culture?

- What do you think the aim of human progress should be?

 Further reading

These two books are quite hefty, but both give interesting perspectives on human development and progress:

Y.N. Harari & D. Perkins (2017). *Sapiens: A Brief History of Humankind*. London: HarperCollins.

S. Pinker (2018). *Enlightenment Now: The Case for Reason, Science, Humanism, and Progress*. New York: Penguin.

2 Progress as a social mobiliser

I am known as a 'first-generation scholar', that is someone who is the first in their family to get a university degree. From my working-class family, I now have a job and income that are categorised as middle class in the UK. In many societies, movement between social classes is seen as progress for individuals, families, or other small collections of people. This is known as social mobility. It is strongest where there are defined class systems, such as in the UK, India, and China. Increased social status, particularly in Western societies, is based on socioeconomic factors: the status of a job or career, the amount of money they have within their family, or the amount of money they earn.

Social mobility is often achieved in many societies through education, whether it be through entrepreneurship, technological skill, or academic success. Indeed, higher qualifications usually equate to higher incomes, which can promote the shift in social status. In the UK and USA, social mobility is high on the political agenda: the desire to have people in employment, to move out of poverty, and be financially better off than their parents. I learned from my time in Beijing that, in some Eastern cultures, progress isn't even a concept, rather a focus on self-fulfilment and self-actualisation.[9]

Compared to looking at the progress of human civilisation, the progress of individuals and families through social structures can be seen within a generation. Education, schools, and teachers can have direct impact on the social mobility of individuals in their society.[10] Not all societies value social mobility; they may focus on finding a space to be productive and contribute to society. There are cultural differences in societies too, which may put emphasis on reproduction and parenthood, piety and religious observance, contribution to the community, career progression, contributing to the economy through paying taxes, status symbols such as watches, cars, and big houses, and, more recently, social media status through popularity, followers, and 'likes' as a form of social capital.[11]

These individual, political, and social values have a direct impact on what is valued in education and schools. It can also be the cause of tension between what schools think their learners need and what learners actually want.

Summary: Progress as a social mobiliser

- Progress through education usually increases life chances with respect to career, future earnings, and opportunities.

- Social mobility can be hindered by a number of factors including postcode/zip code, social class, and socioeconomic factors.

- Different cultures see social mobility in different ways, be it collectivist or individualistic.

---

[9] **H. Garcia & H. Cleary** (2017). *Ikigai: The Japanese Secret to a Long and Happy Life*. London: Hutchinson.

[10] **D.R. Entwisle, K.L. Alexander and L.S. Olson** (2018). *Children, Schools, and Inequality*. Abingdon and New York: Routledge.

[11] **S.P. Borgatti, C. Jones & M.G. Everett** (1998). Network measures of social capital. *Connections*, 21(2), 27–36.

Reflection

- Which inequities do your learners experience?

- To what extent do you, as a teacher, feel you can impact on social mobility?

- What aspects of social mobility are valued in your culture? How do these compare to learners' values?

Further reading

Social mobility via education gets a lot of discussion; these three books explore the main issues and perspectives:

D.R. Entwisle, K.L. Alexander & L.S. Olson (2018). *Children, Schools, and Inequality.* Abingdon and New York: Routledge.

P. Marshall (ed.) (2013). *The Tail: How England's Schools Fail One Child in Five – and What Can Be Done.* London: Profile Books.

R. Wilkinson & K. Pickett (2010). *The Spirit Level: Why Equality is Better for Everyone.* London: Penguin.

3 Progress through education

Having had the good fortune to step beyond the walls of my classroom, I have been able to see education in a variety of schools in a variety of countries. Schools, although seemingly instantly recognisable as institutions, have differing internal and external cultures. Most education systems are controlled by either a national government or at least on local government levels. Globally, there is a movement to standardise education, which has its own opportunities and pitfalls.[12]

Countries now compare themselves to international tables of attainment in education, such as PISA (Programme for International Student Assessment),[13] TIMSS (the Trends in International Mathematics and Science Study) and PIRLS (the Progress in International Reading Literacy Study).[14] This international comparison does appear to compel education authorities to shape their

---

[12] **S.J. Ball** (1998). Big policies/small world: An introduction to international perspectives in education policy. *Comparative Education*, 34(2), 119–130.

[13] **OECD** (n.d.). Programme for International Student Development. Available at: <http://www.oecd.org/pisa/> accessed 3 April 2019

[14] **IEA** (n.d.). TIMSS and PIRLS. Available at: <https://timssandpirls.bc.edu/index.html> accessed 3 April 2019

curricula to help progress up the international comparison tables.[15] When reforming the National Curriculum for England, the then education minister made direct reference to this desire; poor performance in the international tables caused Germany to reform its education policies;[16] and when I worked in Kazakhstan, the education leaders were keen to ensure they were doing things to get them moving up the PISA comparison tables.

The big debate is what learners should be taught in school and what the values of the education system should instil. What is to be learned is often contentious around emotive issues. In some places, there is tension over the teaching of evolution in science, where the school has strong fundamental Christian beliefs.[17] In others, the extent to which sex education is taught in schools, and how it is taught, can be divisive, often based on religious beliefs.[18] How a country's history is taught, particularly in geographic regions with border and military tensions, also gives rise to controversy over which historical perspectives and facts dominate.[19]

Commonly, school curricula are arranged with a dominance of the native language (reading and writing) and mathematics, followed by a series of disciplines such as the sciences, other languages, humanities, the arts, and physical education and sports. This traditional model is being challenged by a call for a curriculum that is more suited to the 'twenty-first century learner' (another controversial term).

Sugata Mitra, a professor in educational technology, argues that schools are actually impeding progress due to their unresponsiveness to embracing technology and the changing landscape in which learners learn.[20] He argues for developing skills such as fast and accurate internet searching, asking good questions, becoming a self-organised learner, and evaluating sources.

---

[15] **S. Grek** (2009). Governing by numbers: The PISA 'effect' in Europe. *Journal of Education Policy*, 24(1), 23–37.

[16] **K. Martens & D. Niemann** (2013). When do numbers count? The differential impact of the PISA rating and ranking on education policy in Germany and the US. *German Politics*, 22(3), 314–332.

[17] **J.D. Williams** (2008). Creationist teaching in school science: A UK perspective. *Evolution: Education and Outreach*, 1(1), 87–95.

[18] **P. Alldred & M.E. David** (2007). *Get Real About Sex: The Politics and Practice of Sex Education*. Maidenhead and New York: Open University Press.

[19] **K. Crawford** (1995). A history of the right: The battle for control of national curriculum history 1989–1994. *British Journal of Educational Studies*, 43(4), 433–456.

[20] **S. Mitra** (2005). Self organising systems for mass computer literacy: Findings from the 'hole in the wall' experiments. *International Journal of Development Issues*, 4(1), 71–81.

There are so many areas that we could value, including knowledge, understanding, skills, processes, motivation, breadth and depth of a topic, social, emotional, or cognitive abilities. Will Ord, an educationalist, captures the crux of this debate with the question, 'Is our progress more towards human doings or human beings?'[21] This, to me, emphasises what we do to actively progress as humans, rather than just existing. In contrast to this argument, there has been a rise in the dominance of the knowledge-based curriculum. Based on advances in cognitive science, it argues that knowledge can be taught in a scientific way and can then be applied to new situations. However, although this is wrapped up in 'science', there is also a sociological argument and a political argument that knowledge curricula create populations with a shared knowledge, shared understanding of history, and therefore, it is argued, a more cohesive society.[22]

Summary: Creating a progress culture through education

- Education is based on values. So, for a teacher to promote a progress culture in the classroom requires an understanding of the values of the education system.

- The policy of education or the written ethos of the school is not always carried through in practice.

- What you say and do as a teacher will reveal your values to your learners.

Reflection

- How do learners progress through education?

- What is the purpose of education in your context?

- What are your thoughts on a knowledge-rich or skills-rich curriculum?

---

[21] **W. Ord** (2017). Chapter 7: What is progress? In I. Wallace & L. Kirkman (eds) (2017). *Progress (Best of the Best)*. Carmarthen: Crown House Publishing, pp. 65–71. Reproduced with permission.

[22] **E.D. Hirsch Jr.** (2016). *Why Knowledge Matters: Rescuing Our Children from Failed Educational Theories*. Cambridge, MA: Harvard Education Press.

Further reading

To explore some of these ideas further, I recommend reading:

B. Lucas & G. Claxton (2010). *New Kinds of Smart: How the Science of Learnable Intelligence is Changing Education.* Maidenhead and New York: Open University Press.

S. Mitra (2006). *The Hole in the Wall: Self-organising Systems in Education.* New York and New Delhi: Tata-McGraw-Hill.

E.D. Hirsch Jr. (2016). *Why Knowledge Matters: Rescuing Our Children from Failed Educational Theories.* Cambridge, MA: Harvard Education Press.

4 Progress through learning

There is much interest in this area of progress, particularly about how learners learn and what the optimal conditions for learning are. Another aspect of this is not only what the optimal conditions are, but also how we can actually accelerate that progress, enabling learners to learn more, faster. In addition, there is interest in developing the skills for learning, for example skills of self-regulation and metacognition.[23] There have been a number of programmes developed to support learners' learning skills, such as Learning to Learn,[24] Habits of Minds[25] and Learning without Limits.[26] These programmes support learners' ability to actively learn, assess their own progress, choose and use techniques to check understanding, and to attend to gaps: ultimately a path to becoming an independent learner.

We also have a number of questions about what learning is and how learners progress in learning. We learn as we experience new things, but this may be on a surface level, where we recognise a new word, a new phenomenon, the title of a new book, or a new equation. Learning is

---

[23] **Education Endowment Foundation** (2018). Metacognition and self-regulated learning report. Available at: <https://educationendowmentfoundation.org.uk/tools/guidance-reports/metacognition-and-self-regulated-learning/> accessed 3 April 2019

[24] **P. Black, R. McCormick, M. James & D. Pedder** (2006). Learning how to learn and assessment for learning: A theoretical inquiry. *Research Papers in Education*, 21(02), 119–132.

[25] **G. Claxton** (2007). Expanding young people's capacity to learn. *British Journal of Educational Studies*, 55(2), 115–134.

[26] **S. Hart, A. Dixon, M.J. Drummond and D. McIntyre** (2004). *Learning Without Limits.* Maidenhead and New York: Open University Press.

making sense of new experiences and remembering that knowledge to apply to new situations.

We have all experienced learners in revision classes saying, 'We've done this before!' and having to tell them that they may *recognise* the subject but not actually *know* or *understand* it. Learning in this way takes energy, commitment, and motivation. However, learners often learn things informally and know the details really well without apparent learning techniques. Global trends such as Pokémon™ and popular computer games such as Minecraft™ seem to capture learners' imaginations and they learn about them in intricate detail without any apparent effort. Get them to learn multiplication tables, the present-tense verbs in French, or the reactions in organic chemistry in a formal classroom setting, and most learners resist, lack motivation, and cannot see the point.

Progress through learning requires a culture in which knowledge is valued and where learning for learning's sake is seen as a challenge and an achievement.[27] This can be best achieved where the teacher allows time to engage in learning, provides a range of tools for learning, and builds resilience through allowing mistakes, taking risks, and self-improvement.[28]

Summary: Towards a progress culture through learning

- Teachers require knowledge of practices such as learning skills and the role of making mistakes, and metacognition and self-regulation.

- Teachers require skills in creating a learning culture that promotes making mistakes, metacognition, and self-regulation.

- Teachers need to value and practise these approaches to learning to provide a learning culture.

⟳ Reflection

- How do learners learn in your phase or subject?

- What methods do you use to support your learners' learning?

- What can you do, as a teacher, to ensure learners make progress through learning?

---

[27] **R.A. Bjork, J. Dunlosky & N. Kornell** (2013). Self-regulated learning: Beliefs, techniques, and illusions. *Annual Review of Psychology*, 64, 417–444.

[28] **J.H. McMillan** (2018). *Using Students' Assessment Mistakes and Learning Deficits to Enhance Motivation and Learning*. Abingdon and New York: Routledge.

Further reading

To explore some of these ideas further, I recommend reading:

P. Black, C. Harrison, C. Lee, B. Marshall & D. Wiliam (2003). *Assessment for Learning: Putting it into Practice*. Maidenhead and New York: Open University Press.

B. Carey (2014). *How We Learn: The Surprising Truth About When, Where and Why It Happens*. London: Macmillan.

P.C. Brown, H.L. Roediger III & M.A. McDaniel (2014). *Make It Stick. The Science of Successful Learning*. Cambridge, MA: The Belknap Press/ Harvard University Press.

5 Progress through pedagogy

Pedagogy is how we teach. How we choose to teach is influenced by a whole range of factors, including personal experiences, professional experiences, assumptions about education, beliefs about our subject, political culture, current local and national policy, and the sociocultural environment. In the middle of my school teaching career, there was a movement in pedagogy of 'sharing good practice'. Teachers shared what worked well for them with other teachers, with the hope good practice would spread. Increasingly, schools and teachers are engaging with evidence-informed strategies and applying peer-reviewed research to the classroom. There is now a movement from doing 'what works' to doing 'what works best'.[29]

Teaching approaches vary from direct instruction to discovery learning; from teaching when a child is ready to accelerated learning strategies; from the emphasis on knowledge to the learning through developing skills. There are also a number of emerging techniques that aim to increase long-term memory. These include making desirable difficulties,[30] promoting the making and correction of mistakes,[31] tackling troublesome

---

[29] **D. Wiliam** (2018). *Creating the Schools That Our Children Need: Why What We're Doing Now Won't Help Much (and What We Can Do Instead)*. West Palm Beach, FL: Learning Sciences International, p.110.

[30] **R.A. Bjork** (2017). Creating desirable difficulties to enhance learning. In I. Wallace & L. Kirkman (2017). *Best of the Best Practical Classroom Guides: Progress*. Carmarthen: Crown House Publishing.

[31] **J.H. McMillan** (2018). *Using Students' Assessment Mistakes and Learning Deficits to Enhance Motivation and Learning*. Abingdon and New York: Routledge.

concepts,[32] spacing and retrieval approaches,[33] interleaving,[34] deliberate practice,[35] and dual coding.[36] I will cover some of these in more detail in Part 2.

All these techniques are about providing the conditions to help learners make progress and sometimes accelerate progress. Teachers have a role in curriculum design, lesson planning, teaching, and assessment that promotes progress. This will set the culture of the learning environment, which is easier to foster if it is a school culture and embedded within society.

Being an effective teacher requires professional knowledge not only of the content that is being taught, but crucially of how it can be taught to all learners. I spent some time with Guy Claxton on an education project in Canada; he illustrates the types of judgements a teacher has to make.[37] If a task is perceived as too easy, it can be seen as boring, but if too hard it can be demoralising. Teachers have to make decisions about what Claxton calls 'the sweet spot' where learning happens. He also contends that nobody knows that sweet spot better than the learners themselves, so a teacher can help find it by supporting learners with 'building learning power'; that is, knowing how to learn, gradually taking on more responsibility for themselves. Claxton promotes the use of activities where difficulty can be adjusted, the 'low threshold, high ceiling' approach.

Summary: Towards a progress culture through pedagogy

- Teachers need to have good subject knowledge, but also good, evidence-based, pedagogical knowledge.

- Teachers need to create a culture that not only promotes the desire to learn, but also the strategies of how to learn.

- Pedagogy is a set of values, beliefs, and skills that can be learned over time.

---

[32] **J. Meyer & R. Land** (eds) (2006). *Overcoming Barriers to Student Understanding: Threshold Concepts and Troublesome Knowledge*. Abingdon and New York: Routledge.

[33] **H.P. Bahrick & L.K. Hall** (2005). The importance of retrieval failures to long-term retention: A metacognitive explanation of the spacing effect. *Journal of Memory and Language*, 52(4), 566–577.

[34] **M.S. Birnbaum, N. Kornell, E.L. Bjork & R.A. Bjork** (2013). Why interleaving enhances inductive learning: The roles of discrimination and retrieval. *Memory & Cognition*, 41(3), 392–402.

[35] **K.A. Ericsson, R.T. Krampe & C. Tesch-Römer** (1993). The role of deliberate practice in the acquisition of expert performance. *Psychological Review*, 100(3), p. 363.

[36] **J.M. Clark & A. Paivio** (1991). Dual coding theory and education. *Educational Psychology Review*, 3(3), 149–210.

[37] **G. Claxton** (2017) Chapter 11: Learning power: Finding your own sweet spot. In I. Wallace & L. Kirkman (eds) (2017). *Best of the Best Practical Classroom Guides: Progress*. Carmarthen: Crown House Publishing.

Reflection

- What does pedagogy mean to you?

- To what extent does your pedagogy support progress?

- Are some teaching approaches more focused on promoting progress than others?

 Further reading

To explore some of these ideas further, I recommend reading:

G. Claxton (2002). *Building Learning Power*. Bristol: TLO Ltd.

H.L. Andrade & M. Heritage (2018). *Using Formative Assessment to Enhance Learning, Achievement, and Academic Self-regulation*. Abingdon and New York: Routledge.

J.H. McMillan (2018). *Using Students' Assessment Mistakes and Learning Deficits to Enhance Motivation and Learning*. Abingdon and New York: Routledge.

6 Progress through assessment

I find it helpful to imagine that teaching, learning, and assessment are the trilogy that make progress happen (see Figure 1.1). Assessment can, if used appropriately, enhance progress and if used without care, it can hinder progress or just be pointless.[38] All teachers assess their learners, which can inform both next steps in teaching and next steps in learning, as illustrated in Figure 1.1.

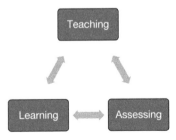

Figure 1.1: The 'Teaching–Learning–Assessing' triangle. How do the three points interact?

---

[38] **P. Black & D. Wiliam** (1998). Assessment and classroom learning. *Assessment in Education: Principles, Policy & Practice*, 5(1), 7–74.

For example, if assessment is limited to just summative assessment, the influence on learning is minimal. However, good formative assessment can improve teaching and learning.

Without some sort of brain scanner from the future, we have limited ways to understand exactly what learners have learned in school. We can only assess them by what they speak, write, or can do. This is a proxy of what they actually know and understand, as we cannot see each other's mental models. We can only express them verbally, through writing or drawing.

The default way to assess and compare learners' knowledge, understanding, and skills is through a standardised test. That way, we can see what they can and can't do, give them a grade corresponding to their response, and compare that to other learners in the same cohort. Most tests require written responses, but some language exams have a spoken component and others can have a practical component, such as practical work in Science, painting or sculpture in Art, and performances in Drama and Music.

Standardised testing dominates most countries' education policy to monitor and evaluate teaching and learning in schools. This form of assessment is seen by most as fair, rigorous, accurate, and valid. However, the purpose of such tests, how the results are used, and the value of the outputs are often highly trusted by the public, but highly contested by education professionals and researchers.

The dominance of formal testing within schools and the use of the data continues to be challenged by educational researchers and many education professionals.[39] Formative assessment in schools has been on the increase in many countries since 1998, when the Assessment for Learning (AfL) movement started.[40] AfL is based on the idea that assessment is used to help learners to progress by helping them become aware of where they are, where they want to be, and how to get there. It moves the assessment away from being something that is done to learners by teachers, to being a joint endeavour where assessment is actually part of the learning process.[41]

Although formative assessment approaches, including feedback,[42] have been shown to be significantly effective, due to the insistence of governments and educational authorities wanting to measure, monitor, and control education,

---

[39] **W. Mansell** (2011). Improving exam results, but to what end? The limitations of New Labour's control mechanism for schools: Assessment-based accountability. *Journal of Educational Administration and History*, 43(4), 291–308.

[40] **P. Black & D. Wiliam** (1998). Assessment and classroom learning. *Assessment in Education: Principles, Policy & Practice*, 5(1), 7–74.

[41] **W. Harlen** (2007). *Assessment of Learning*. London: Sage.

[42] **J. Hattie & H. Timperley** (2007). The power of feedback. *Review of Educational Research*, 77(1), 81–112.

summative assessment remains the main mode of assessment. However, day-to-day in schools, formative assessment can dominate in classrooms and support learning.[43]

 Reflection

- What types of assessment take place in your context?
- How does compulsory assessment impact on what and how you teach?
- How does compulsory assessment impact on how you assess formatively?

 Further reading

To explore some of these ideas further, I recommend reading:

P. Black, C. Harrison, C. Lee, B. Marshall & D. Wiliam (2003). *Assessment for Learning: Putting it into Practice*. Maidenhead and New York: Open University Press.

D. Christodoulou (2016). *Making Good Progress? The Future of Assessment for Learning*. Oxford: Oxford University Press.

A. Chandler-Grevatt (2018). *Oxford Teaching Guides: How to Assess your Students. Making Assessment Work for You*. Oxford: Oxford University Press.

Summary: Towards a progress culture through assessment

- Teachers need to have good understanding of assessment: the purposes, uses, and interpretation of both formative and summative assessment.

- Teachers need to create a culture that promotes personal progress, not comparative outcomes.

- The way we assess learners and what we assess influences our classroom culture.

7 Progress as a management tool

A few years ago, some of my trainees were telling me that their placement schools were expecting them to demonstrate progress every ten minutes in lessons. This expectation appeared to arise from nowhere. What possibly could be the reason behind this?

---

[43] **P. Black** (2015). Formative assessment – an optimistic but incomplete vision. *Assessment in Education: Principles, Policy & Practice*, 22(1), 161–177.

In many countries, education is under enormous scrutiny by the government. Schools are accountable for learners' grades and progress through school. Authorities monitor school effectiveness and make judgements on that effectiveness based on learner outcomes. These judgements impact the jobs of the school leaders, the financial support of the school and, in some cases, the very future of the existence of the school.[44]

In addition, the English school inspectorate, Ofsted, uses this data to judge schools and decide whether the school is outstanding, good, or requires improvement.[45] The terms by which the school is judged impact on what school management want their teachers to do, often leading to performances rather than embedding of good practices. Myths arise and schools put their staff and pupils through 'mocksteds' (pretend inspections), 'learning walks' (where senior managers drop in on lessons) and performance management focused on inspection outcomes.

Interestingly, one of the dominant myths[46] created around Ofsted is that teachers have to demonstrate learners' progress every ten minutes in a lesson. This, it seems, originated from the observation that an inspector will spend an average of ten minutes within a lesson and will need to see 'evidence for progress' within that time. There was a proliferation of, usually ineffective, strategies and lesson plans to achieve this. When 'progress' becomes a tool by which to manage teachers, teaching, and learners, there are serious implications for the very purpose of teaching, learning, and education.

Instead of final outcomes of learners in exams, some governments are interested in the progress made by learners during the school experience.

 Reflection

- To what extent is progress used for management in your context?

- What impact does management have on learner outcomes?

- What impact does management have on the culture of your classroom and your approach to teaching?

---

[44] **W. Mansell** (2007). *Education by Numbers: The Tyranny of Testing*. London: Politico's Publishing.

[45] **Ofsted** (n.d.). <https://www.gov.uk/government/organisations/ofsted> accessed 3 April 2019

[46] **Ofsted** (2018). Guidance: Ofsted inspections: myths. Available at: <https://www.gov.uk/government/publications/school-inspection-handbook-from-september-2015/ofsted-inspections-mythbusting> accessed 3 April 2019

In some cases, this has led governments to impose a set of regular tests to check that all learners are making the required progress. For example, England uses 'Progress 8' or 'Value Added' statistics that are intended to show the progress that learners make in school.[47]

 Further reading

To explore some of these ideas further, I recommend reading:

S.J. Ball (2017). *The Education Debate*. 3rd edition. Bristol: Policy Press.

W. Mansell (2007). *Education by Numbers: The Tyranny of Testing*. London: Politico's Publishing.

A. Hargreaves & D.L. Shirley (eds) (2009). *The Fourth Way: The Inspiring Future for Educational Change*. Thousand Oaks, CA: Corwin Press.

1.3 What are the features of a progress culture?

Having explored a range of perspectives on progression and education, we are now ready to consider some of the key questions concerning progress and go into deeper detail that is directly relevant to progress in school. These I have identified as:

- Ready to progress? Starting points

- Progress towards what? Meaningful destinations

- How does progress happen? Models for progress

- Observable progress: What does progress look like?

- Role of the teacher.

Ready to progress? Starting points

In this section, I argue that it is important for teachers to understand and take into account the cultural factors in the classroom, so that all learners, whatever their background, may have a chance to progress in school.

---

[47] **Department for Education** (2019). Guidance: Secondary accountability measures (including Progress 8 and Attainment 8). Available at: <https://www.gov.uk/government/publications/progress-8-school-performance-measure> accessed 3 April 2019

Before we start, have a go at the assumptions analyser (Table 1.1). Once you have read the section, revisit it to see if any of your assumptions have been challenged.

Table 1.1: Assumptions analyser: Ready to progress?

	Strongly agree	Tend to agree	Neither agree nor disagree	Tend to disagree	Strongly disagree
1 Home life has significant influence on how a child will progress at school.					
2 As long as they work hard, all learners have the same opportunity to progress at school.					
3 Teachers can have significant influence on the progress a child makes at school.					
4 Particular groups in society have less chance of progressing at school due to cultural differences.					
5 The way the curriculum is taught can disadvantage some learners in making progress.					
6 Testing learners when they start school means we can accurately measure their progress through school.					

Analyse your assumptions

Now you have thought about your assumptions, read this section and see how these ideas fit together.

For systems that attempt to measure progress, it would be really useful if all learners started school having the same experiences, knowledge, understanding, and skills. However, they do not, and in fact the experiences that learners have before starting school can be disparate, vast, and have significant impact not just on their starting point in education but on their ability to learn. Teachers and school are only one aspect of learners' lives, and if learners are to make progress at school, there are foundations that need to be in place outside of and before schooling.

In this section, I will consider the influences of home life and school life on a child's potential to progress in school. I will then look at the impact on progress of starting school and the transitions learners make within the school system.

Home life

Home life has significant influence on how a child makes progress at school. There are key factors that a child has no influence over; these include where the child was born (for example, the postcode and zip code effect in the UK[48] and the USA respectively[49]), the socioeconomic situation the child grows up in, their social class,[50] their race, and their gender.[51]

In many cultures, people do not progress through merit, but based on their social class. Privilege such as this happens in societies where there is a class system, such as in the UK.[52] School systems are arguably set up to promote cultural bias through practices such as setting within schools, having catchments that separate learners from different postcodes or districts, and social segregation based on selection carried out by faith schools and private schools. Parts of the UK have a grammar-school system that is based on learners' ability to do an exam at age 11; Kazakhstan has the Nazarbayev Intellectual Schools based on scholarships and common schools for the rest of the learners in the country.[53]

Parents can have a huge influence on whether a child will progress at school. For example, the more parents read to their child, the wider the child's vocabulary and the greater chance they have of being ready to start school (look up Fry's words if you are interested in this[54]). Similarly, pre-school experiences of mathematics influence future progress.[55] If parents do not 'speak the language of schooling', they can disadvantage their child's progress.[56]

---

[48] **K.E. Stanovich** (1986). Matthew effects in reading: Some consequences of individual differences in the acquisition of literacy. *Reading Research Quarterly*, 21, 360–406.

[49] **M.L. Kornhaber, K. Griffith & A. Tyler** (2014). It's not education by zip code anymore – but what is it? Conceptions of equity under the Common Core. *Education Policy Analysis Archives*, 22, 4.

[50] **R. Breen & J.O. Jonsson** (2005). Inequality of opportunity in comparative perspective: Recent research on educational attainment and social mobility. *Annual Review of Sociology*, 31, 223–243.

[51] **S.F. Krein & A.H. Beller** (1988). Educational attainment of children from single-parent families: Differences by exposure, gender, and race. *Demography*, 25(2), 221–234.

[52] **S.J. Ball** (2007). *Education plc: Understanding Private Sector Participation in Public Sector Education*. Abingdon and New York: Routledge.

[53] **D. Bridges** (ed.) (2014). *Education Reform and Internationalisation: The Case of School Reform in Kazakhstan*. Cambridge: Cambridge University Press.

[54] **E. Fry** (1957). Developing a word list for remedial reading. *Elementary English*, 34(7), 456–458.

[55] **E.C. Melhuish, K. Sylva, P. Sammons, I. Siraj-Blatchford, B. Taggart, M. Phan & A. Malin** (2008). Preschool influences on mathematics achievement. *Science*, 321(5893), 1161–1162.

[56] **J. Hattie** (2009). *Visible Learning: A Synthesis of Over 800 Meta-analyses Relating to Achievement*. Abingdon and New York: Routledge.

I have also experienced, both in England and abroad, the impact of being in a minority group and progress in schooling. The UK has a population of traveller families, who by law have to send their children to school when they settle somewhere for a short time. It means that a child from a traveller family can experience many schools in many different places during their childhood, often leading to a fragmented experience of schooling and a negative impact on qualifications when leaving school.[57] In Canada, I met young people from the aboriginal groups. Some of these learners found that their parents' cultural values differed from the values of formal schooling, meaning that, at home, educational opportunities were not prioritised for them.[58] When young people chose to follow formal schooling, they did so with the disapproval of their families. These are examples of significant cultural clashes that have an impact on some learners' progress in school.

In John Hattie's collection of meta-analyses, he ranked features of home life in the top 50 factors that affect learners' achievement at school. Most influences in the top 50 were factors associated with the learner, the teaching approach, and the school. 'Home environment' and 'socioeconomic status' come in at 31 and 32 respectively, followed by 'parental involvement' at number 45. Each of these had significant size-effects of 0.57, 0.57 and 0.51 respectively, meaning that they are all influences that have the greatest impact on learners' achievements.[59]

As a teacher, being aware of a child's starting points will help you to understand if a child is 'school ready'. Important factors include: how often the child is read to, or reads on their own at home, or has regular opportunities to experience numbers in everyday life. In addition, parents need to present a positive experience of school and have academic aspirations for their children. Teachers, however, can make a difference to learners' school lives and ability to progress in the way we choose to teach them and help them progress within school. For example, if teachers feel that a particular learner's parents are not engaged with school or schooling, with the support of the school, parent engagement programmes can be put in place.

---

[57] **C. Kiddle** (2000). Partnerships depend on power-sharing: An exploration of the relationships between Fairground and Gypsy Traveller parents and their children's teachers in England. *International Journal of Educational Research*, 33(3), 265–274.

[58] **B. Schissel, T. Wotherspoon & J.W. Friesen** (2002). The legacy of school for Aboriginal people: Education, oppression, and emancipation. *Canadian Ethnic Studies*, 34(2), p.129.

[59] **J. Hattie** (2009) *Visible Learning: A Synthesis of Over 800 Meta-analyses Relating to Achievement*. Abingdon and New York: Routledge, pp.19 and 33.

School life

When I was training a group of teachers in China, many of them put their heads on the desks to sleep after lunch. I found out during my stay that many school teachers take a post-lunch nap, with the learners doing the same. As a keen napper, I think this is a great idea. However, there are perhaps some real learning benefits.

Day to day, learners need to be ready for school and ready to learn, thus to make progress. To be ready to learn, there are basic needs that must be satisfied: getting enough sleep and being fed and watered. Tired, hungry, thirsty learners do not learn well. They need to feel safe at home, outside, and at school, as well as having someone who loves and cares for them and friends who allow them to belong. When these things are in place, a child will have self-esteem, confidence, and self-respect, allowing them to be ready to learn. This, in essence, is what Maslow's hierarchy of needs offers as the conditions for an optimal sense of self (see Research 1.1 below), and it is often used to justify the basic requirements for learners to be in a position to learn. As with all theories, they have their limitations and undergo critique. Whether or not these factors are a hierarchy, there are certainly individual factors that do impact on a child's ability to learn.

The links between sleep and learning are becoming increasingly apparent from neuroscience and psychology, specifically the role of sleep in remembering, forgetting, and conceptualising.[60] During sleep, after a day of learning, these essential learning processes occur. Sleep does more than just making you feel less tired! Food is seen as so essential to learning that in some areas of poverty, schools provide breakfast clubs before classes begin, to feed those unable to have breakfast at home.[61] In addition, the government in England has provided free school meals to some learners, based on parental income, to ensure they have at least one good meal a day.[62]

---

[60] **M.P. Walker** (2017). *Why We Sleep: The New Science of Sleep and Dreams.* New York: Allen Lane.

[61] **D. Simpson** (2001). The impact of breakfast clubs on pupil attendance and punctuality. *Research in Education*, 66(1), 76–83.

[62] **S. Gorard** (2012). Who is eligible for free school meals? Characterising free school meals as a measure of disadvantage in England. *British Educational Research Journal*, 38(6), 1003–1017.

Research

1.1 Basic needs: biology, psychology, and motivation

A.H. Maslow (1943). A theory of human motivation. *Psychological Review*, 50(4), 370–396.

I have chosen this very old paper because Maslow's theory pervades many disciplines, including education. It has been developed since its first publication, critiqued thoroughly, and continues to resonate with the classroom teacher.

Abraham Maslow was a psychologist who was interested in how some people become fully 'self-actualised'. Through biographical analytical research of 18 people he considered to be self-actualised, he was able to develop a pyramid that illustrated a hierarchy of needs for an individual to be motivated and achieve self-actualisation.

Figure 1.2: Maslow's hierarchy of needs

Limitations

Some critiques have expressed concern of the methodology that Maslow used. Specifically, the small sample size, the qualitative and subjective nature of biographical research, and the sampling technique being skewed towards men.

There has also been some discussion of whether these needs are really a hierarchy and whether all people need to fulfil all levels before reaching self-actualisation. Finally, the concept of self-actualisation has been interrogated as difficult to define, although attempts have been made to develop the term.

For me, Maslow's hierarchy of needs is a useful reminder of the basics that are needed for a child to even have a chance of being motivated to learn. Since Maslow wrote this first paper, we have developed a more sophisticated understanding of the impact of physiological deficiencies on development and learning in learners and through to adulthood, including nourishment and sleep. Motivation theory has also come a long way, particularly that of mindsets, self-regulation, and metacognition, and their roles in effective learning. If you read Maslow's list of characteristics and behaviours of 'self-actualised' people,[63] there are many in common with those with a growth mindset[64] and characteristics that are promoted in self-regulation.[65]

See Section 3.6 for more guidance on taking a critical approach to academic research.

Starting at school

For a child, starting out at school and their readiness to start school are dependent on these pre-school experiences, as well as the experiences that continue at home throughout school. Teachers who teach learners in this situation need not only good skills in pedagogy, but also a good understanding of the social and cultural influences on the learners and their families. Schools need flexibility to provide for all learners with a range of experiences when they first walk through the school gates.

Transitions between phases

Most learners go through different phases of schooling. In most situations, this next stage is seen as going up a year. There are few places in the world where learners are held back a year if they have not progressed enough; most learners just have to plough on to the next year regardless of how far they have progressed.

The transition between phases within a school can sometimes be an issue. A well-documented phenomenon in England was the Key Stage 3 'wasted years'.[66] Key Stage 3 is the phase for 11–14-year-olds, and progress slowed

[63] **A.H. Maslow** (1970). *Motivation and Personality*. New York: Harper & Row.

[64] **C. Dweck** (2017). *Mindset: Changing the Way You Think to Fulfil Your Potential*. Updated edition. London: Robinson.

[65] **M. Boekaerts & L. Corno** (2005). Self-regulation in the classroom: A perspective on assessment and intervention. *Applied Psychology*, 54(2), 199–231.

[66] **Ofsted** (2015). Key Stage 3: The Wasted Years? Available at: <https://www.gov.uk/government/publications/key-stage-3-the-wasted-years> accessed 10 March 2019

down in these years between primary school and starting GCSEs (the final qualifications). Among the findings were:

- The phase (KS3) was not a high priority for many secondary-school leaders in timetabling, assessment, and monitoring of pupils' progress.

- Teaching in MFL (Modern Foreign Languages), History, and Geography at Key Stage 3 does not lead to good levels of achievement.

- Leaders prioritise the pastoral over the academic needs of pupils during transition from primary school.

- Many secondary schools do not build sufficiently on pupils' prior learning.

Competing priorities in schools can mean that some aspects of the curriculum are given more attention and resources are unevenly distributed. Interestingly, a lot of attention is given to a smooth transition for learners between their primary and secondary schools. This is often focused on the child's well-being, with often their previous achievements in primary school being ignored, which leads to the issues surrounding transition between schools.

Transitions between schools

There are two types of transitions between schools: the planned between phases, such as between primary and secondary school, and the unplanned, such as when families relocate and learners have to start a new school.

Change will always hinder progress, but its effect can be reduced if opportunities are put in place to visit the new school ahead, connections are made between the new teachers and other learners, a transition and hand-over period is in place, and teachers have a good understanding of what the learner knows, understands, and can do before the learner starts the new school, and building from that.[67]

Towards a progress culture: starting points

In a progress culture, teachers must:

- develop awareness of how different social backgrounds have different learning experiences; hence teachers need to know that learners will have different starting points

- know that some learners will be less prepared to start school or transition between schools than others, based on home experiences and psychological factors

[67] **D.W. Test, C.H. Fowler, S.M. Richter, J. White, V. Mazzotti, A.R. Walker, P. Kohler & L. Kortering** (2009). Evidence-based practices in secondary transition. *Career Development for Exceptional Individuals*, 32(2), 115–128.

- recognise that the actions of a school and a teacher can have significant impact on improving a learner's progress.

> ## Reflection
>
> Reflect on these questions after reading this section:
>
> - In your context, what are the cultural and social differences between the learners you teach?
> - What are the home life and school life factors that will impact on learners' progress?
> - What can a teacher do to ensure all learners start school or a new phase 'ready to progress'?

Progress towards what? Meaningful destinations

This book is focused on the term 'progress' within the context of school education. To be useful, the practical examples to support a progress culture will be presented in Part 2.

Analyse your assumptions

Before you read this section, have a go at the assumptions analyser (Table 1.2). Once you have read this section, revisit it to see if any of your assumptions have been challenged.

Table 1.2: Assumptions analyser: Progress towards what?

	Strongly agree	Tend to agree	Neither agree nor disagree	Tend to disagree	Strongly disagree
1 The purpose of school is to get good grades and good qualifications.					
2 The grades learners get in school are essential for success in life.					
3 Schools should focus only on what it takes to help a learner progress to get good grades.					
4 It is a teacher's responsibility to ensure learners learn what they are taught.					
5 A teacher's job is to teach the curriculum.					
6 A teacher's job is to design the curriculum.					

Now you have thought about your assumptions, read this section and see how these ideas fit together.

If we consider all the aspects in which learners make progress during their 10–12 school years, they are diverse and numerous. Physically, a child will grow and mature; psychologically, they will develop their personality, learn social skills, form their own interests, and recognise their own abilities; academically, they will increase their vocabulary, their mathematical skills, and knowledge and understanding of the sciences, humanities, and arts; they will develop skills in dance, drama, sports, and team playing; spiritually, they will develop thoughts on ethics, religion, and justice. I suspect you can think of several more. These all play a role in a learner's identity, who they feel they are, and how they are perceived by others.

However, among all of these aspects of being human, very few actually are measured or assessed in the final year of school. Instead, we assess a narrow range of subjects using a restricted range of assessment strategies, reducing this progress to a list of grades. In fact, the list of grades at the end of schooling tells us nothing about a child's progress. It just tells us what they have managed to attain, often compared to others in their year group. These grades represent the learning through a curriculum of a selected range of subjects and that's it. It is the curriculum that determines what is valued through what is taught and how it is assessed. So, it is necessary to consider the range of curricula available and their relationship with progress in school. Progress through the curriculum will allow learners to achieve their grades.

Ultimately, progress in school is summarised as a list of grades at the end of compulsory schooling. School leavers may also have a pile of certificates to show achievements or proficiencies in particular areas, such as swimming lengths of a pool, riding a bike, first aid, etc. Grades are the currency for the next step of life, whether it is going into the workplace, taking on an apprenticeship, or continuing in formal education.

This assumes that school examinations that are based on a curriculum hold useful information for all learners about the next steps into the world of work or further education. So, what are the features of a good curriculum for progress?

From his meta-analyses, John Hattie concludes that aspects of the curriculum that have a positive influence on learning include:[68]

- developing a curriculum that aims for the best balance of surface and deep understanding

- ensuring a focus on developing learning strategies to construct meaning

---

[68] **J. Hattie** (2009). *Visible Learning: A Synthesis of Over 800 Meta-analyses Relating to Achievement*. Abingdon and New York: Routledge, p. 35

- having strategies that are planned and deliberate

- having explicit and active programmes that teach specific skills and deeper understanding.

The whole premise of John Hattie's *Visible Learning* is that learners can see how learning takes place, the processes are explicitly taught, so these features of a curriculum focus on *understanding (surface and deep)*, *meaning construction* and *specific skills in learning*. However, not all curricula include these features and even fewer contain all three.

The curriculum is not a neutral or objective document; whether produced by a school, an education authority, or a national government, a school curriculum is underpinned by the values, beliefs, and assumptions made by the writers. Currently, in the United States and in England, there is a movement towards a 'knowledge-based' or 'knowledge-rich' curriculum. This is based upon educational research within the cognitive psychology domain, which includes Daniel Willingham,[69] who advocates that the focused learning of knowledge leads to deeper understanding, and E.D. Hirsch's ideology of a 'cultural literacy',[70] which contends that equality and social cohesion can be achieved through everyone having a shared 'common knowledge'.

When I first started teaching, the National Curriculum was, for me, the list of content and skills that I had to cover in my teaching. I knew nothing of the type of curriculum we were using, nor did I have any idea about how to critique it. A.V. Kelly, a leading academic who has produced several editions of a textbook about the theory and practice of school curricula since 1977, reveals the complexities of studying and understanding the curriculum.[71] The curriculum can be studied in terms of philosophy of education, sociology of education, psychology of learning, and the politics of education.

Table 1.3 summarises some of the aspects of curriculum that Kelly describes. I have summarised what I consider to be the key points, but you may want to read further. The purpose is to illustrate the complexity of curriculum and what exactly we want learners to achieve in school, and what they actually achieve during their experience at school.

Curriculum coherence, the 'why, what and how' to curriculum design and delivery, has been brought into sharp focus in England recently. The concept

---

[69] **D.T. Willingham** (2009). *Why Don't Students Like School? A Cognitive Scientist Answers Questions About How the Mind Works and What it Means for the Classroom*. San Francisco: Jossey-Bass.

[70] **E.D. Hirsch, J.F. Kett & J.S. Trefil** (1988). *Cultural Literacy: What Every American Needs to Know*. New York: Vintage.

[71] **A.V. Kelly** (2009). *The Curriculum: Theory and Practice*. 6th edition. London: Sage.

of a 'Coherent Curriculum Programme' has been advocated by policymakers[72] and this has been explored further by Mary Myatt, who tries to bridge the understanding of 'knowledge' and 'curriculum'.[73]

Table 1.3: Manifestations of the curriculum[74]

Curriculum type	A description
Educational	How a curriculum is planned, and why it is planned. What is to be taught and why.
Total	Beyond just 'what is taught', the total curriculum is the overall justification of how and why a curriculum should be taught.
Hidden	The things learners learn at school because of the way the curriculum is planned, organised, structured, and delivered. These are often unconscious, such as propagating gender stereotypes.
Planned	The curriculum laid out in a syllabus, specification, or prospectus. The intended learning.
Received	The actual curriculum that learners experience, compared to the planned curriculum.
Formal	The timetabled subjects, lessons, and teaching that are formally identified, in which to deliver the curriculum.
Informal	The 'extracurricular' activities that are not explicitly part of the formal curriculum, but indeed have educational value.

Schmidt and Prawat describe the coherent curriculum as:

> '... a precise technical term: a national curriculum should have content arranged in an order which is securely based in evidence associated with age-related progression, and all elements of the system (content, assessment, pedagogy, teacher training, teaching materials, incentives and drivers etc.) all line up and act in a concerted way to deliver public goods.'[75]
>
> **W.H. Schmidt & R.S. Prawat** (2006).
> Curriculum coherence and national control of education:
> Issue or non-issue?

[72] **J. Blake** (2018). *Completing the Revolution: Delivering on the Promise of the 2014 National Curriculum*. London: Policy Exchange. Available at: <https://policyexchange.org.uk/wp-content/uploads/2018/03/Completing-the-Revolution.pdf> accessed 10 March 2019

[73] **M. Myatt** (2018). *The Curriculum: Gallimaufry to Coherence*. Woodbridge: John Catt Educational.

[74] **Adapted from A.V. Kelly (2009)**. *The Curriculum: Theory and Practice*. 6th edition. London: Sage, pp. 5–12.

[75] **W.H. Schmidt & R.S. Prawat** (2006). Curriculum coherence and national control of education: Issue or non-issue? *Journal of Curriculum Studies*, 38(6), 641–658.

Coherence is an attempt to align all the aspects of curriculum, perhaps ensuring all the various aspects in Table 1.3 are addressed. Schools, teachers, and learners will understand the purpose and expected outcome for the curriculum. There will be a smaller gap between the planned curriculum and the received curriculum. The formal and informal curricula become the total curriculum, and at least then the hidden curriculum may become more transparent.

Progress through any curriculum depends on what features of the curriculum are measured and how. The types of assessment will no doubt drive a difference between the planned curriculum and the received curriculum.

Key points

For learners to progress, we must have a clear idea of where we want them to be.

- A curriculum that focuses on learning has these features: *understanding (surface and deep)*, *meaning construction*, and *specific skills in learning.*

- Curriculum design and curriculum enactment are different, influenced by political perspectives, social norms, and values, and the views of those who are teaching it.

- Curriculum coherence may reduce some differences between the planned and received curriculum and the formal and informal curriculum, but still has potential to be skewed by how it is assessed.

 Reflection

Reflect on these questions after reading this section:

- How would you describe the curriculum in your context?

- What are the differences between the planned and received curriculum in your context?

- To what extent does assessment affect the received curriculum in your context?

How does progress happen? Models for progress

Most teachers have a mental model of progress for how learners learn. They are likely to hold a theory of learning that they can apply when teaching whole classes and individuals. They use this model of progress and theory of learning to plan, assess, and respond to learners' needs.

> **Reflection**
>
> - How do you think learners progress in your school phase or subject?
> - What is your mental model of progress? Try to draw it.
> - What is your theory for learning? How do you think learners learn in your context?

Before we get too excited about this, a couple of working definitions are in order. The terms 'development' and 'learning' could be used interchangeably, and often are. In this section, I will be considering both processes, though our definition of progress is defined with a school system.

- Development is the biological and psychological changes that occur in a child.

- Learning is the process of accumulating knowledge, understanding, and skills, either through informal experiences or through formal school-based learning experiences.

It is also easy to see that these two processes are linked, as quite possibly more learning experiences may speed up development.

Analyse your assumptions

Respond to the questions in Table 1.4, to discover your assumptions about a child's progress with regard to development and learning.

Now you have thought about your assumptions, read this section and see how these ideas fit together.

Metaphors for progress

We often think in metaphors of how progress may happen. There are four models that are often used, which provide a framework for discussion:

- progress as 'climbing a ladder'

- progress as 'a jigsaw puzzle'

- progress as 'training for a marathon'

- progress through the 'waves' model.

Table 1.4: Assumptions analyser: How does progress happen?

	Strongly agree	Tend to agree	Neither agree nor disagree	Tend to disagree	Strongly disagree
1 Learners' development happens in distinct stages.					
2 Learners become ready to learn some concepts before other concepts.					
3 You can teach learners aged between 5 and 11 any concept if you know the right way.					
4 Progress happens when learners make connections between knowledge or skills.					
5 Learners' learning is a patchy, unpredictable process that depends on the child's own lived experience.					
6 Most learners at the same age learn and make similar progress each year.					
7 Learners have a better chance of progressing when a teacher teaches them knowledge in small chunks.					

The first three I came across in a Science education curriculum document[76] and I was introduced to the final model by David Didau.[77] I have built on these as I have discussed them with teachers, embellished them, and considered them in light of educational theories. Let's consider each of these in turn.

Climbing a ladder

The model of the ladder suggests that learners move through conceptual steps of gaining knowledge, understanding, and skills. In its purest form, it relies on the assumption that these things are hierarchical, that you need to have achieved one step before attempting the next. This is often seen as a good enough model for science and humanity subjects, where concepts are built up. For example, in Chemistry, the concept of matter as solids, liquids, and gases needs to be understood before an understanding of the concepts of particle behaviour, and so on (see Case study 1.1). If we are to consider the role of the teacher in this model, it would be to put in place smaller steps, so

---

[76] **W. Harlen** (ed.) (2010). *Principles and Big Ideas of Science Education*. Hatfield: Association for Science Education.

[77] **D. Didau** (2017). Chapter 5: The real shape of progress. In I. Wallace & L. Kirkman (eds) (2017). *Best of the Best Practical Classroom Guides: Progress*. Carmarthen: Crown House Publishing, pp. 49–55.

that the learner can make it to the next significant rung. However, many of the mastery models of learning use this idea of steps.

The ladder model is the one I have often used to develop pathways for learning key concepts and skills in secondary Science (see Case study 1.1). The model has its roots in early cognitive development theories such as that of Jean Piaget (see Research 1.2). This is the theory that we develop in stages; that, biologically and psychologically, we are only ready for the next stage after a period of time or a set of experiences. A sequence of set developmental steps allows us to reach a stage of 'thinking adult'.

1.1 Progress in Chemistry

 **Case study**

In Chemistry, we teach that all matter is made of atoms. However, in reality matter is made up of subatomic particles that behave according to quantum mechanical laws. Logically, we could build a school curriculum that starts with fundamental quantum mechanics in primary school and build up from there. However, we don't. Five-year-olds haven't got the conceptual understanding for these abstract concepts, so instead we start with what learners know about: the materials around them. We start from the premise that there are different types of materials with different properties, then that materials have three states of matter. Thus, water can be in one of three states: solid, liquid, or gas. Not until around age 11 do we start to explain the properties of water in solid, liquid, and gas using particle models. Then later, we learn that the particles are atoms or molecules, that elements are made up of the same type of atom, that elements are organised on the periodic table. These elements can be joined up in numerous ways by chemical reactions; they can join using different types of bonds, which dictates their properties. The structure of each atom itself is made of protons, neutrons, and electrons. It's often not until after compulsory education that learners will learn about quantum particles.

This can be seen as a very structured pathway, where learners have to experience one step before the next. There is a logical sequence of conceptual development.

 Research

1.2 Cognitive development

Jean Piaget is the best-known theorist for using a staged model, where learners develop through a set of stages. In Piaget's theory, learners move from sensorimotor to pre-operational thinking stages between the ages of

2 and 7 years. Then, aged 7–12 years, they reach the concrete operational stage, and finally aged 12 onwards they enter the formal operational phase.

We are familiar with the first stage, where babies and toddlers are focused on their perceptions and actions. For example, if they want their mother's keys, they will reach for them. During this stage, they develop object permanence; that is, the child understands that when the keys are in a pocket, they still exist. Younger learners just think the keys have vanished when they can't see them. In the next stage, learners start to use symbols to think about things; for example, the word 'keys' represents their mother's bunch of keys, but they are still focused on their own needs. The next stage is characterised by learners thinking through problems in their head, rather than having to physically try them out. They know that keys open doors, and perhaps which key will open which door, based on the shape of the keyhole. Finally, at the formal operational stage, at age 11 plus, most people are able to think about abstract concepts, think logically, and test hypotheses.

Although Piaget's methods and aspects of his theories have been contested,[78] there are neo-Piagetian theorists who have taken the first ideas of cognitive science and used them to understand child development, applying them to learning.[79] The key aspect of Piaget's ideas is that development has a strong biological influence: we are innately 'programmed' to develop over time. This has implications for teaching learners.

Key applications of Piaget's stage theory

Piagetian programmes score very highly in John Hattie's meta-analyses, particularly in mathematics, but also in reading, ranking second of the most effective strategies (effect size d = 1.28 d = 0.44 respectively).[80]

The idea of 'readiness' for learners to engage or learn specific concepts has implications for curriculum design and timing of formal instruction. If there are biological and psychological constraints on the capacity to learn, then teachers need to account for these.

In Science, where learners encounter abstract concepts such as forces and particles, the concrete operational stage and formal operational stage indicate the need to consider how to support learners' thinking from the concrete to the

[78] **M. Donaldson** (1978). *Children's Minds*. Glasgow: HarperCollins.
[79] **A. Karmiloff-Smith** (1995). *Beyond Modularity: Developmental Perspective on Cognitive Development and Conceptual Change*. Massachusetts: MIT Press.
[80] **J. Hattie** (2009). *Visible Learning: A Synthesis of Over 800 Meta-analyses Relating to Achievement*. Abingdon and New York: Routledge, p. 43.

abstract; for example, water is wet and runny (concrete) because it is made of particles that flow around each other (abstract). So, sequencing of lessons and curriculum design can draw on Piaget's, or at least neo-Piagetian, ideas of stages.

Piaget also came up with a theory of schemata, which we shall visit later in a more relevant section (see Research 1.3).

Jigsaw puzzle

In contrast, the 'jigsaw puzzle' model does not necessarily take a linear approach. Instead, 'pieces' of knowledge, understanding, and skills are slowly pieced together. Sometimes certain blocks grow faster than others, occasionally one developed patch of fitted jigsaw pieces will make a connection with another well-developed patch of pieces. Just one new piece of knowledge or concept can link two separate bodies of knowledge together. In psychological terms, the brain does seem to hold 'schemas' of knowledge, often unconnected, sometimes conflicting, until there is a gestalt moment of understanding when two schemata are joined together, or one is rejected to be replaced by another (see Research 1.3). The role of the teacher here is to find pieces that make the links, or offer strategies for completing the jigsaw (group pieces of the same colour together, find the edge pieces first).

1.2 Learning another language    Case study

Learning another language involves learning both its grammar and its vocabulary. Learning languages in school is usually done in discrete lessons, spread over a week. Some teachers use the target language throughout the lesson and others use a mixture of the native language and the target language using exercises.

Language is taught using four domains: listening, speaking, reading, and writing. A large proportion of time is spent learning vocabulary and phrases. Within these is the learning to use different tenses, e.g. present, past, and future.

Some language teachers find that the 'jigsaw' metaphor resonates with their experiences of teaching, where the pieces (vocabulary) are built up using listening, speaking, reading, and writing, then placed into sentences as the schema grows and links are made between the different approaches to tenses. Others prefer the 'marathon metaphor', where different skills (listening, speaking, reading, and writing) are continually developed for using the vocabulary. Then these skills are brought together to be able to have a conversation or write an essay in the target language.

Research

1.3 Piaget's schema

Piaget started this idea and it has been developed by others. The theory is that a building block of knowledge known as a 'schema' (plural: schemata) can be composed of objects, actions, and concepts. Learning is the connections between schemata. As we develop and learn, schemata become more elaborate and connected.

Schemata are created by a process of adaptation to a new situation. When presented with a new 'unit of knowledge' we can 'assimilate' it into a current schema; if that schema does not exist, we 'accommodate' it by changing an existing schema or creating a new one. 'Equilibration' is the phenomenon that drives progress in learning, where the unpleasant feeling of new knowledge 'not fitting' into our existing schemata is 'disequilibration', so effort is made to restore the balance by accommodation.[81]

Limitations

We know that Piaget focused on the individual, personal constructivism, ignoring the input from social interaction and cultural influences. Other relevant limitations include:

- At the time, Piaget did not have any influence of neurobiology. What happens in the brain? Is the physiology correct?

- Schemata are poorly defined. What does a schema look like? What is it made up of? Where is it located?

Work building on Piaget's schema

There are several teaching programmes based on Piagetian models that appear to have significant impact on attainment.[82] There are many studies that continue to utilise and adapt Piaget's schema of development,[83] taking sociocultural perspectives on areas such as reading development.[84]

---

[81] **J. Piaget & M. Cook** (1952). *The Origins of Intelligence in Children*. New York: International Universities Press. Vol. 8, No. 5, p.18.

[82] **J. Hattie** (2009). *Visible Learning: A Synthesis of Over 800 Meta-analyses Relating to Achievement*. Abingdon and New York: Routledge. p. 43.

[83] **S.J. Derry** (1996). Cognitive schema theory in the constructivist debate. *Educational Psychologist*, 31(3–4), 163–174.

[84] **M.B. McVee, K. Dunsmore & J.R. Gavelek** (2005). Schema theory revisited. *Review of Educational Research*, 75(4), 531–566.

Cognitive studies and neurobiological understanding do deal with specific regions of the brain, how we learn, and how neurons develop and link to create and connect memories. Perhaps schemata are more than a metaphor for these cellular and chemical workings in our brains.[85]

Training for a marathon

The 'training for a marathon' model is based on the approach of building different skills. Apparently, marathon runners never do the full 26.4 miles before the actual race. Instead, they work on building up various aspects of fitness.[86] Training involves a mixture of easy runs, steady runs, hill runs, interval runs and marathon pace runs, regular rests, stretching and core exercise, and attention to diet. It is not until the big day that all these attributes come together and hopefully help the runner to complete the full race. (When discussing these ideas with teachers, there seems to be a lot of contention about exactly how marathon runners train!)

This model assumes that the teacher has the role of a coach, assisting the learner with making decisions on what to work on, when, and how often.

Daisy Christodoulou uses a marathon-runner metaphor for educational progress, recognising that although some exercises that lead to an improvement in the time taken to run a marathon are clearly related to marathon running, such as running a half-marathon, others, such as strength and conditioning exercises, do not look anything like the final outcome.[87] All are important.

Waves on a beach (ebb and flow)

Based on the idea that learners often use a range of approaches to learning over a period of time, development can be imagined as the ebb and flow of overlapping waves where alternative ways of thinking change in frequency. This model suggests that instead of using one mode of development, learners use multiple ways of thinking, and instead of substituting each step of development, cognitive change is a series of continuously changing frequencies of a range of ways of thinking.[88]

---

[85] **D. Eagleman** (2015). *The Brain: The Story of You*. Edinburgh: Canongate Books.

[86] **Virgin Money London Marathon** (2019) Training plans. Available at: <https://www.virginmoneylondonmarathon.com/en-gb/trainingplans/> accessed 10 March 2019

[87] **D. Christodoulou** (2016). *Making Good Progress? The Future of Assessment for Learning*. Oxford: Oxford University Press, pp.156–157.

[88] **R.S. Siegler** (1996). *Emerging Minds: The Process of Change in Children's Thinking*. Oxford: Oxford University Press, pp. 86–90.

What do these metaphors tell us?

These four models do have their limitations. The ladder assumes a linear model of learning, which is often contested. Learning is multifaceted, multimodel, and highly complex. However, the ladder can provide a framework in which to work, an approximate pathway of development through which teacher and learner can have a mutual understanding of where to go next and how to get there. So, it can be argued that the jigsaw puzzle represents a more realistic model for progress in a subject, where fragments of knowledge, understanding, and skills are developed independently and sometimes get links between them. It demonstrates that messy, non-linear aspect of learning. It lacks a direction; instead it just accumulates. In this model, the 'what next' is harder for a teacher to define, whereas the marathon-training model presents several strands of progress, with a sense of direction to an end point. The strands on their own do not necessarily look like the final end point, but all build towards it.

This exercise of integrating the four models reveals some of our general assumptions about the nature of making progress within a subject. First, although we accept that progress is not made in a linear way, in most subjects there is a sense of direction, a destination, in mind. Second, different disciplines have different skill sets and pathways that can be developed over time. Finally, the assumptions of these metaphors reveal our assumptions about progress:[89] linear, building blocks, patchworked, pathways, complex, and irregular.

So, what can these metaphors or models for progress tell us about developing a progress culture? Teachers undoubtedly have their own mental models that they have developed tacitly through experience and, depending on their phase and subject, they may have different assumptions.

All these models are simplifications of development and progress, whether we learn through building blocks, steps on a ladder or staircase, or like a jigsaw puzzle, building domains that occasionally join up, or using multiple strategies where as we develop there comes a threshold moment where development moves onto a next stage. Development and learning are complex; learners' learning is particularly complex because they are developing as well as learning.

---

[89] **G. Lakoff & M. Johnson** (2003). *Metaphors We Live By*. Chicago: University of Chicago Press.

Key points

- Most teachers have a professional model for how learners progress within their phase or subject. This may or may not be informed by theory and evidence.

- Learners are developing into adults. Therefore, they are primed for learning, but are also to some extent limited by the constraints of biological and sociological development.

- Metaphors or frameworks that help teachers understand how learners progress have their limitations, but they can be useful for 'visualising' progress qualitatively.

- Teachers' assumptions about how learners progress will influence how they plan, teach, and assess.

 Reflection

- Which metaphor for progress do you most relate to in your school phase or subject?

- How is that metaphor useful for planning, teaching, and assessing?

- Which educational theories inform your understanding of progress? Why?

- Reflect on your responses in Table 1.4, and reflect upon how your assumptions may have been challenged.

Observable progress: What does progress look like?

> 'The narrative is one about the growth of knowledge over time.'
>
> **R. Duschl, S. Maeng & A. Sezen** (2011). Learning progressions and teaching sequences: A review and analysis. *Studies in Science Education, 47(2), p.123.*

Having considered how progress might happen, it is now useful to think about what progress looks like. I have a niece and nephew who live in Wales, and I only see them a few times a year. Each time I see them, I notice how much they have developed, changed, matured. These changes could be considered progress in their personal, social, and intellectual development. These snapshots into their lives make their progress through childhood noticeable because there is a significant time between each visit and childhood has particularly fast developmental changes.

Reflection

- What does your phase or subject focus upon in the curriculum?
- What proportion do knowledge and skills take up in teaching your phase/ subject?
- What are the main debates in your phase/subject about what is taught and how it is taught?
- What is your personal preference? Why?

Analyse your assumptions

Respond to the questions in Table 1.5 to see what your assumptions are.

Table 1.5: Assumptions analyser: What does progress look like?

	Strongly agree	Tend to agree	Neither agree nor disagree	Tend to disagree	Strongly disagree
1 Learners have made progress when they can apply their knowledge to everyday living.					
2 Learners have made progress when they can achieve their predicted grade in an examination.					
3 Learners have made progress when they know, understand or can do something new (to them).					
4 Learners have made progress when they can apply new knowledge, understanding, and skills to a new context.					
5 It is impossible to map out how a learner might make progress within a subject.					

Learning progressions

Learners are innately programmed to develop fast and progress towards adulthood, taking on new experiences and acquiring new knowledge, understanding, and skills. They grow rapidly, go through puberty, and become adults. We can see differences as they develop. When it comes to learning, there are two problems. The first is how we define progress and the second, how we see evidence for it.

Defining progress in school is a curriculum issue. As discussed earlier, curriculum design is a contested enterprise. There are many influences of political and social control; it is in itself not a neutral document. The main argument from governments in England and the United States is that we need a knowledge-based curriculum. However, there is much debate about what that looks like on paper and in the classroom. To illustrate this, I have put together three case studies of the main debates about the curriculum and how learners progress. These case studies have a focus on literacy in primary schools, secondary Mathematics, and primary and secondary Music. By presenting these case studies, I hope to reveal some of the tensions about agreeing on exactly what learners should be taught and what success looks like.

1.3 What does progress look like in primary literacy education?

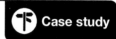 Case study

A primary-school teacher told me that when learners make progress they become happier and more confident. What interested me was that the teacher did not focus on the National Curriculum descriptors, the assessment grades, or qualification, just two human characteristics: happiness and confidence.

In England, the primary curriculum focuses learning to read using 'synthetic phonics',[90] which is tested in Key Stage 1 (ages five to six). The introduction of phonics over morphological approaches was controversial, as it is seen as politically driven rather than evidence based.[91] The research community and many teachers still question this approach.[92] Phonics does appear to increase the accuracy of reading, but not the comprehension.[93]

Progress in reading has become progress in phonics due to that being measured. It may have its limitations and, despite the policy agenda, primary teachers still look at whether a child has progressed in reading by how much more confident and happy they are.

[90] **Department for Education/Standards Testing Agency** (2014). Teaching phonics: information for schools <https://www.gov.uk/government/collections/phonics> accessed 10 March 2019

[91] **J. Soler & R. Openshaw** (2007). To be or not to be? The politics of teaching phonics in England and New Zealand. *Journal of Early Childhood Literacy*, 7(3), 333–352.

[92] **S. Ellis & G. Moss** (2014). Ethics, education policy and research: The phonics question reconsidered. *British Educational Research Journal*, 40(2), 241–260.

[93] **Education Endowment Foundation** (n.d.). Phonics: Moderate impact for very low cost, based on very extensive evidence. Available at: <https://educationendowmentfoundation.org.uk/evidence-summaries/teaching-learning-toolkit/phonics/> accessed 28 March 2019

1.4 How do learners progress in secondary Mathematics education?

 Case study

The pedagogy of Mathematics teaching is hotly contested.[94] In the briefest sense, there are those who argue that learners learn best in lessons that concentrate on individual repetition and practice, and those who argue that learners should learn through problem-solving and collaboration. There are deeply held views on both side of the debate.

Professor Jo Boaler, who now works at Stanford University, was incidentally my supervisor for my doctorate. Since then I have followed Boaler's career and seen the ferocity of feeling between the tribes on Mathematics teaching. Boaler is seen as a 'progressive' and has a prolific peer-reviewed evidence base,[95] and a huge following from Mathematics teachers in the USA and around the world who apply and develop her ideas.[96]

It comes down to the purpose of teaching Mathematics, perspectives on the discipline of Mathematics, and the need for everybody to be numerate, challenging cultural assumptions about Mathematics teaching and learning, and tackling inequalities of gender and other minorities from the 'hidden' curriculum.

1.5 What does progress look like in Music education?

 Case study

Should we be giving learners the experience of playing as many musical instruments as possible? Or should we allow them to get very good at one instrument at the expense of experiencing others? Could it be somewhere in between, where learners try a range of instruments until they find one that they like and then take that further?

Learning to play a musical instrument is not the same as learning about music. What could be included in the curriculum? What should learners be learning?

- The history of music? Which history?

- The global history of music or the cultural musical heritage?

---

[94] **P. Wright** (2012). The math wars: Tensions in the development of school mathematics curricula. *For the Learning of Mathematics*, 32(2), 7–13.

[95] **J. Boaler** (2015). *The Elephant in the Classroom: Helping Children Learn and Love Maths*. London: Souvenir Press.

[96] **J. Boaler** (2016). *Mathematical Mindsets: Unleashing Students' Potential Through Creative Math, Inspiring Messages and Innovative Teaching*. San Francisco: Jossey-Bass.

- The genres of music?

- Reading music or music by ear?

- Song writing?

Is Music education about becoming a musician or knowing about music?

Primary schools often have a strong musical presence with daily songs, regular use of percussion instruments, and rhythms. However, the quality of this will depend on the teachers' expertise and confidence to teach Music. This often diminishes to just one hour a week in secondary school for most learners, unless they pursue an instrument in parallel.

In response to curriculum change in England and the removal of any assessment guidance for teachers, the Incorporated Society of Musicians (ISM) put together a rubric to help teachers plan for progress in Music and assess the progress of their learners in primary[97] and secondary[98] Music. Their view is that:

> 'Assessment of musical learning should be rooted in the reality of musical activity that the young people undertake. Consequently, assessment should be of the musical attainment they have evidenced in a range of learning activities in which they have been singing, playing, performing, improvising, composing, and critically engaging with music. Progress is made over time, and evidence from ongoing musical assessments should be used to show this.'
>
> **A. Daubney & M. Fautley** (2019). *The National Curriculum for Music: A Revised Framework for Curriculum, Pedagogy and Assessment in Key Stage 3 Music.*

---

[97] **A. Daubney & M. Fautley** (2019). *The National Curriculum for Music: A revised framework for curriculum, pedagogy and assessment across primary music.* London: Incorporated Society of Musicians. Available at: <https://www.ism.org/images/images/ISM_The-National-Curriculum-for-Music-booklet_Primary_2019_digital.PDF> accessed 15 July 2019

[98] **A. Daubney & M. Fautley** (2019). *A Revised Framework for Curriculum, Pedagogy and Assessment in Key Stage 3 Music.* London: Incorporated Society of Musicians. Available at: <https://www.ism.org/images/images/ISM_The-National-Curriculum-for-Music-booklet_KS3_2019_digital.pdf> accessed 15 July 2019

These three case studies illustrate the tensions between what should be taught and how it should be taught in specific subjects and phases of schooling. Tensions include:

- Do we teach about a subject or how to become a practitioner of the subject; for example, are we teaching learners about science or how to be scientists? Are we teaching them about history or how to be historians? Or if both, what proportion of each?

- Do we teach knowledge/content or skills; for example, do we teach Science without being in a laboratory, learn how to play football without actually playing a game? Or if both, what proportion of each?

- Do we teach for knowledgeable citizens who share an understanding of their cultural heritage, or do we attempt to teach without context; for example, Science without the scientist who made discoveries, History without critique? Or if both, what proportion of each? Do we teach in general, surface terms or specific, deep ways? Or if both, what proportion of each?

Curricula usually focus on what is to be taught, not how or in what order. If teachers are the architects of the curriculum, then they need to have an idea of what progress looks like through the subject. I would go as far to argue that the curriculum should be written with progress in mind.

In perfunctory terms, teachers make everyday professional decisions about the order in which to teach their subject. Primary teachers will either tacitly or formally know which learners' reading books are best to read next; they will have an order of books in mind that increases in challenge and complexity. There are a number of commercial companies that produce books on just such progressions. Based on their knowledge of their subject, teachers will plan their teaching and assessment based on a progression of some kind, whether it is an accumulation of knowledge, understanding, and skills, or an increasingly complexity of knowledge, understanding, and skills.

I have a passion for learning ladders in Science education. There was a learning ladder that was generic, composed of general descriptors that could be used as activities to design learning ladders for specific activities. If the tasks were carried out over time, the learner would have regular opportunities to try out the generic knowledge, understanding, and skills in various specific situations.

Learning progressions are a hot topic in education research. They are called various terms: learning trajectories, learning pathways, and roadmaps. I will call these learning progressions for the rest of this book.

Purpose of learning progressions

Learning progressions have a particular purpose in education:

- to order knowledge, understanding, and/or skills into a logical sequence
- to use the sequence to plan teaching, formative, and summative assessment
- to have shared understanding of expectations, progress, and next steps
- to communicate a sense of progress over time.

I have always designed learning progressions to make sense of the curriculum; that is, what must be taught and my understanding of how knowledge and understanding develop in my subject. I draw on a range of sources including evidence from learning theories, such as concrete and abstract ideas and the 'sweet spot' for learning, and specific research papers based on how learners learn particular knowledge or concepts. In addition, I draw on my professional knowledge of what learners commonly struggle with. There are, of course, other constraints of the school year (such as school timetables and whether one or more teachers teach the same class) that will determine whether that sequence will be best for a particular learner or group of learners. However, for my subject, Science, I have a number of assumptions about progress that I know are different from those of teachers of other phases and subjects.

 Research

1.4 Progression pathways and educational research

The construction, purpose, and use of learning pathways in the school setting is still hotly debated in the academic world. Part 2 of this book is informed by much of the discussion that has been taking place in peer-reviewed journals over the past 15 years. A lot of energy has been put into the construction of learning progressions, particularly in subjects like Science[99] and Mathematics. The main purpose is for the development of learning environments that bring together curriculum, learning, and assessment.[100] In addition, language learning has an accepted agreement

---

[99] **M.J. Ford** (2015). Learning progressions and progress: An introduction to our focus on learning progressions. *Science Education*, 99(3), 407–409.

[100] **R. Duschl, S. Maeng & A. Sezen** (2011). Learning progressions and teaching sequences: A review and analysis. *Studies in Science Education*, 47(2), p.124.

on what progression in language learning looks like.[101] The playing of musical instruments also has a pathway set out in 'grades' in the UK,[102] with similar examination pathways in other countries.

The assumptions of learning progressions

Learning progressions have a number of assumptions that are worth considering:

- Learning knowledge, understanding, and skills is approximately linear.

- All learners follow a very similar pathway in their learning.

- Starting points and end points for all learners are approximately the same.

- At the very least, all learners pass through specific milestones or display key indicators at particular points in their learning.

- Learning starts with simpler knowledge, understanding, and skills, and works towards more complex knowledge, understanding, and skills.

Linking back to the metaphors for progress

If we think about which metaphor for how learners progress is most relevant to the idea of learning progressions, immediately the ladder metaphor seems obvious. Although a learning progression sets out a pathway for learning, it does not determine *how* the learning takes place through that pathway. Going back to our metaphors for how learners make progress (the ladder, jigsaw, marathon, and waves), they reveal some of the assumptions we make about what a learning progression should or should not include.

- The metaphor of the ladder suggests a linear progression, but when we use a ladder we can go up as well as down: backward steps are common in learning, or just hanging around for a bit before the next step. We know learning is not linear, but having a set of likely steps is useful in order to know where we are going. It also has a dimension of time, or at least expected time, in which to reach some of the steps.

---

[101] **Council of Europe** (n.d.). Common European Framework of Reference for Languages (CEFR). Available at: <https://www.coe.int/en/web/common-european-framework-reference-languages/level-descriptions> accessed 10 March 2019

[102] **S. Holland** (2017). How to get a music exam distinction – Part 2. Available at: <https://serenademagazine.com/series/music-education/get-music-exam-distinction-part-2/> accessed 10 March 2019

- The jigsaw metaphor moves away from the linear and more towards a web of knowledge: clusters of facts and concepts, and their connections. This could be presented as a big concept map, with the nodes being discrete knowledge or concepts. Learning takes place as connections between nodes are made.

- The marathon, on the other hand, suggests a similar situation to the ladder. However, the significance here is that those steps or building blocks may not look anything like the final knowledge, understanding, or skill. Advocates of a knowledge-based curriculum argue for breaking complex tasks into simpler units, which may not look like the final skill;[103] for example in Music, learning scales, to read music, and to play an instrument before playing a complicated piece of music. These blocks all need to be accessible and they will need an opportunity to be put together some time. Is that before or at the exam?

- Finally, the ebb and flow of waves works well, with several opportunities to engage with the same concept or skill set. This is possibly superior to the ladder model because it allows for the fuzzy nature of learning, approximate steps, and slow accumulation of knowledge, understanding, and skills, moments of it all coming together, and allowance for backward steps, several steps forward, and several steps back at a time. I imagine several ladders on a sandy beach, their bottom rung just at the water line, the top at the upper end of the beach. As the tide washes in, it laps up and down the rungs of each ladder. At any given point, each ladder will have a different number of rungs submerged, some will be regularly wetted by an incoming wave, others, higher up, only occasionally get wet. Once the tide is in, the tops of most of the ladders are reached. Progress has been made with a random overall forward movement, with plenty of setbacks along the way.

⟳ Reflection

- Reflect on your responses in Table 1.5 and how your assumptions may have been challenged.

- How do learners progress in your subject?

- What are the advantages and disadvantages of learning pathways?

---

[103] **D. Christodoulou** (2016). *Making Good Progress? The Future of Assessment for Learning.* Oxford: Oxford University Press.

Role of the teacher

Having now considered the different ways in which we can consider progress to be understood in education, and looked specifically at the aspects of progress through an educational curriculum in school, it is time to consider the role of the teacher.

A lot of things are done to teachers, particularly policy is imposed by educational authorities and within the school or college where they work. Teachers often see the requirement to enact the curriculum and use the school policies as part of their professional duties. However, teachers are also people who have deeply held beliefs in education based on their own educational experiences; so while most professional teachers do adapt their practice, many will rightly question new initiatives. The space where a teacher has most control is in their classroom, where they can choose to enact imposed policy.

The role of a teacher in developing a 'progress culture' is two-fold: first to learn about it, then to live it in the classroom. These things are best done concurrently with a cycle of try, reflect, adapt, try again. This is a common approach to action research. As I pointed out earlier, teachers and teaching methods have a significant impact on learners' school achievement despite other factors such as home life. We can make a difference to individuals; there is a real 'teacher effect'.

Analyse your assumptions

Respond to the questions in Table 1.6 below to see what your assumptions are.

Table 1.6: Assumptions analyser: The role of the teacher

	Strongly agree	Tend to agree	Neither agree nor disagree	Tend to disagree	Strongly disagree
1 Teachers have only a small effect on the progress of the learners they teach.					
2 Teachers have little influence on the curriculum.					
3 Teachers have a big influence on how the curriculum is taught.					
4 Teachers can improve their practice through reading and using educational theory.					
5 Teachers can improve their practice by carrying out educational research.					

The following sections of this book will show you how you can develop a 'progress culture' in your classroom, your attitudes, values, and behaviours, and how you can encourage learners to develop those same attitudes, values, and behaviours. Part 2 is a practical toolkit of how to use various strategies to create a progress culture. Part 3 is a guide for you to improve your assessment literacy, with a series of activities to understand progress in your phase and subject.

The teacher effect

Sir John Jones, a British educationalist, uses his personal and professional experiences as a headteacher to promote the idea that schooling can transform the lives of young people, because of the human impact of teachers as role models and inspiration and aspiration raisers. He believes in the 'teacher effect' that can take learners from all backgrounds and transform their lives. His book on this subject is itself inspiring and transformative. In an era of teacher-knocking and political interference in education, John Jones reminds us of the huge impact a good teacher can have on a learner, even when their early experiences are in deficit when they start school.[104]

Teachers can have a big influence on learners' progress within school. Teachers themselves, the methods they employ to teach, the curriculum employed, and the school structures can all have a greater influence on progress than the home life of a learner. Above, I drew on the influences from home that are from John Hattie's meta-analyses.[105] The top 30 largest effects are all school-centred, before the home environment. The take-home message is that teachers can and do make a difference in the choices they make. In Part 2 of this book, I will illustrate a range of ways of promoting progress, all of which are classroom-focused. However, a note of caution with Hattie's work is that it is a purely quantitative integration of quantitative studies that has squeezed out any social or cultural context in the analysis.

As we have seen, the curriculum is a complex document and it does require expertise to design. However, when it is in isolation from teachers, the intended curriculum can be different from the enacted curriculum, meaning that the original intentions are lost. By involving teachers in curriculum design, the political agenda could be lost and politicians' influence

---

[104] **J. Jones** (2010). *The Magic-weaving Business: Finding the Heart of Learning and Teaching.* London: Leannta Education.

[105] **J. Hattie** (2009). *Visible Learning: A Synthesis of Over 800 Meta-analyses Relating to Achievement.* Abingdon and New York: Routledge.

reduced.[106] However, how could we agree on a curriculum, particularly a coherent curriculum?[107]

There are many teachers who now use educational research to directly inform their practice, as well as schools that take on research-based initiatives. In England, there is the emergence of research schools that focus on using educational research, being subjects for educational research, and where teachers become education researchers themselves.[108]

 Reflection

- When have you felt, as a teacher, that you have had a particular impact on a learner?
- How is your time best used as a teacher to maximise effect?
- What impact would having a role in curriculum design have on your teaching and learning?

Summary: What are the features of a progress culture?

From the discussions in Part 1, we now have some key characteristics of a progress culture that teachers can develop. These are as follows.

- Teachers need to understand the starting points of all their learners, particularly social and cultural differences.
- Learners need to feel free to make mistakes, improve, and move on. Teachers can create that classroom culture.
- Teachers and learners need a clear understanding of shared goals.
- A teacher should have a deep understanding of how learners progress in their subject and how best to assess that progress.
- Teachers and learners need some sort of learning pathway that allows them to understand where they are, where they should be next, and how to get there.
- Teachers need to be able to select and use valid and appropriate methods of assessment.

[106] **C.J. Craig** (2012). 'Butterfly under a pin': An emergent teacher image amid mandated curriculum reform. *Journal of Educational Research*, 105(2), 90–101.

[107] **M. Priestley, R. Edwards, A. Priestley & K. Miller** (2012). Teacher agency in curriculum making: Agents of change and spaces for manoeuvre. *Curriculum Inquiry*, 42(2), 191–214.

[108] **Research Schools Network** (n.d.). <https://researchschool.org.uk/> accessed 29 March 2019

Part 2

How to ensure learners make progress

What teachers do, the strategies they employ, and how they use those strategies are the catalyst for the progress of all their learners. In this part of the book, I introduce and provide some guidance on how to use the approaches to five aspects of ensuring progress in learning:

- models of progress

- measuring progress

- communicating progress

- teaching for progress

- feedback and intervention.

Building on the metaphors for progress in Part 1, I introduce some established models for progress that teachers use to help ensure that learners understand what progress and success look like. Measuring progress is becoming increasingly questioned as a valuable endeavour in teaching, but I describe the approaches that teachers commonly use and their advantages and disadvantages. I contend that good communication about progress actually improves progress, which links into how teachers can teach for progress and the way they feed back and intervene.

Each section has a practice analyser at the beginning. This will give you a more targeted reading focus if you don't have time to read the whole section. If you find something you want to try, I would recommend consulting the relevant recommended reading, as I only offer a brief introduction to each strategy.

Additionally, when you want to try something new, keep it contained. Choose one class to trial it with, over a finite time period. Regularly reflect upon and refine the strategy. If it doesn't work for you the first time, try it again with another group. Often new strategies take at least three attempts before they are most effective. Working with other teachers is also helpful: if you all decide to trial a strategy and work together on the reflection and refinement process, the collaboration will help you evaluate the success of the approach on progress.

Finally, everything we do in the classroom should be done with a critical eye. Evaluate the evidence and the applicability to your context. Part 3 has a useful section on just this: 3.6 Critical engagement with assessment theory, policy, and practice. Use the exercises in that section to make your professional pedagogical decisions.

2.1 Models of progress

Introduction: Visualising progress

In Part 1, I described teachers' metaphors for progress. There are, however, a number of established models for learning and understanding progress. What they all have in common is a shared structure and language that teachers and learners understand and can use to visualise what progress looks like. In Part 3, there are exercises to help teachers visualise progress.

Be aware that each model has its advantages and limitations. In this section, I ask you to reflect upon your current practices and consider improving your current approach, or consider alternatives. The models I explore are:

- Bloom's taxonomy
- SOLO taxonomy
- learning pathways
- learning ladders
- mastery approaches.

 Consider

- How do you visualise progress in your phase or subject?
- What external models of progress inform your practice?
- What are the advantages and limitations of your current practice?

Analyse your practice

Use Table 2.1 to rate your experience of using each model of progress.

Table 2.1: Practice analyser: Models of progress

	Never heard of it	Heard of it	Have tried it	Used it sometimes	Confidently apply
1 Bloom's taxonomy					
2 SOLO taxonomy					
3 Learning pathways					
4 Learning ladders					
5 Mastery approaches					

Of course, you can read about each model in order, but if you wish to focus on one, then skip ahead to the relevant 'how to' section to learn a bit more about the strategy and how to apply it to your practice. There are references in each section and additional reaction at the end of this section. After reading this section, you may want to reflect on what you have learned.

1 How to use Bloom's taxonomy

US psychologist, Benjamin Bloom, first constructed a hierarchy of learning outcomes in the 1950s.[1] It was widely adopted across universities and examination systems, then came to inform teachers and learning. Bloom's taxonomy dominates assessment theory and practice.

The theory behind Bloom's taxonomy is as follows. There are some skills that are cognitively easier to perform than others. For example, recalling a fact is easier than describing something, which is easier than explaining something, and so on. These terms have been categorised and ranked into increasing cognitive demand. There are also taxonomies for two other domains, 'affective' (emotional) and 'psychomotor' (actions), which can be more applicable in arts and physical subjects respectively. The cognitive domain is made up of six categories: knowledge, comprehension, application, analysis, synthesis, evaluation. These were often presented as a pyramid, with knowledge forming the foundation.

Bloom's taxonomy was revised in 2001 by a team of authors who made the following changes to it:[2] they changed the nouns to verbs, which emphasises 'doing', and they replaced 'synthesis' with 'create', and demoted 'evaluation'

---

[1] **B.S. Bloom** (1956). *Taxonomy of Educational Objectives, Handbook 1: Cognitive Domain*. New York: David McKay.

[2] **L.W. Anderson, D.R. Krathwohl, P.W. Airasian & B. Samuel** (2001). *A Taxonomy for Learning, Teaching, and Assessing: A Revision of Bloom's Taxonomy of Educational Objectives*. New York: Longman.

to below 'create'. They were also more explicit about the types of knowledge (factual, conceptual, procedural, and metacognitive) and presented them in a table like Table 2.2.

Table 2.2: Revised Bloom's taxonomy with knowledge dimensions[3]

The knowledge dimension	Remember	Understand	Apply	Analyse	Evaluate	Create
Factual						
Conceptual						
Procedural						
Metacognitive						

Bloom's taxonomy has many applications throughout education, including defining learning outcomes in lesson planning, planning verbal and written questions, in learning ladders and rubrics (see Section 2.1, *4 How to use learning ladders*), and in the design and writing of a range of examinations.[4]

Like all frameworks, Bloom's and its application have been critiqued since its creation, including the nature of the taxonomy, its subjectivity, and even the direction of the pyramid.[5] Despite this healthy discussion, Bloom's has had significant staying power within the education systems of the world. It forms the foundations of most examination systems and reaches many teachers in their day-to-day lesson planning and teaching. As a framework for supporting progress, it is the dominant framework from which many other models have developed. In the following sections, SOLO taxonomy and mastery approaches are both developments from Bloom's original work in the 1950s and 1960s.

Anderson *et al.*'s revised Bloom's taxonomy book presents a series of vignettes that illustrate how Table 2.2 can be used in teaching and learning. The example in Table 2.3 is one for report writing for fourth-grade students in the USA. It is accompanied by a commentary on how the table was used to adapt the original objectives into more challenging ones and align the objectives,

---

[3] **L.W. Anderson, D.R. Krathwohl, P.W. Airasian & B. Samuel** (2001). *A Taxonomy for Learning, Teaching, and Assessing: A Revision of Bloom's Taxonomy of Educational Objectives.* New York: Longman.

[4] **L. Yew-Jin, K. Mijung & Y. Hye-Gyoung** (2015). The intellectual demands of the intended primary Science curriculum in Korea and Singapore: An analysis based on revised Bloom's taxonomy, *International Journal of Science Education*, 37(13), 2193–2213.

[5] **S. Wineburg & J. Schneider** (2009). Was Bloom's taxonomy pointed in the wrong direction? *Phi Delta Kappan*, 91(4), 56–61.

Table 2.3: Exemplar of the revised Bloom's taxonomy with knowledge dimensions[6]

The knowledge dimension	The cognitive process dimension					
	1 Remember	2 Understand	3 Apply	4 Analyse	5 Evaluate	6 Create
A Factual knowledge	*Lesson 2 activities*					**Objective 3; Objective 4** *Lessons 17–20 activities; Lessons 21–30 activities* Assess F1, F2
B Conceptual knowledge	*Lesson 1 activities*	*Lesson 2 activities*		**Objective 1; Objective 2** *Lessons 3, 4 activities* Assess In2, In3	*Lesson 4 activities; Lessons 17–20 activities*	**Objective 3; Objective 4** *Lessons 17–20 activities; Lessons 21–30 activities* Assess F1, F2
C Procedural knowledge			*Lessons 3, 4 activities; Lessons 9–14 activities; Lesson 16 activities* Assess In1, In3			
D Meta-cognitive knowledge						

[6] **L.W. Anderson, D.R. Krathwohl, P.W. Airasian & B. Samuel** (2001). *A Taxonomy for Learning, Teaching, and Assessing: A Revision of Bloom's Taxonomy of Educational Objectives.* New York: Longman.

Table 2.3: (*continued*)

> **Key**
>
> Objective 1: Select sources of information related to writing a report on a famous person in American history.
>
> Objective 2: Select information about a famous person in American history that is relevant to the purposes of students' written and oral reports.
>
> Objective 3: Write informative text that communicates to classmates and other appropriate audiences in the school important aspects of the life of a famous person in American history and that includes students' opinions of how the famous American's contributions impacted society.
>
> Objective 4: Deliver a talk to the class about a portion of the written report.
>
> Assess In1, In2, and In3 refer to three separate informal assessments; assess F1 (written report) and F2 (oral presentation) refer to the two formal assessments.
>
> Note: As discussed in the text, activities related to Lessons 5–8 and 15 are not analysed in terms of the taxonomy table.
>
> Dark shading indicates the strongest alignment – an objective, an instructional activity, and an assessment are all present in the same cell. Lighter shading indicates two of the three are present.

learning activities, and assessment activities over the learning period. This table is for the teacher only; the learning activity materials and assessment rubrics are made separately in learner-friendly language. It is worth reading the whole book to get the benefit of understanding the process.

Using Bloom's allows teachers to have a sense of progress through cognitive thinking. It can be used as a framework within each domain to guide the demand in thinking. Common examples include:

- planning learning intentions
- planning learning outcomes
- planning questioning
- assessing prior knowledge, understanding, and skills
- setting targets for progress through knowledge, understanding, and skills
- designing low-, medium- and high-demand test questions when writing tests.

2 How to use SOLO taxonomy

SOLO taxonomy is an offspring from Bloom's taxonomy, an abbreviation of Structure of Observed Learning Outcomes (SOLO).[7] As shown in Figure 2.1, there are five categories of taxonomy represented by helpful symbols:

---

[7] **J. Biggs & K. Collis** (1989). Towards a model of school-based curriculum development and assessment using the SOLO taxonomy. *Australian Journal of Education*, 33(2), 151–163.

prestructural, unistructural, multistructural, relational, and extended abstract. It is used as a common language of learning where learners' responses to tasks can be categorised and improvements can be identified. For example, work in which a learner lists the factors that contribute to global warming can be described as 'multistructural', and work that explains the causes of global warming would be considered as 'relational'.

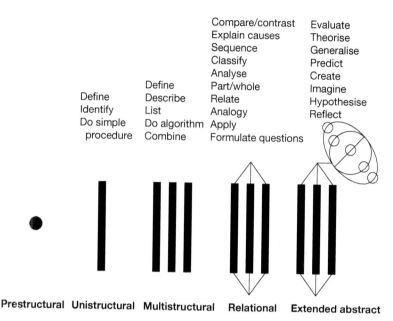

Figure 2.1: SOLO taxonomy with symbols and links to Bloom's taxonomy

This can be used at most stages of education, from primary to higher education. I have seen it used in A-level lessons as a way of improving conceptual understanding. With younger learners, some teachers have actions associated with categories, to strengthen the communication of progress.

There are three benefits of this approach:

• It provides a structure for planning learning intentions.

• It can support progress through identifying starting points and suitable learning strategies.

• It uses common language so that both teachers and learners can understand the next steps to improve.

The common language of SOLO taxonomy allows meaningful communication about teaching and learning, and it focuses on assessment of the work, not the learner themselves. Importantly, this approach promotes deeper learning to reach the higher categories.

While Bloom's taxonomy is particularly popular in the UK, Europe, and the USA, SOLO taxonomy is widely used in New Zealand and in some Australian states. Pam Hook and her colleagues have been particularly productive in developing SOLO taxonomy and associated activities.[8] They have produced a range of material to support a number of subjects including English, Mathematics,[9] Science, Geography,[10,11] History and Physical Education.

Teachers can use SOLO taxonomy in the planning and teaching of lessons, including to:

- create a common understanding and language of progress within a lesson
- plan lessons so that all learners can make progress
- assess learners' work and suggest next steps
- support learners with assessing their own work and next steps.

There are a number of exercises and activities provided in SOLO taxonomy publications that promote the making of connections, knowledge organisation, and progress through the stages.

3 How to use learning pathways

Learning pathways are usually evidence-based sequences for learning, devised as a guide for teachers and learners to understand what to teach or learn next. Variations are known as learning trajectories or learning progressions. These pathways are intended to support teachers and learners in their next steps in learning within a concept, skill, or topic.[12]

A key aspect, often missed in schools, is that these pathways are based on what we know about the development of most learners. They are not straitjackets, but rather approximations of concept and skill development. Pathways should only be used as guidance; they should be used along with professional pedagogic knowledge to be the most useful. There will always be some learners who deviate from the path.

[8] **P. Hook & J. Mills** (2011). *SOLO Taxonomy: A Guide for Schools. A Common Language of Learning* (Book 1). Laughton: Essential Resources.

[9] **H. Chick** (1998). Cognition in the formal modes: Research mathematics and the SOLO taxonomy. *Mathematics Education Research Journal*, 10(2), 4–26.

[10] **T.D. Courtney** (1986). The significance of the SOLO taxonomy for learning and teaching in geography. *Geographical Education*, 5(2), 47–50.

[11] **E. Munowenyu** (2007). Assessing the quality of essays using the SOLO taxonomy: Effects of field and classroom-based experiences by 'A' level geography students. *International Research in Geographical & Environmental Education*, 16(1), 21–43.

[12] **P. Sztajn, J. Confrey, P.H. Wilson & C. Edgington** (2012). Learning trajectory based instruction: Toward a theory of teaching. *Educational Researcher*, 41(5), 147–156.

In general terms, learning pathways usually move:

- from concrete ideas to more abstract ideas
- from the simple to the complex
- from single steps to multisteps
- from the basic to the detailed
- from the familiar to the less familiar.

A number of subjects have developed learning pathways, including Mathematics,[13] Geography (REF)[14] and Science.[15] Below, I illustrate examples from Chemistry and History.

Example of a learning pathway: Chemistry

Science topics need to be taught in a sequence to aid conceptual development. Although there are debates over how and when particle theory should be taught, there is a general consensus that is shown in Figure 2.2.

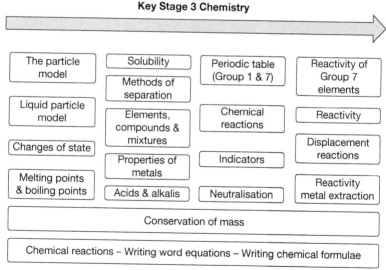

Figure 2.2: An example pathway from Key Stage 3 Chemistry

[13] **A. Noyes & P. Sealey** (2011). Managing learning trajectories: The case of 14–19 Mathematics, *Educational Review*, 63(2), 179–193.

[14] **Niem Tu Huynh, Michael Solem & Sarah Witham Bednarz** (2015), A Road Map for Learning Progressions Research in Geography, *Journal of Geography*, 114:2, 69–79.

[15] **R. Duschl, S. Maeng & A. Sezen** (2011). Learning progressions and teaching sequences: A review and analysis, *Studies in Science Education*, 47(2), 123–182.

In Figure 2.2, the general direction of progress is shown by the arrow at the top. There could be arrows between the boxes to show the links between them, but they are all linked to some degree. In Chemistry particularly, there are a couple of concepts that can be developed across the key stage: conservation of mass (that particles cannot be made or destroyed) and chemical reactions (types and nomenclature).

Example of a learning pathway: History

A common approach to History teaching is that of historical skill development, one in particular being historical interpretation. Figure 2.3 shows an example, based on wide evidence of what these skills are.

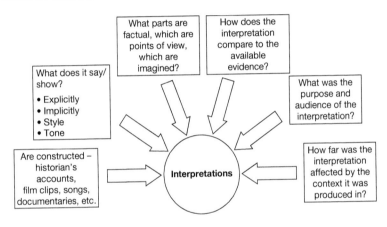

Figure 2.3: An example pathway from History[16]

In Figure 2.3, the features of historical interpretations are identified and lessons are planned that develop these skills.

Experienced teachers develop their own learning pathways based on their experience of the subject, the constraints of the curriculum, and professional experience of teaching. This relates directly to the teacher's progress map (see Part 3).

Teachers can use learning pathways:

- as structures from which to plan their lessons

- as guides for improving learners' knowledge, understanding, and skills

- for deciding upon next steps in learning in informal teaching situations.

---

[16] **R. McFahn** (2017), https://www.historyresourcecupboard.co.uk/dont-tell-interpretations-difficult-key-stage-3/ (accessed 22/05/2019)

4 How to use learning ladders

Like learning pathways, learning ladders are usually evidence-based but focus on a specific concept or skill (or a few), in isolation from the wider subject. Learning ladders are usually shared with learners, and are made up of increasingly demanding outcomes for the same open-ended tasks. They became particularly popular in England in 2005–2014 in a number of primary and secondary subjects. I wrote a lot of these for secondary Science.[17] They feature widely in the USA, more frequently in the form of rubrics. Rubrics are usually a matrix of learning areas against learning outcomes.[18] Some learning ladders can be generic; that is, they can be applied to a specific skill whenever that skill is being used. Table 2.4 is a learning ladder for Science investigations that acts as a guide for the type of skills and the level of skill learners can carry out, and the skills they can develop. Table 2.5 shows a learning ladder for a specific task; however, the task was written to help develop transferable skills as well.

Table 2.4: A generic learning ladder: Science investigations

To get Level:	You might:
3	Planning: • Plan a simple experiment. Obtaining: • With help, take three observations or measurements. • With help, put some results in a simple table. • With help, plot a simple chart or graph. Considering: • With help, state the pattern from your evidence. • With help, state your conclusion. Evaluating: • Suggest an improvement to the investigation.

---

[17] **A. Grevatt** (2006). *Badger Key Stage 3 Science Year 7 Levelled Investigation Tasks*. Stevenage: Badger Publishing.

[18] **E. Panadero & A. Jonsson** (2013). The use of scoring rubrics for formative assessment purposes revisited: A review. *Educational Research Review*, 9, 129–144.

Table 2.4: (*continued*)

To get Level:	You might:
4	**Planning:** • Plan an experiment to answer the question, selecting suitable equipment. • Identify the factors that you will change, measure, and control (keep the same). • Describe how you will make sure you are safe while doing the investigation. • State a simple prediction with a reason. **Obtaining:** • Follow instructions carefully; make at least three observations or measurements. • When told, take action to keep yourself safe during the investigation. • Record data in a simple table. • Draw a simple graph or chart, with some help with scales. **Considering:** • With some help, state the pattern from your evidence. • With some help, state your conclusion. • With some help, explain your conclusion using simple scientific ideas. **Evaluating:** • Suggest improvements to the investigation with reasons.
5	**Planning:** • Plan an experiment to answer your question (step-by-step instructions). • Select suitable equipment, giving some reasons for your choices. • Identify the factors that you will change, measure, and control. • Describe how you will make sure the investigation is safe for you and others. • State a prediction with a scientific reason. **Obtaining:** • Make a series of observations or measurements systematically. • Design a simple results table and record your evidence clearly in the table. • Present your results in a simple graph or chart. **Considering:** • Describe the pattern from your evidence. • State your conclusion, using scientific knowledge and understanding. • Explain your conclusion using scientific words and units. **Evaluating:** • Suggest how the investigation could be improved with scientific reasons.

Table 2.5: A specific learning ladder[19]

Check	The types of things you can do:
Advanced	You will have written a detailed report, drawing on detailed scientific knowledge and understanding. • Explain how the amount of water available is limited, and how it is circulated and processed both by natural means and artificial means. • Explain the ways we waste water, giving figures that suggest how much wastage occurs. • Explain in detail how water shortages affect the environment, giving details of examples of water shortages and their effects worldwide. • Evaluate different water wastage prevention methods, giving evidence or case studies about each. • Use a range of scientific words, symbols, and units accurately.
Confident	You will have written a report, drawing on scientific knowledge and understanding. • Explain how the amount of water available is limited, and how it is processed before we can use it. • Explain the ways we waste water. • Explain how water shortages affect the environment. • Explain methods we can use to prevent water waste, giving advantages and disadvantages to these. • Use a range of appropriate scientific words, symbols, and units.
Establishing	You will have written a basic report, drawing on some scientific knowledge and understanding. • Describe how water moves through the water cycle and how we obtain it. • Describe some ways we waste water. • State two or three effects of water shortages. • Describe two or three ways to save water/prevent wastage. • Use some appropriate scientific words, symbols, and units.

Learning ladders can be used as a guide for planning, classroom assessment, and feedback. Sometimes teachers can have generic learning ladders that are brought out whenever learners are performing a certain activity, such as a particular type of writing (e.g. argumentative, persuasive, instructional) or a specific approach to presenting data, where a learning ladder for 'Drawing a good graph' can be used.

Learning ladders can used to support progress:

• by having a shared understanding about what progress looks like

• by identifying where learners are, where they need to get to, and how to get there

• providing the basis of discussion for improvement.

---

[19] **A. Chandler-Grevatt & V. Stutt** (2014). *ACE Science: Science Tasks with Learning Ladders: Chemistry Homework Book*. Stevenage: Badger Publishing.

5 How to use mastery approaches

Mastery learning attempts to ensure that learners have 'mastered' a particular set of knowledge, understanding, and skills before they move onto the next set. It is a teaching and learning approach that relies on carefully placed assessments and interventions. It originates from the 1950s when Benjamin Bloom and co-workers came up with the 'Learning for Mastery'[20] approach with which most classroom teachers are familiar.[21] The premise is that a learner's ability is not fixed, but rather learning requires time and persistence under the guidance of an expert teacher. The expert teacher is able to break complex ideas into more manageable 'chunks' and present these to learners in a variety of ways so that the learner can learn them. Importantly, the teacher is skilled enough to produce individual meaningful feedback and 'corrective' information from a formative assessment.[22]

How do we know that a learner has mastered something? In typical mastery models, they need to have achieved 80 per cent or more in the test. However, the fact that a learner scores 80 per cent does not mean they will retain that information. What would happen if they are tested a week later, a month later, a term later? This is an essential part of mastery: the fluency. Fluency is achieved through practice and retesting at intervals.[23]

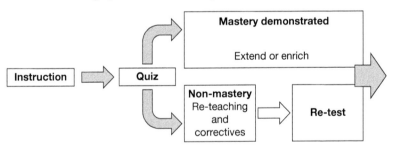

Figure 2.4: A generalised approach to mastery

The assumptions with mastery include the following. Everyone can reach that step in mastery; there are no limitations beyond practice, repetition, and new explanations. All complex knowledge, understanding, or skills

[20] **T.R. Guskey** (2007). Closing achievement gaps: revisiting Benjamin S. Bloom's 'Learning for Mastery'. *Journal of Advanced Academics*, 19(1), 8–31.

[21] **B.S. Bloom** (1968). Learning for mastery. Instruction and Curriculum. Regional Education Laboratory for the Carolinas and Virginia, Topical Papers and Reprints, Number 1. *Evaluation Comment*, 1(2), n2.

[22] **T.R. Guskey** (2010). Lessons of mastery learning. *Educational Leadership*, 68(2), 52.

[23] **C. Binder, E. Haughton & B. Bateman** (2002). Fluency: Achieving true mastery in the learning process. *Professional Papers in Special Education*, 2–20.

can be broken down into more manageable units. The mastery approach requires expert teachers teaching to a high quality, along with time spent on acquiring new knowledge, understanding, or skills.

Some of the issues with mastery approaches include the fact that many school systems are not structured to allow mastery. All learners are expected to reach a certain level of knowledge, understanding, and skills at specific points within the school year. Curriculum topics have a finite time allocated to them, and often whole classes move on to the next topic, whether or not everyone has mastered it.

 Discuss

- Which models of progress do you find most useful to your phase or subject?

- To what extent are learning pathways useful to your teaching and learning?

- What do you think mastery means in your context?

 Reflection

Revisit the practice analyser: Models of progress (Table 2.1).

- How have you progressed?

- What will you do to improve your own practice?

- How will you check any measures have been effective?

 Further reading

To explore some of these ideas further, I recommend reading:

P. Hook & J. Mills (2011). *SOLO Taxonomy: A Guide for Schools. A Common Language of Learning (Book 1)*. Laughton: Essential Resources.

J.B. Biggs & K.F. Collis (2014). *Evaluating the Quality of Learning: The SOLO Taxonomy (Structure of the Observed Learning Outcome)*. New York: Academic Press.

H. Drury (2018). *Oxford Teaching Guides: How to Teach Mathematics for Mastery*. Oxford: Oxford University Press.

Also see

This section also links to:

Part 1: 1.3, section on Metaphors for progress

Part 3: 3.3, 2 How to create a mental model of progress in your phase
or subject

3.6 Critical engagement with assessment theory, policy,
and practice

2.2 Measuring progress

Introduction: Words and numbers

'Not everything that can be measured matters and not everything that matters can be measured.'

Interestingly, this quote is often mistakenly attributed to the physicist Albert Einstein, but was most likely first said by a sociologist: William Bruce Cameron. Einstein is firmly associated with numbers and Cameron is associated with words. However, both recognised that neither numbers nor words alone can describe or explain human nature. Measuring progress is particularly problematic; however, we do attempt to do this in various ways.

Walking into a school for the first time and getting to grips with assessment can be daunting. When sending my trainee teachers into schools, I ask them to try to establish the following to help them start to develop their understanding for progress in their phase/subject:

- expectations of the curriculum

- expectations of age/phase

- understanding of the individual learners

- the assessment system used by the school

- any statutory assessments (tests/exams) the learners take.

These form the underpinning of what we understand about progress and how we may be able to measure it.

In this section, I will explore how we attempt to measure progress using simple statistics, assessment criteria, norm-referencing, a no-grade approach, and finally comparative judgement.

Consider

For your context, which of these questions can you answer?

- What baseline data is available (if any)?
- What target data is available? What type of target?
- What individual data (such as special educational needs) is available?
- How is progress measured (if at all)?
- How relevant is the data to your phase/subject/class?

Analyse your practice

Use Table 2.6 to rate your experience of using each approach to measuring progress.

Of course, you can read about each of these in order, but if you wish to focus on one, then skip ahead to the relevant 'how to' section to learn a bit more about the strategy and how to apply it to your practice. There are references in each section and additional reading at the end of this section. After reading this section, you may want to reflect on what you have learned.

Table 2.6: Practice analyser: Measuring progress

	Never heard of it	Heard of it	Have tried it	Used it sometimes	Confidently apply
1 Simple statistics					
2 Assessment criteria					
3 Norm referencing					
4 No grades					
5 Comparative judgement					

1 How to use simple statistics

I have always used simple statistics in various forms to measure, record, and communicate progress, mostly from formal topic tests. It is not the same for all teachers in all phases and subjects, but at various points assessments are carried out to check progress. In secondary schools, it is common for regular topic assessments or tests to occur every few weeks or at least once a term. Here, I look at three approaches I have used or seen used: percentages, distance from target, and improvement.

Percentages

Each test score can generate a percentage. Even if each test has a different number of questions, converting the raw score into a percentage can help compare consecutive test scores over time. This relies on the tests not differing too much in length, difficulty, and range of difficulty. When I design tests now, I make sure that they are the same length, with a similar style of questions, and finally the same distribution of low-demand, medium-demand, and high-demand questions. This can improve the comparability between tests.

Distance from or towards?

If we want to capture and communicate progress, we can try to measure either from a starting point or how near to a target. I have done this previously in an attempt to value progress being made, rather than summative marks.

For example, if each learner starts the year with a particular grade, they can then aim to improve on that grade in all assessments. Note, grade D is lower than grade B in this situation. So, imagine my class of learners is made up of those starting with grades D, C, and B. In a test, Rosie, who started with a D, achieves a B, whereas Lily, who started with a C, also scores a B. Although both learners have scored a B, Rosie has made more progress than Lily.

Many schools set learners target grades to achieve at the end of a phase or at the end of schooling. In a similar way to the approach described above, we can record how far from their target each learner is, based on their performance in an assessment. This keeps the target in mind and gives learners something to aim for.

Things to consider

This approach depends on a number of factors: that each test or assessment is producing reliable results, that consecutive tests or assessments are comparable, that the baseline score is reliable, and that the target grade is realistic.

It is surprisingly hard to ensure all these factors are accounted for. On reflection, when I have been making these judgements with my classes, that judgement was often based on just a few marks within each grade range. The reliability of such tests is low, and any small change between the tests could be just by chance. However, learners who rarely showed any improvement could be identified and supported, and those who showed significant progress could be stretched. The focus on improvement rather than attainment means that every learner is on a level playing field at the start, giving everyone the opportunity to feel success.

Data, data, everywhere

Having used all of these approaches at various times, I have found them useful for having a conversation with learners who are performing below or beyond their expectations. If a whole class has done particularly poorly or well in a test, it could be that the test is comparatively too hard or too easy, respectively. Tests could be adjusted to be more in line with other tests. However, most tests were on new topics, where a majority of the content was new, so expecting improvement test on test was rather unrealistic.

In recent times, using test data in this way has been called into question.[24] Although many schools continue to use this approach, as part of improving a teacher's assessment literacy (see Part 3), existing practice can be and should be critiqued and, if necessary, improved.

2 How to use assessment criteria

The use of assessment criteria is usually based on an underlying model of progression, as described in Section 2.1. The criteria describe the expected outcomes in the form of descriptors against which the assessor makes a judgement. If more than one criterion is used for a given piece of work, then an overall best-fit judgement can be made.

Criteria-based assessments have advantages in that there is a shared language that both learners and teachers can understand. The criteria can be used to inform learning intentions, progress, and feedback. If a grading system is associated with the rubric, grades can be assigned and used to identify progress.

In everyday lessons, rubrics used as criteria can ensure that teachers and learners are looking for progress in specific areas, whether using something more generic like SOLO taxonomy (see Figure 2.1) or something more specific in a learning ladder (see Table 2.4). When necessary, the teacher can justify their judgement with a learner. When criteria-based assessment is used in high-stakes assessment, the subjectivity can be reduced through processes such as moderation. This involves other teachers looking at samples of marked work and making decisions on how well the criteria have been interpreted.

A limitation of using criteria-based assessments is that they are subjective. It is difficult to make judgements against criteria. It becomes problematic

---

[24] **R. Allen** (2018). Meaningless data is meaningless. Available at: <https://rebeccaallen.co.uk/2018/11/05/meaningless-data-is-meaningless/> accessed 29 March 2019

when several domains are being assessed and a 'best-fit' assessment has to be made. This means that reliability can be an issue, although it can be improved with moderation processes. Another limitation is that the criteria mean that learners are expected to converge on predetermined expectations: there is no space for creativity beyond the criteria. In addition, some claim that criteria limit learners' opportunity to progress beyond them, and therefore repress progress. Of course, this latter argument can be used for examinations and tests that have mark schemes with expected responses.

3 How to use norm referencing

The basic approach to norm referencing is that all learners sit an exam. The raw marks are then collected and ranked from highest to lowest. The same approach is used for subsequent tests, and the same process is carried out. Individual learners will go up, stay the same, or decrease within the ranking. If one learner moves up, another will have to move down.

The next step in norm referencing is to allocate grade boundaries. This can be done by dividing the number of grades into equal proportions. For example, grades A–E are made up of five grades. So, if dividing the cohort equally, the top 20 per cent will achieve an A, the next 20 per cent a B, and so on. In this way, whenever a learner gets an A grade, we know that they are in the top 20 per cent of the cohort.

Computer spreadsheets can do this very easily for each test, and graphs can be produced to map the progress of an individual learner against the rest of the class or cohort. The larger the cohort, the better this approach. The ranking of a class of 30 learners would be improved by ranking them within a cohort of more than 100 learners, and even better if taken into a national sample.

In high-stakes examinations, there is a process of mark checking and then a standardisation process in which the current cohort is compared to previous cohorts before the grade boundaries are decided. Statistics are used to achieve this. However, grade boundaries often come down to human judgement; even in official examinations, committees will, with the assistance of statistics, make decisions on grade boundaries.

The limitations of norm referencing include the underlying assumptions used in the design of the test or examination. The test has to be written using good practice in selecting questions of a suitable range of demand and a mark scheme that is reliable, particularly when there are teams of people marking the tests. In addition, a test that covers the full range of outcomes can be very long. To mitigate this, tests can be divided into tiers: for example, two tiers with one paper having low- and medium-demand questions, and a more challenging paper containing the medium- and higher-demand questions. This can have disadvantages if learners sit the wrong paper. If they sit the lower paper, their result can be capped, and if they sit the higher paper, they may not reach the minimum mark to get a score.

Norm referencing of low-stakes tests can be used in everyday classrooms to monitor progress of learners within a class or cohort.

4 How to use no grades

Culturally, grades are often part of educational systems. Learners and their parents want grades to understand how they are doing. However, it has long been known that giving grades for specific pieces of work has negative effects on motivation for learning compared with feedback comments alone.[25] There are also concerns about the whole educational structure being dependent on grades and the effect on the well-being of learners.[26] Some schools and even universities have been experimenting with no-grade policies.[27]

An approach that can be effective, even in a graded system, is 'best work comparisons', also known as ipsative assessment.[28] This approach moves the emphasis from comparison with other students to just competing against oneself: use 'best' work comparisons at particular points in time and aim to beat your personal best.[29]

Most computer games rely on ipsative assessment: always trying to beat your previous personal best. In the same way, many classroom strategies can be employed, including ungraded learning ladders (see *How to use learning ladders* in Section 2.1), using words rather than numbers (see *How to use words and numbers* in Section 2.3), and verbal feedback (see *How to feed back verbally in Section 2.5*).

[25] **R. Butler** (1987). Task-involving and ego-involving properties of evaluation: Effects of different feedback conditions on motivational perceptions, interest, and performance. *Journal of Educational Psychology*, 79(4), p. 474.

[26] **J. Bower & P.L. Thomas (eds)** (2016). *De-testing and De-grading Schools: Authentic Alternatives to Accountability and Standardization*. Oxford: Peter Lang.

[27] **C. McMorran, K. Ragupathi & S. Luo** (2017). Assessment and learning without grades? Motivations and concerns with implementing gradeless learning in higher education. *Assessment & Evaluation in Higher Education*, 42(3), 361–377.

[28] **G. Hughes** (2014). *Ipsative Assessment: Motivation Through Marking Progress*. New York: Springer.

[29] **M. Waters** (2017). Chapter 6: Doing well for your age. In I. Wallace & L. Kirkman (eds) (2017). *Best of the Best Practical Classroom Guides: Progress*. Carmarthen: Crown House Publishing, pp. 56–64.

5 How to use comparative judgement

This is a relatively new addition to classrooms in the UK, although the concept of comparative judgement has been around for several decades.[30] I felt that I needed to include this approach due to its more recent adaptation[31] and increasing presence in some schools, but I have no direct experience of it in my own practice. I have, however, attended a training session led by Daisy Christodoulou,[32] read some academic research, and gathered a range of opinions from teachers who are trialling it.

Marking extended writing is very time-consuming and can be more subjective than marking short-answer questions. It can be particularly problematic in the assessment of examination scripts. In addition, as shown in the previous sections, examinations are constraining as they are based on a mark scheme, so it does not allow for learners to demonstrate their knowledge and skills beyond a specific point. Comparative judgement provides a solution.[33] It can be used for a variety of subjects, including problem-solving in Mathematics.[34]

The simplest approach to comparative judgement is to take the essays of a class or whole cohort and compare them, ranking them in order of quality.[35] This is done without a mark scheme, rubric, or learning ladder. However, in order to make it more reliable, if a number of teachers judge a sample of the submitted work by judging them side by side, the essays (or other work) can be ranked further. This approach has been digitised so that essays can be scanned in, randomly displayed side by side, and compared by the teachers. The ranking is produced by this comparison and the scores are adjusted to make them relative.[36]

---

[30] **L.L. Thurstone** (1927). A law of comparative judgment. *Psychology Review*, 34, 273–286.

[31] **A. Pollitt** (2012). The method of adaptive comparative judgement. *Assessment in Education: Principles, Policy & Practice*, 19(3), 281–300.

[32] **No More Marking** (2018) No more marking: Using comparative judgement to provide a quicker, more reliable method of assessment. Available at: <https://www.nomoremarking.com/> accessed 26 February 2019

[33] **D. Christodoulou** (2018). *Making Good Progress? The Future of Assessment for Learning*. Oxford: Oxford University Press.

[34] **I. Jones, M. Swan & A. Pollitt** (2015). Assessing mathematical problem solving using comparative judgement. *International Journal of Science and Mathematics Education*, 13(1), 151–177.

[35] **A. Pollitt** (2012). The method of adaptive comparative judgement. *Assessment in Education: Principles, Policy & Practice*, 19(3), 281–300.

[36] **A. Pollitt** (2012). Comparative judgement for assessment. *International Journal of Technology and Design Education*, 22(2), 157–170.

There are, however, a number of limitations, or at least problems to solve. The importance of the expertise of the assessors involved is a particular issue. I'm also concerned that as a process, it removes the human aspect of the teacher–learner relationship. But let's watch this space.

 Discuss

- How do you currently measure and record progress? What are the advantages and limitations of this approach?

- How comparative are the tests or assessments that you use? Could this be improved?

- To what extent do your tests or assessments help to measure progress?

 Reflection

Revisit the Practice analyser: Measuring progress (Table 2.6).

- How have you progressed?

- What will you do to improve your own practice?

- How will you check any measures have been effective?

 Further reading

To explore some of these ideas further, I recommend reading:

D. Christodoulou (2018). *Making Good Progress? The Future of Assessment for Learning.* Oxford: Oxford University Press.

 Also see

This section also links to:

Part 1: 1.2, section on Progress through assessment

Part 3: 3.4 Knowledge of requirements of (statutory/standard) assessments

3.6 Critical engagement with assessment theory, policy, and practice

2.3 Communicating progress

Introduction

A shared understanding is an important part of communicating assessments and progress. Having to communicate between learners, teachers, and parents, who all have different expectations and needs, can be particularly troublesome.

Teachers usually talk about a learner's attainment and progress in terms of whether it is in line with what is expected of that learner. Learners want to know if they are doing what they should be, and parents often want to know not how well their child is doing, but how well they are doing, compared with others.

A shared language in assessment is important for communication between teachers, learners, and parents. In a classroom where learning expectations and expected outcomes are shared, it is important that learners and teachers both understand what success looks like. Teachers often give regular oral and written feedback as part of everyday teaching to their learners. In early years and primary school settings, teachers often have opportunities to communicate with parents on a daily basis, but this becomes less frequent once a learner moves to secondary education, where most communication takes place via reports and parent–teacher meetings.

Analyse your practice

Use Table 2.7 to rate your experience of using each strategy for communicating progress.

Table 2.7: Practice analyser: Communicating progress

	Never heard of it	Heard of it	Have tried it	Used it sometimes	Confidently apply
1 Using words and numbers to communicate progress					
2 Communicating progress to learners					
3 Communicating progress to parents					
4 Communicating progress to other teachers					
5 Using reports on progress					

Of course, you can read about each of these in order, but if you wish to focus on one, then skip ahead to the relevant 'how to' section to learn a bit more about the strategy and how to apply it to your practice. There are references in each section and additional reading at the end of this section. After reading this section, you may want to reflect on what you have learned.

 Consider

- To what extent are attainment and progress effectively communicated to parents, teachers, and learners?

- What are the barriers to communicating progress?

- What could be done to improve communication and understanding of progress?

1 How to use words and numbers

What does a grade mean? We know an A is good. What do teachers understand by the grade? What about the learner who has received that grade? And what about the parent(s) of that learner? A grade A has a lot of associations. It's perceived as a high grade: getting an A makes us feel pleased, we feel we have done well, our parents will be proud. It might mean that you can get onto the course you want to or gain entry to a university or job that you have applied for. But do we know what a learner that achieves an A grade actually knows, understands, and can do?

When a learner achieves a grade A, we need to understand whether the grade is criterion-based or norm-referenced. Achieving an A based on a set of criteria gives a clear indication of what that learner has demonstrated they know, understand, and can do. Achieving the same grade based on norm referencing means that the learner has achieved that grade compared to the other learners in their cohort. It usually shows that out of all the learners who took that test, the learner achieved a grade that was, for example, in the top 15 per cent of the cohort. This can mean that cohort is not necessarily comparable to one in previous years. However, several examination boards use statistics to minimise this.

When communicating progress, we can use two modes, 'words' or 'numbers', and often a combination of both. The use of words is very transparent in what a learner knows, understands, and can do, and what they should try to do next. Words may be spoken or written, and allow instant or delayed feedback (see Section 2.5 for more detail on how to feed back). They are useful for clarifying meaning, sharing understanding, and ascertaining where a learner is, where they need to be, and how to get there. The disadvantage of words is that they can be time-consuming, so that we find short cuts to summarise learning. This can be done using encapsulating terms such as 'developing', 'secure' and 'extending'. This allows a learner and teacher to understand that, at a particular point, a learner's progress is below, at, or beyond the expectation. Further still, we can use numbers (or letters) to abbreviate attainment (and perhaps show progress), such as a numbered grading system. However, the further we abbreviate, the less specific and less meaningful the communication becomes.

As a halfway house, many teachers use scales, learning ladders and progress charts based upon criteria in the form of a rubric (see Section 2.2, *Measuring progress*). With descriptors for particular levels of attainment or grades, these can be used to show where a learner is, where they need to be, and what to do to get there.

In summary, to be able to communicate progress you need to have:

- a starting point, a target, and a current position
- a shared understanding of progression and attainment
- a progression and attainment system based on broad descriptors
- a combination of words and numbers.

2 How to communicate progress to learners

Building on the previous section, it is useful for learners to know where they are and how they have improved, so they can make progress. For that, it is helpful to have a common understanding of what progress looks like. SOLO taxonomy or rubrics (grade descriptors) can be useful for creating a shared meaning (see Section 2.1, *2 How to use a SOLO taxonomy*).

There are different times when we give feedback: in everyday lessons, at the end of an assessment period, and at the end of a learning phase. During everyday lessons, verbal feedback to the whole class and to individuals is the main mode of assessment to assist progress. During an assessment phase, it is more common to get written feedback with comments and/or a grade. It is favourable for learners to have the opportunity to respond to these assessments and make improvements in preparation for an assessment.

3 How to communicate progress to parents

I was taught from the start of my teaching career that parents should feature strongly in the three-way relationship between teacher, learner, and parent. Parents are anxious to know how well their child is doing and often how well they are doing compared to other children. However, considering the complexities of measuring, communicating, and understanding progress in education, it is common for parents to feel frustrated by school reports that do not appear to make sense.

Tom Sherrington, an experienced headteacher, concludes that reporting to parents is a combination of three elements:[37]

- stating the child's performance as a raw score (for each subject area)

- a comparison to the cohort or class, for example, report a year group's or class's average

- a teacher's judgement on the child's progress. This can be done using a comment bank, simple free-text comment, or a set of codes.

Some schools provide a legend or glossary, with examples of what is 'expected' at particular points. The advice is to keep it simple but sophisticated. Make sure there is an underlying logic and rigour to the progress, but minimise the information you share.

4 How to communicate progress to other teachers

Teachers communicate progress to other teachers in several ways and at key points in a learner's education. Again, this is best achieved if all teachers have a common understanding of assessment. When communicating between teachers as learners move classes in the same school or move up a year, teachers have a shared understanding of the assessment system and what good progress looks like. However, caution is needed when a learner moves between schools, as different schools and different education authorities may have different assessment systems that are difficult to compare.

---

[37] **T. Sherrington** (2018). How can we measure and report progress meaningfully? Available at: <https://teacherhead.com/2018/06/18/how-can-we-measure-and-report-progress-meaningfully/> accessed 26 February 2019

5 How to use reports on progress

Reports are often a point in time when a summative summary of a learner's performance is given. However, there are approaches to sharing the progress made. I have discussed the issues with using test scores as comparisons. The following could be used:

- rank position within class or cohort; this can show the changing position within the class

- competency descriptors on ladders; these can show a starting position and the current position

- descriptions of achievements, listing achievements over a set time.

 Discuss

- How do you communicate progress to each stakeholder: learners, parents, and teachers?

- What challenges do you have communicating between schools or districts? What common benchmarks are there?

- What is the most effective way for you to communicate with your learners?

 Reflection

Revisit the Practice analyser: Communicating progress (Table 2.7).

- How have you progressed?

- What will you do to improve your own practice?

- How will you check any measures have been effective?

 Also see

This section also links to:

Part 1: 1.1 What do we mean by 'progress'?

Part 3: 3.6 Critical engagement with assessment theory, policy, and practice

2.4 Teaching for progress

Introduction: A classroom culture

Teaching for progress relies on a classroom culture that fosters beliefs, attitudes, and practices that support improvement. I call this a 'formative culture'.[38] A summative classroom culture values the importance of outcomes, prioritises attainment, and assessment is done *to* the learner. In contrast, a formative classroom culture fosters strategies of learning, making progress, improvement, and assessment is done *with* the learner. The classroom culture is ideally driven by the ethos of the school, but a teacher has significant influence on the culture, based on how they communicate their expectations and what practices they use to teach and learn.

 Consider

- To what extent do you foster a formative culture in the classroom?
- What practices do you use to help your learners make progress?
- How could you improve your approaches to support progress through your teaching?

Analyse your practice

Use Table 2.8 to rate your experience of using each strategy for teaching for progress.

Table 2.8: Practice analyser: Teaching for progress

	Never heard of it	Heard of it	Have tried it	Used it sometimes	Confidently apply
1 Improving learner self-regulation					
2 Tackling troublesome knowledge					
3 Improving memory					
4 Accelerating learning					
5 Planning for progress					

If you wish to focus on one part in particular, skip ahead to the relevant 'how to' section to learn more about the strategy and how to apply to your practice.

---

[38] **A. Chandler-Grevatt** (2018). *How to Assess Your Students*. Oxford: Oxford University Press.

1 How to improve learner self-regulation

If we consider the types of progress from Section 1.1, a set of knowledge, understanding, and skills in self-regulation and metacognition provides personal resources that can aid learning for examinations as well as life within school. It can be essential in ensuring that a learner has strategies to improve and make progress independently.

More recently, through their extensive research, it has been shown by Professor Heidi Andrade and Margaret Heritage that self-regulated learners tend to learn more effectively because they have a powerful combination of learning strategies, self-control, and motivation.[39] The principles of self-regulation have been considered important enough to be taken forward into a toolkit for teachers, which shows these three components can be nurtured:[40]

- cognition: the metal processes of learning

- metacognition: knowing how to learn

- motivation: the willingness to learn.

These components manifest themselves in a variety of ways; here are some examples of how to nurture them:

- Provide learners with opportunities to identify strengths and areas for development in their work.

- Guide metacognitive process on personal levels, task level, and a learning strategy level (for example, opportunities to reflect on how they felt about the task, how they completed the task, and how they tackled the task, respectively).

- Facilitate learners in planning, monitoring, and evaluating their learning.

Teachers need to understand the principles of self-regulation and metacognition, and provide regular opportunities to foster these skills with their learners. A few examples follow.

- Plan opportunities and provide strategies for learners to self-regulate.

- Provide opportunities for learners to plan their learning, choose strategies to solve problems, and select resources to support their work.

---

[39] **H.L. Andrade & M. Heritage** (2017). *Using Formative Assessment to Enhance Learning, Achievement, and Academic Self-regulation.* New York and Abingdon: Routledge, p.13.

[40] **Education Endowment Foundation** (2017). Metacognition and self-regulation. Available at: <https://educationendowmentfoundation.org.uk/evidence-summaries/teaching-learning-toolkit/meta-cognition-and-self-regulation/> accessed 26 February 2019

- Model how to monitor learners' progress; for example, checking back to the task or question, ensuring they are heading in the right direction, and identifying any difficulties or obstacles.

- Evaluation can be modelled by simple reflections on 'what went well?' and 'what could be improved?', exploring how learners overcame obstacles and what they learned from the process. Encourage talk between learners to share these reflections.

- Teachers modelling self-regulation and metacognition can be very effective in improving these skills in learners.[41]

2 How to tackle troublesome knowledge

Some ideas and concepts are harder to learn than others. The term 'troublesome knowledge' was coined by those studying threshold concepts. There are three main aspects to this: the notion of threshold concepts, responding to different types of mistakes, and desirable difficulties.

For each topic or concept, ask yourself:

- What's hard to learn or understand?

- What's hard to teach and understand?

- Why are they so difficult to understand?

- How did you come to understand these?

- What interventions work?

- Do they work for everyone?

- Will understanding this improve understanding?

According to Professor James H. McMillan, research on learners' mistakes is carried out from a variety of research areas including mindset, text anxiety, achievement motivation, behaviourism, goal orientation, self-regulation (see previous section), and neurology.[42] I believe this illustrates what a complex issue mistake-making and learning is. Below I consider how threshold concepts, responding to mistakes, and desirable difficulties are applicable to classroom teaching.

---

[41] **D.H. Schunk** (2003). Self-efficacy for reading and writing: Influence of modeling, goal setting, and self-evaluation. *Reading & Writing Quarterly*, 19(2), 159–172.
[42] **J.H. McMillan** (2017). *Using Students' Assessment Mistakes and Learning Deficits to Enhance Motivation and Learning*. Abingdon and New York: Routledge, pp. 45–47.

Threshold concepts

According to Mayer and Land,[43] threshold concepts are areas of a discipline that are particularly troublesome to learn. Based on my research, I find a good way to explain threshold concepts is by likening them to a portal to new knowledge and understanding. By way of analogy, I have described the portal in the movie and TV series *Stargate*. The Stargate is a portal in time (and space) that is a large hoop with symbols around it that can be arranged into different orders. The adventurers have to arrange the symbols around the portal to get access to a particular time and location.[44] During learning, the prior knowledge (symbols) has to be in the correct order to fully understand the threshold concept and open access to the new applications of that concept.

Threshold concepts have been mostly studied at the level of higher education, looking at the key knowledge and concepts that are needed to fully understand a subject discipline. For example, what key concepts do you need to understand physics or economics? According to Meyer and Land, a threshold concept represents a transformed way of understanding, or interpreting, or viewing something without which the learner cannot progress.[45]

Meyer & Land (2003) originally proposed these characteristics of a threshold concept:

'a) *Transformative,* in that, once understood, its potential effect on student learning and behaviour is to occasion a significant shift in the perception of a subject, or part thereof.

b) Probably *irreversible,* in that the change of perspective occasioned by acquisition of a threshold concept is unlikely to be forgotten, or will be unlearned only by considerable effort.

c) *Integrative*; that is, it exposes the previously hidden interrelatedness of something.

---

[43] **J. Meyer & R. Land** (2006). *Overcoming Barriers to Student Understanding: Threshold Concepts and Troublesome Knowledge.* Abingdon and New York: Routledge.

[44] **A. Chandler-Grevatt** (2015). Challenging concepts in chemistry, *Education in Chemistry*, December. Available at: <https://eic.rsc.org/feature/challenging-concepts-in-chemistry/2000069.article> accessed 4 April 2019

[45] **J. Meyer & R. Land** (2003). Threshold concepts and troublesome knowledge: Linkages to ways of thinking and practising within the disciplines. Occasional Report 4. Edinburgh: ETL Project, University of Edinburgh. Available at: <http://www.etl.tla.ed.ac.uk/docs/ETLreport4.pdf> accessed 4 April 2019

d) Possibly often (though not necessarily always) *bounded* in that any conceptual space will have terminal frontiers, bordering with thresholds into new conceptual areas.

e) Potentially (and possibly inherently) *troublesome.*'

J. Meyer & R. Land (2003). *Threshold concepts and troublesome knowledge: Linkages to ways of thinking and practising within the disciplines.*

While threshold concepts are a useful aspect of understanding concepts within disciplines, I do wonder how applicable they are to school curriculum knowledge.

Responding to mistakes

Learners make mistakes in their learning for a number of reasons. Often out of carelessness, but equally due to a learning deficit or error such as:[46]

- application error

- incorrect identification

- confusion

- misunderstanding

- learning error

- memory deficit

- partial understanding

- misconception.

A simplified version of this has been developed by Professor Keith Taber for Science education, where he recognises the type of mistake and the type of intervention needed.[47] I took this idea and developed something called 'pinch point' activities.[48] Threshold concepts to me seem too complex for concepts in the school curriculum. I perceive curriculum concepts to be 'sub' concepts of threshold concepts and have identified these as pinch points within the

---

[46] **J.H. McMillan** (2017). *Using Students' Assessment Mistakes and Learning Deficits to Enhance Motivation and Learning*. Abingdon and New York: Routledge, p.15.

[47] **K.S. Taber** (2014). *Student Thinking and Learning in Science: Perspectives on the Nature and Development of Learners' Ideas*. New York and Abingdon: Routledge.

[48] **A. Chandler-Grevatt** (2017). How to make effective interventions. Education in Chemistry, December. Available at: <https://eic.rsc.org/ideas/how-to-make-effective-interventions/3008224.article> accessed 30 March 2019

curriculum. Although they are being used in Science subjects, pinch points are equally applicable to other subjects and seem to be called 'gateway topics'.

Pinch points focus on chunks of knowledge and understanding, rather than small units. Making learners aware of pinch points can provide opportunities to engage with them, rather than ignore them. Engaging with pinch points could lead to 'mastery' or 'deep learning'. So, once understood, pinch points allow learners to apply the concept confidently to new situations. Identifying pinch points allows diagnosis and application of specific interventions.

Taber's four main mistakes – lack of knowledge, missing connection, misconception, and misunderstanding – each require a different type of intervention to aid correction (Figure 2.5). These are a making-good activity, a connecting activity, a dissociating activity, and a correcting activity, respectively.

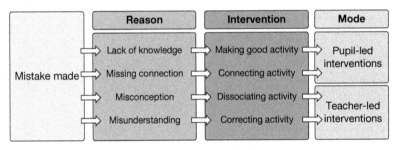

Figure 2.5: Mistakes, reasons, and interventions[49]

The types of intervention that can be used for each activity include:

- Making-good activities:

  - Key words and meanings

  - Comprehension questions

  - Revisit specific knowledge or concepts

  - Identification of key processes

- Connecting activities:

  - Compare and contrast

  - Concept maps

  - Sequencing events

---

[49] Adapted from **K.S. Taber** (2014). *Student Thinking and Learning in Science: Perspectives on the Nature and Development of Learners' Ideas*. New York and Abingdon: Routledge, p. 208.

- Correcting activities:
  - Demonstration with questioning
  - Same questions asked differently
  - Spoken and written explanations
- Dissociating activities:
  - Compare and contrast
  - Concept maps
  - Sequencing events.

Pinch-point activities combine a diagnosis of the type of mistake made and the intervention activity based on the type of mistake. This completes a feedback loop (see Figure 2.6 in Section 2.5, *Feedback for progress*).

Desirable difficulties

Desirable difficulties are features that teachers can add to a learning task to make it more challenging and therefore more memorable.[50] Robert Bjork has been studying the environmental context of memory-making for a number of decades[51] and more recently this concept has been applied to classroom learning.[52] Interestingly, this is at odds with some of the Cognitive Load Theory ideas discussed in the following section on how to improve remembering and memory. Desirable difficulties can be created, which on the surface appear to slow down learning, but in fact improve long-term memory and transfer.[53] Strategies that can be used in the classroom include the spacing effect and interleaving (described in the next section) and also:

- *Variation*: Variation in the ways a teacher approaches their teaching (didactic, project-based, examples given) and changes in the learning environment (layout of classroom, place where learning takes place, and even the smell of the room) can create a greater number of unique situations and therefore better learning.

[50] **R.A. Bjork & J.F. Kroll** (2015). Desirable difficulties in vocabulary learning. *The American Journal of Psychology*, 128(2), p. 241.

[51] **S.M. Smith, A. Glenberg & R.A. Bjork** (1978). Environmental context and human memory. *Memory & Cognition*, 6, 342–353.

[52] **R. Bjork** (2017). Chapter 9: Creating desirable difficulties to enhance learning. In I. Wallace & L. Kirkman (eds) (2017). *Best of the Best Practical Classroom Guides: Progress*. Carmarthen: Crown House Publishing, p. 83.

[53] **N.C. Soderstrom & R.A. Bjork** (2015). Learning versus performance: An integrative review. *Perspectives on Psychological Science*, 10, 176–199.

- *Encouraging active engagement*: Engaging in materials in a number of different ways, which have an element of challenge, helps learners retain long-term memory and retrieval. Quizzes, puzzles, and simple problem-solving all add a desirable difficulty that can improve learning.

- *Creating order from (a little) chaos*: Instead of providing learners with information that is easily understandable, have it slightly disorganised, so they have to organise it for themselves. This includes extracting information from more than one source, selecting relevant information from extended text, or providing information in different forms such as video, written text, and diagrams.

3 How to improve remembering and memory

Our understanding and classroom application of cognitive science is increasing greatly. There are two areas that can be applied to classroom practice; both are designed to help increase memory formation and memory retention.

Cognitive science works on the understanding that learning is memory-forming: if facts are remembered and accessible, they can be applied to new situations. This approach is still in its infancy, but is currently popular and heralded to influence evidence-based teaching and instruction.[54]

An important part of memory formation is that of forgetting. The brain receives a lot of information and chooses which information to store for the long term and which to forget. The forgetting curve itself is not new; Hermann Ebbinghaus first produced it experimentally in the late 1800s, showing how retention of 'facts' is reduced over time.[55] More recently, the experiment has been repeated with similar results,[56] so a lot of research and pedagogical practice has been focused on reducing forgetting.

Spaced retrieval and interleaving

Interleaving and spacing are two techniques that teachers use to help reduce forgetting and to secure long-term memory. The premise is that if new information is to be remembered, then the retrieval of that information will

---

[54] **F. Paas, A. Renkl & J. Sweller** (2003). Cognitive load theory and instructional design: Recent developments. *Educational Psychologist*, 38(1), 1–4.

[55] **Classics in the History of Psychology** (n.d.) *Memory: A Contribution to Experimental Psychology*, Hermann Ebbinghaus (1885). Available at: <http://psychclassics.yorku.ca/Ebbinghaus/index.htm> accessed 26 February 2019

[56] **J.M.J. Murre & J. Dros** (2015). Replication and analysis of Ebbinghaus' forgetting curve. *PLoS ONE*, 10(7), e0120644.

be strengthened if it is regularly repeated, reducing the effect of forgetting.[57] The second is 'interleaving'; that is, mixing up learning so that it is not confined to a topic. For example, facts from last week, last month and last term are tested regularly, interleaved with the most recent facts to learn. Interleaving has been shown to have a positive impact on long-term memory storage.[58] This can be achieved in a number of ways in the classroom.

The simplest version of this is the 'Read-Write-Review' method used by teachers around the world. I remember doing this for learning spellings: read it, write it (without looking), and check you've got it right. Move on to the next one. Keep going through the list until you get them all correct.

Low-tech approaches include flashcards – cards with a question on the front and an answer on the back. These are then mixed up to self-test. Regular practice, such as the next hour, the day, the next two days, the next week, and so on, checks if the learner has retained the memory. The very act of doing this increases the chance of long-term memory storage. This works well with learning vocabulary, particularly in language-learning, as well as learning 'facts and figures'. There are also a number of 'hi-tech' approaches, including software applications that use these techniques by regular self-tests and interleaving information recall.

Cognitive load theory

We know that there is a limit to how much new information we can hold in our head at a particular time, for example, a short list of numbers or the items of a shopping list. After five or six items, we start to forget. This is due to the capacity of our working memory. Our long-term memory, however, is constructed of schemata. Schemata are collections of information that represent concepts in our minds (see Research 1.3: Piaget's schema in Section 1.3).

Cognitive load theory (CLT) is a framework within which teachers can present information to optimise learning, taking into account the amount of information our working memory can deal with.[59] John Sweller has been central to the application of CLT to the classroom.[60]

---

[57] **J.D. Karpicke & H.L. Roediger** (2008). The critical importance of retrieval for learning. *Science*, 319(5865), 966–968.

[58] **M.S. Birnbaum, N. Kornell, E.L. Bjork & R.A. Bjork** (2013). Why interleaving enhances inductive learning: The roles of discrimination and retrieval. *Memory & Cognition*, 41(3), 392–402.

[59] **J. Sweller** (1988). Cognitive load during problem solving: Effects on learning. *Cognitive Science*, 12(2), 257–285.

[60] **J. Sweller** (1994). Cognitive load theory, learning difficulty, and instructional design. *Learning and Instruction*, 4(4), 295–312.

There are three types of cognitive load:

- intrinsic cognitive load: the demand of the learning task itself

- extraneous cognitive load: the demand unrelated to learning

- germane cognitive load: attention on activities that promote learning.

As teachers, CLT says that we should manage the intrinsic cognitive load, minimise the extraneous cognitive load, and maximise the germane cognitive load. Teachers need to consider how can they maximise the incorporation of new information into existing schemata and support the creation of new schemata. There are a number of classroom techniques that can be used to support this. Here I describe three approaches:[61] worked examples, split attention, and reducing interactivity of the task:

- *Worked examples*: The explicit teaching or modelling of how to solve a problem or approach a task is highly effective in helping learners access and become successful in learning. This is common in Mathematics and Science, but can be effective in analysing texts as well as a host of other situations.

- *Split attention effect*: To help learners concentrate on the learning, visual representations can be more effective by reducing the extraneous cognitive load. Diagrams should have text integrated into them rather than separated in a key. This reduces split attention.

- *Reducing interactivity of the task:* Interactive textbooks and webpages can increase the extraneous load, so CLT suggests that simplifying these activities can increase learning.

4 How to accelerate progress

Many of the interventions we have considered so far are designed to improve the efficiency of learning. However, there is a movement to accelerate learning in schools. A number of programmes aim to achieve the same amount of learning in a shorter period of time. Sometimes such courses are called 'intensive learning'. Some degree courses are attempted in two years, instead of the usual three, using this approach. However, the area I want to highlight here is the acceleration of cognitive development.

---

[61] **P.C. Brown, H.L. Roediger & M.A. McDaniel** (2014). *Make It Stick*. Cambridge, MA: Harvard University Press.

There are three programmes that have been developed at King's College London since the 1980s,[62] one for Science, one for Mathematics and one for the arts:

- CASE: Cognitive Acceleration through Science Education
- CAME: Cognitive Acceleration through Mathematics Education
- Cognitive Acceleration through the Arts.

Cognitive acceleration is heavily dependent on an approach to teaching that challenges learners' prior knowledge, encourages the social construction of learning, metacognition, and finally 'bridging' between skills. Each programme is built on these principles and depends on the regular use of the activities. An essential factor is the training of teachers using the programme to ensure they are competent at supporting learners' cognitive acceleration. These programmes are still in use in schools.[63]

These cognitive acceleration programmes have shown a positive impact on attainment[64] (claims of 25–50 per cent of learners showing cognitive acceleration compared to a control group) and motivation.[65] There have inevitably been critiques of the approach and the outcomes, particularly the need for a specific pedagogical approach and a whole-school approach to get full benefit. With respect to those learners who do not appear to benefit, it has been suggested that this can be explained by motivational differences between learners, essentially the difference between a fixed and a growth mindset.[66]

The basic approach to these programmes is the creation of cognitive conflict situations, through which learners make sense of the situation by working together and finally supporting metacognitive approaches to understand how learning has happened.

---

[62] **King's College London** (n.d.) Cognitive acceleration (CASE and other projects). Available at: <https://www.kcl.ac.uk/ecs/research/research-centres/crestem/research/past-projects/cognaccel> accessed 10 July 2019

[63] **Let's Think** (n.d.) <https://www.letsthink.org.uk/> accessed 26 February 2019

[64] **P. Adey & M. Shayer** (2016). *Really Raising Standards: Cognitive Intervention and Academic Achievement.* Abingdon and New York: Routledge. (Originally published in 1994.)

[65] **T. Finau, D.F. Treagust, M. Won & A.L. Chandrasegaran** (2018). Effects of a mathematics cognitive acceleration program on student achievement and motivation. *International Journal of Science and Mathematics Education*, 16(1), 183–202.

[66] **E.L. Leo & D. Galloway** (1996). Conceptual links between cognitive acceleration through science education and motivational style: A critique of Adey and Shayer. *International Journal of Science Education*, 18(1), 35–49.

5 How to plan for progress

Planning is a key part of helping learners make progress through the curriculum. The previous three points: self-regulation, troublesome knowledge, and improvement of memory, can be integrated into long-, medium- and short-term planning.

Long-term planning

Long-term planning is based on the curriculum as a whole. As well as knowledge, understanding, and skills, the wider educational experience and outcomes are considered. Teachers have the opportunity to share expectations of learning and learning approaches. If your school's assumption of progress is focused solely on examination success, or it has a broader perspective on educational progress, then appropriate activities can be planned. How progress will be communicated is an essential part of long-term planning. It forms the foundations of a progress culture.

Medium-term planning

Within units of learning, plan in opportunities for tackling and addressing troublesome knowledge, practising techniques, and explicitly modelling approaches to learning.

If you are using a mastery approach, this needs to be part of the medium-term planning. Teachers need to work out when learners will be tested and how those who 'pass' can continue to learn, while the remainder have time to master that set of knowledge.

Short-term planning

Lesson-by-lesson planning is based on assessment of learners at the end of the previous lesson to inform the next lesson. Integrating opportunities for self-regulation, practice, and challenging troublesome knowledge are all part of short-term planning. The teacher's assessment literacy can help them to use unplanned, informal, formative assessment practices.

 Discuss

- Is there a single most effective way to promote progress?
- What factors affect how a learner makes progress?
- What factors affect how effective a teacher is at promoting progress?

Reflection

Revisit the Practice analyser: Teaching for progress (Table 2.8).

- How have you progressed?

- What will you do to improve your own practice?

- How will you check any measures have been effective?

 **Further reading**

To explore some of these ideas further, I recommend reading:

J. Meyer & R. Land (2006). *Overcoming Barriers to Student Understanding: Threshold Concepts and Troublesome Knowledge*. Abingdon and New York: Routledge.

P.C. Brown, H.L. Roediger & M.A. McDaniel (2014). *Make It Stick*. Cambridge, MA: Harvard University Press.

 Also see

This section also links to:

Part 1: 1.3, section on Observable progress: What does progress look like?

Part 3: 3.3 Interpretation of student responses and appropriate interventions

3.6 Critical engagement with assessment theory, policy, and practice

2.5 Feedback for progress

Introduction: The loop

The cycle of 'Where am I now? Where do I want to be? How do I get there?' relies on feedback at specific points. Learners rely on teachers to help them understand where they are and what their goals are, and to support them in getting there (Figure 2.6).

Figure 2.6: The feedback loop[67]

Like an electrical circuit, in order to work, the loop needs to be complete. Giving feedback is a complex process that relies on many factors to be successful. If any of these factors is missing, the effectiveness of the feedback will be reduced. In addition, if the opportunity to improve is not explicitly offered and valued, then the loop is not closed. Feedback is useless if nothing is done in response to the feedback.

The key part of feedback is effective communication. The teacher and learner must both understand what the other is talking about. There needs to be a shared language about progress. There then needs to be a shared understanding of what success looks like and shared values and motivation to improve. The interventions provided need to not only offer strategies on what to improve, but how to improve. This will ensure that the feedback loop is closed.

In this section, we look at five practical approaches to give feedback to learners. The first three consider modes of feedback: verbal, through intervention activities, and through marking work. The other two consider the use of data and strategies to plan feedback.

 Consider

- When do you feed back to learners?

- How do you feed back to learners?

- How do you plan to feed back?

---

[67] Adapted from **P. Broadfoot, R. Daugherty, J. Gardner, W. Harlen, M. James & G. Stobart** (2002). *Assessment for Learning: 10 Principles. Research-based principles to guide classroom practice Assessment for Learning*. London: Assessment Reform Group. <www.aaia.org.uk/news/article/assessment-for-learning-10-principles> accessed 10 July 2019

Analyse your practice

Use Table 2.9 to rate your experience of using each strategy for giving feedback for progress.

Table 2.9: Practice analyser: Feedback for progress

	Never heard of it	Heard of it	Have tried it	Used it sometimes	Confidently apply
1 Verbal feedback					
2 Using effective interventions					
3 Marking effectively					
4 Using data to feedback					
5 Planning for feedback					

Of course, you can read about each of these in order, but if you wish to focus on one, then skip ahead to the relevant 'how to' section to learn a bit more about the strategy and how to apply it to your practice. There are references in each section and additional reading at the end of this section. After reading this section, you may want to reflect on what you have learned.

1 How to feed back verbally

John Hattie[68] identifies three types of feedback, which I have linked to the feedback triangle (Figure 2.6):

- Feed up (Where do I want to be?)
- Feed back (Where am I now?)
- Feed forward, the next steps (How do I get there?)

For each of these types, we can feed back at four levels:

- *Task*: focused on how learners are approaching the activity – 'That's the right answer.' 'Spend a bit more time on Section 3.'
- *Process*: focused on the processes the learner uses to achieve the task – 'Why have you used that strategy to solve the problem?' 'Which devices could you use to improve this section of your essay?'

---

[68] **J. Hattie** (2008). *Visible Learning: A Synthesis of Over 800 Meta-analyses Relating to Achievement*. Abingdon and New York: Routledge, p.176

- *Self-regulation*: encourages evaluation of the task and the learner coming up with their own feed forward.

- *Self-level*: praise the individual, rather than the work – 'What a good student you are!'

Teachers can become skilful at choosing the type and level of verbal feedback, depending on the activity, situation, and the learners' needs. Verbal feedback can be very effective because it is instant and dialogue can take place. However, it is time-consuming and is difficult to sustain with large classes of learners.

Like all feedback, verbal feedback is most effective when it is specific and positive. There are a lot of emotions associated with receiving feedback, whether it is positive or negative. Skilled teachers know their learners and how they may respond to feedback. There has been some interesting research looking at the emotional effects of feedback and showing that if it is anticipated – that is, if the learner knows they will get feedback on the task or activity – they are more likely to respond to it positively.[69]

2 How to use effective interventions

Interventions are responses or activities that help a learner progress. They have two main motives: correcting or improving. Correcting interventions identify mistakes and aim to challenge them; improving interventions identify a successful step in learning and aim to identify and support the next steps for the learner. Intervention is the 'how do I get there?' part of the cycle (Figure 2.6) and can be addressed in many ways. I have come to realise that 'intervention' is 'teaching'; it's not an add-on, something done outside lessons, or as extra lessons. It is an intrinsic part of teaching and learning.

Five features of effective interventions are as follows.

Interventions are planned

Knowing when, how, and why you are intervening are factors that allow feedback to be effective. Although there is value to 'responsive feedback' (see the previous section, *1 How to feed back verbally*), planned interventions allow time to be given for improvement by using specific activities and approaches.

---

[69] **R. Pekrun, A. Cusack, K. Murayama, A.J. Elliot & K. Thomas** (2014). The power of anticipated feedback: Effects on students' achievement goals and achievement emotions. *Learning and Instruction*, 29, 115–124.

In addition, anticipated feedback can increase the chances of learners having a positive emotional response to the feedback (see Section 2.4, *1 How to feed back verbally*).

Interventions are valued

Valuing intervention is a signal to learners that a teacher places importance on the act of intervention and the response to that intervention. If learners are asked to respond to feedback or carry out an intervention activity in their own time, or as homework, there is no real incentive to do so. It also sends the message that intervention is an afterthought, rather than an important part of the learning process. Increasing the value of an intervention can take several forms.

In response to a test, learners can be given specific areas to revise and revision techniques to learn as homework, then retested in the next lesson. This shows that the teacher values the intervention and will follow it up. This is time-consuming, though. If time can be given to attempt the intervention during a lesson, this holds greater value with the teacher and the learner. Flipped learning[70] is a specific method whereby learners engage with the knowledge at home, then the lesson is composed of activities to apply the knowledge and interventions. This, of course, requires disciplined learners and works well in post-compulsory education.

Interventions are focused

Feedback is more effective if it is focused. This means that both teacher and learner must know how the task will be assessed. This can be achieved through sharing learning objectives or learning intentions from the start of an activity, and then providing feedback on just those. Sometimes, if an assessment activity has been carried out before and a relevant target was given, this could be addressed in a new activity at a later date to see if it has improved.

Interventions are timely

Although there is a range of research on the relationship between the effectiveness of feedback and the delay in receiving it, there is no clear advice. I use the general rule of giving feedback as soon after the assessment event as possible. Most schools have a turnaround of assessment marking and feedback of less than a week. This is practical and probably worthwhile.

---

[70] **AdvanceHE** (2018) Flipped Learning. Available at: <https://www.heacademy. ac.uk/knowledge-hub/flipped-learning-0> accessed 26 February 2019

Often, emotionally, learners need time between an assessment and the feedback to be able to reflect and take on that feedback. However, the longer that time, the less they will remember about the assessment.

Interventions are personalised

The more meaningful the feedback is to a learner, the greater the chance that it will be received positively and acted upon effectively, thus facilitating progress. Although it can seem overwhelming for teachers to personalise feedback, I find there are some techniques that can achieve this. Often there are only three to five areas that need improvement in a lesson. Intervention activities can be provided for each of these, plus an extension activity. Giving learners a choice of which they think is most useful to them, based on the feedback the teacher gives them, helps them value the activity they are doing.

3 How to mark effectively

In most subjects, marking learners' work is a traditional practice carried out by teachers, often in the form of marking exercise books. Although parents like to see that their child's book has been marked, research suggests that teachers checking or marking books has little impact on learners' progress. Instead, there are a number of alternative approaches that can be more effective:

Checking books

Often feedback in books is managerial,[71] focusing on the presentation of the work rather than the learning. Presentation of work in books does not in itself improve progress, but taking pride in and having an understanding of presentation are good qualities to foster. Promoting these expectations, teachers can do spot checks during lessons and outwardly praise for good presentation. In addition, marking can be speeded up using marking codes. A shared list of presentation expectations and errors can be prepared and shared. Codes for spelling mistakes, sentence structure, and punctuation errors can be used to reduce the amount of time teachers spend writing:

- T: Write a title and underline it

- D: Date your work

- S: Spelling error

- P: Punctuation error.

---

[71] **P. Black & D. Wiliam** (1998). Assessment and classroom learning. *Assessment in Education: Principles, Policy & Practice*, 5(1), 7–74.

To close the feedback loop, learners can be given time to make the corrections and improvements.

Live marking

Live marking combines oral feedback (see Section 2.4, *1 How to feed back verbally*) with book checking (above). The teacher spends a few minutes with each learner and 'checks and feeds back'. This can happen more easily in primary classes when a teacher spends a larger period of the day with the class. A section of a lesson can be used during one-hour lessons to feed back to a few learners. Over a week or two, every learner has received some live feedback. Live marking is particularly common in more physical subjects such as Physical Education, Drama, and Dance.

Focused feedback

If feedback is given on pre-agreed objectives, it can be focused on these shared outcomes. This works well on extended writing and projects where a rubric is provided that matches the learning aims of the activity. Rubrics are helpful as they often require only highlighting or ticking the descriptors that have been met (see Table 2.10).

Table 2.10: An example of a rubric for a religious festivals project

	Not met	Met	Exceeded
Described the country and its religious festivals		Yes *Good use of calendar of the festivals*	
Explained the features of the festival			Yes *Excellent detail*
Spelling, punctuation and grammar	*Proofread your work, correcting spellings and punctuation*		

Whole-class feedback

When going through a set of books or assignments to mark, some teachers write a list of the common successes and mistakes they come across. They then present this to the class in a lesson, where the learners respond to their specific issues. This is a more efficient way of marking, feeding back, and giving time to respond. It's a method I use when marking a set of postgraduate assignment drafts, as it consolidates the common errors and allows time for them to be challenged before the final draft is completed.

4 How to use data to feed back

In Section 2.2, I spent some time discussing the opportunities and limitations of using data to measure progress. There are, however, some practical uses of data in giving feedback.

A common feature of mastery approaches to learning is that regular low-stakes tests are used to assess a learner's knowledge, understanding, and skills. Often the 'pass mark' is 80 per cent of the questions correctly answered. This is part of the mastery feedback loop: if a learner achieves 80 per cent or more, they can move on; if they fall below 80 per cent they need to revisit and retest. The test checks 'Where am I now?', the 80 per cent threshold is 'Where do I want to be?' and the intervention is 'How can I get there?'.

High-stakes, well designed tests on a mixture of topics can be useful to check on progress at key points in the school year, though I discussed the cautions of using these in Section 2.2. However, when tests are used to generate data, it is important for both teacher and learner to know what the result means and ideally have a way to communicate what and how to improve.

5 How to plan for feedback

As I have established, feedback is an essential part of the assessment loop in enabling learners to make progress. Knowing how and when you will feed back is helpful for both teacher and learner. The feedback model you choose to use will help you to decide how and when you will feed back.[72] However, there are a number of strategies that can be used.

Feedback in lessons can be categorised as that which is planned and that which is responsive.[73] Planned feedback can happen within a lesson, across a number of lessons (often during a topic), and often at the end of a learning episode.

In the classic three-part lesson, the feedback often takes place in the plenary section, where learners reflect upon the learning intentions and, ideally, work out what they need to do next. Teachers sometimes gather their responses to inform planning of the next lesson. Using a mastery approach, there is a specific feedback point in the form of a low-stakes test. The very nature of

---

[72] **J. Hattie** (2008). *Visible Learning: A Synthesis of Over 800 Meta-analyses Relating to Achievement*. Abingdon and New York: Routledge. p. 176.

[73] **B. Bell & B. Cowie** (2001). *Formative Assessment and Science Education*. Dortrecht: Kluwer Academic Publishers, pp. 91–94.

teaching and learning is that some aspect of assessment is taking place most of the time, whether it's establishing where the learners are now, where they need to get to, or how to get there.

Informal, unplanned feedback happens frequently in lessons through teacher–learner interactions. Opportunities within lessons to feed back in response to learners' ongoing performance should be maximised, as it is instant and can be effective if specific and positive. However, this requires a teacher to have a well-developed assessment literacy (see Part 3).

 Discuss

- Is it always essential to complete the feedback loop?
- What proportion of feedback should be focused on doing a task compared to the strategies used to achieve the task?
- How can feedback be linked to developing metacognitive strategies?

 Reflection

Revisit the Practice analyser: Feedback for progress (Table 2.9).

- How have you progressed?
- What will you do to improve your own practice?
- How will you check any measures have been effective?

 Further reading

To explore some of these ideas further, I recommend reading:

M. Gershon. (2017) *How to Use Feedback and Marking in the Classroom: The Complete Guide.* Volume 10 in the How to... Great Classroom Teaching Series. CreateSpace independent publishing platform.

J. Hattie & S. Clarke (2018). *Visible Learning: Feedback.* Abingdon and New York: Routledge.

R. Morrison McGill (2016). *Mark. Plan. Teach.: Save time. Reduce workload. Impact learning.* London: Bloomsbury.

Also see

This section also links to:

Part 1:   1.3, Ready to progress? Starting points

Part 3:   3.2 Knowledge of common mistakes, misunderstandings, and misconceptions

3.3 Interpretation of student responses and appropriate interventions

3.6 Critical engagement with assessment theory, policy, and practice

Improving progress through teacher assessment literacy

So far we have considered, in Part 1, what progress in education is and what it could be. Then, in Part 2, I presented practical ways of supporting children in making progress. Finally, in Part 3, I want to concentrate on teachers' assessment literacy and how to improve it.

3.1 Teacher assessment literacy

'Teacher assessment literacy' is a phrase used mostly in academic literature, but I feel it is important to make this visible to teachers in the hope that they can actively make some changes to their own practice and improve their knowledge, understanding, and skills.

Teachers' professional knowledge is often described as 'pedagogical content knowledge' or PCK.[1] Subject knowledge alone is not enough to be an effective teacher; even the most knowledgeable people may not be able to communicate or teach someone what they know. Teachers also have 'pedagogical' knowledge, which includes how we teach, when to teach, how learners learn, and so on.[2] This is often presented as a Venn diagram (Figure 3.1), showing that where subject knowledge and pedagogical knowledge overlap is where PCK exists.

---

[1] **S.K. Abell** (2008). Twenty years later: Does pedagogical content knowledge remain a useful idea? *International Journal of Science Education*, 30(10), 1405–1416.

[2] **S. Gudmundsdottir & L. Shulman** (1987). Pedagogical content knowledge in social studies. *Scandinavian Journal of Educational Research*, 31(2), 59–70.

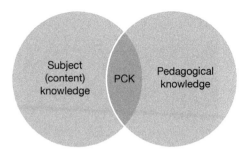

Figure 3.1: Pedagogical content knowledge (PCK)[3]

Subject knowledge is what we teach, which includes:

- knowledge and understanding of the discipline

- skills of the discipline

- applications of the discipline.

Pedagogical knowledge is how we teach, which includes:

- knowledge and understanding to teach the discipline

- how the discipline is taught within the curriculum context

- how learners learn the discipline.

An important part of pedagogical knowledge is assessment literacy. This refers to the set of professional knowledge, understanding, and skills that a teacher uses in assessing and assessment in order to support their learners in making progress. In this context, it will usually, but not always, be progress through the curriculum and assessment via a standard exam. More pertinently, another definition for assessment literacy is 'the knowledge about how to assess what students know and can do, interpret the results of those assessments, and apply the results to improve student learning and program effectiveness'.[4]

Based on my experiences of training teachers, I have formulated a set of features of an assessment-literate teacher. Reflecting on what is required to improve each of these will help you develop and improve your own assessment literacy and thus have the tools to improve learners' progress.

---

[3] Adapted from **S. Gudmundsdottir & L. Shulman** (1987). Pedagogical content knowledge in social studies. *Scandinavian Journal of Educational Research,* 31(2), 59–70.

[4] **N.R. Elshawa, C.S. Heng, A.N. Abdullah & S.M. Rashid** (2016). Teachers' assessment literacy and washback effect of assessment. *International Journal of Applied Linguistics and English Literature*, 5(4), 137.

The key features of an assessment-literate teacher I have identified are:

- knowledge of common mistakes, misunderstandings, and misconceptions
- interpretation of student responses and appropriate interventions
- knowledge of requirements of (statutory/standard) assessments
- knowledge of exam technique
- critical engagement with assessment theory, policy, and practice.

In this part of the book, I will deal with each one. Presenting you with a practice analyser and some practical approaches to improve your practice will, I hope, impact on your teaching and your learners' progress. Many of the practical suggestions include strategies from Part 2, which I will refer you to when they come up.

Each section will provide activities for you to try, to improve your assessment literacy. These activities are intended to help improve different aspects of your assessment literacy. Over time, they will increase your knowledge, and your confidence in applying that knowledge and developing a critical perspective on assessment theory, policy, and practice. The activities do require short periods of work, ranging from 30 minutes to a couple of hours.

This is not supposed to be a one-time activity; instead it is a process that develops over time, deepening knowledge, understanding, and skills associated with assessment literacy. Figure 3.2 attempts to illustrate this continual development.

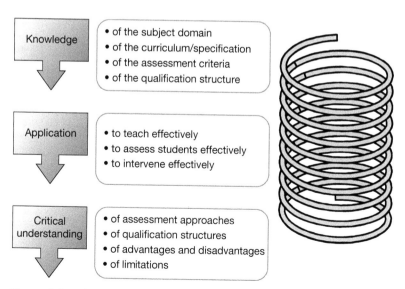

Figure 3.2: A framework for assessment literacy

Research

3.1 Research in assessment literacy

R.J. Stiggins (1991). Assessment literacy. *Phi Delta Kappan*, 72(7), 534–539.

Assessment literacy of teachers and other education professionals is severely lacking; here is what we could do about it.

Richard Stiggins, an assessment researcher and trainer, first argued for the importance of assessment literacy in teachers in 1991. Since then, he and his colleagues have developed strategies to improve teacher assessment literacy. This is based on education in the United States, but my experience tells me that this is something recognised in the UK, Kazahkstan, Canada, and China, and I suspect worldwide. The paper has, to date, been cited in other peer-reviewed journals over 300 times.

In the article, he argued that important instructional and policy decisions were based on student achievement data, recognising that good decisions lead to student benefits, but bad decisions lead to student harm. He claims that currently 'we are a nation of assessment illiterates… a society that has come to care very much about high standards of achievement, but we are a society that is incapable of understanding whether those standards are being met' (p. 535).

What is assessment literacy?

Two key questions:

- What does this assessment tell students about the achievement outcomes we value?
- What is the likely effect of this assessment on students?

Assessment literates:

- know what constitutes high-quality assessment
- know the importance of using an assessment method that reflects a precisely defined achievement target
- realise the importance of sampling performance fully
- are aware of extraneous factors that can interfere with assessment results
- know when the results are in a form they can understand and can use.

How assessment literate are we?

Stiggins highlights that assessment literacy is important for all those making decisions about education, including education officials, policymakers, and school boards, as well as teachers. He argues that the only people who have the basic requirements are those practitioners and scholars of educational measurement and assessment.

Stiggins asserts that as a society we do not really care about the quality of the assessments, and we rarely offer teachers training in assessment to improve their assessment literacy. He highlights that education policymakers have little or no training or knowledge about assessment processes.

> 'My point is that we spend all of our available resources to train teachers and administrators to produce learning and to put that training to work in schools. Then we allocate virtually no resources to train practitioners or interested others in sound methods of assessing the outcomes of those efforts.'
>
> **R.J. Stiggins** (1991). Assessment literacy. *Phi Delta Kappan*, 72(7), p. 539.

This paper raises the importance of the assessment literacy of teachers and educational professionals. Since then, several researchers have developed this concept.

Research since this article

Educational research on teacher assessment literacy appears to have concentrated on the following areas over the past few decades:

- the assessment literacy of pre-service teachers
- the assessment literacy of teachers
- particular interest in the assessment of English as a foreign language.

The AfL movement from 1998 definitely increased teachers' understanding of formative assessment, but, as has been noted, often formative assessment is tokenistic rather than fully embedded into classroom practice.

A useful review of 100 research papers on teacher assessment literacy and teacher education was written by researchers in New Zealand, but drawing on international research:

Y. Xu & G.T.L. Brown (2016). Teacher assessment literacy in practice: A reconceptualization. *Teaching and Teacher Education*, 58, 149–162.

From this review, they identified seven areas that teachers should develop during training and into their careers:

'1 choosing assessment methods appropriate to instructional decisions

2 developing assessment methods appropriate for instructional decisions

3 administering, scoring, and interpreting the results of both externally produced and teacher-produced assessment methods

4 using assessment results when making decisions about individual students, planning teaching, developing curriculum, and school improvement

5 developing valid pupil grading procedures

6 communicating assessment results to various stakeholders

7 recognising unethical, illegal, and inappropriate assessment methods and uses of assessment information.'

Y. Xu & G.T.L. Brown (2016). Teacher assessment literacy in practice: A reconceptualization. *Teaching and Teacher Education*, 58, 149–162.

As is often the case, this research is not 'joined up', with the research being limited to certain researchers in particular places. There is a lot more room to develop this concept and implement change in education policy, teacher training, and teacher in-service training.

Application to progress

Supporting learner progress hinges on teachers understanding the purposes and applications of assessment practices. In the wider sense, this means having an idea of how learners progress, identifying the obstacles they face in learning and the interventions required to move them on. In a more focused sense, it means the mechanics of assessments, how to maximise success in examinations, and develop appropriate assessments.

It seems to me that assessment literacy is key to a teacher's professional repertoire, and identifying its importance will help teacher educators and teachers themselves to develop the knowledge, understanding, and skills needed to understand the practice and use of assessment techniques.

3.2 Knowledge of common mistakes, misunderstandings, and misconceptions

Introduction

I once set a homework activity for a Year 7 class (11–12-year-olds) to make a model of a plant cell. I provided some instructions and some examples of previous models that could be made. I wanted to see the main parts of the cell including the cell membrane, the cell wall, the nucleus, cytoplasm, and chloroplast. Among the various creations, which included a plasticine model, several shoebox versions, and an impressive (and tasty) cake, Tracy presented a piece of carpet with a hole cut in it containing a small flower pot and a seedling. Tracy had clearly misunderstood the task; it was an error that I could not have predicted, but it did reveal that I needed to help Tracy understand what was expected and the details of a plant cell.

Part of an experienced teacher's repertoire, beyond subject knowledge, is a knowledge of the common mistakes made by learners within their phase or subject. Awareness of many of these mistakes increases with teaching experience, but teachers can improve their knowledge of mistakes by reading relevant research and through engaging with more experienced practitioners.

Often, teachers respond to mistakes in an undifferentiated way, trying different methods to help learners understand. However, learners make mistakes for many reasons. Professor James H. McMillan at Virginia Commonwealth University, USA, identifies a variety of types of being wrong that include: careless mistake, application error, incorrect identification, confusion, misunderstanding, learning error, memory deficit, partial understanding, and misconception.[5]

Professor Keith Taber, of Cambridge University, has identified four possible reasons for mistakes:[6]

- a lack of knowledge

- a missing connection

- a misunderstanding

- a misconception.

---

[5] **J.H. McMillan** (2018). *Using Students' Assessment Mistakes and Learning Deficits to Enhance Motivation and Learning*. Abingdon and New York: Routledge, p.15.

[6] **K.S. Taber** (2014). *Student Thinking and Learning in Science: Perspectives on the Nature and Development of Learners' Ideas*. New York and Abingdon: Routledge, p. 208.

He goes on to discuss ways in which to address each type of mistake. Lack of knowledge requires an activity to update that missing knowledge; a missing connection requires strategies to make those connections; a misunderstanding needs a correction activity; and a misconception requires an activity to undo that wrong connection.

Knowing the type of mistake made and the reason for that mistake being made can help a teacher select an appropriate intervention.

 Consider

- What are the most common mistakes learners make in your phase/subject?
- How do you deal with mistakes?
- Do you pre-empt mistakes? If so, how?

Analyse your practice

Use Table 3.1 to establish your current practice concerning mistakes and misconceptions.

Table 3.1: Practice analyser: Knowledge of common mistakes, misunderstandings, and misconceptions

	Regularly	Often	Sometimes	Rarely	Never
1 I recognise when a learner makes a mistake and am able to challenge it.					
2 I can predict the common mistakes learners make in my phase/subject.					
3 I am aware of the common misconceptions learners have in my phase/subject.					
4 I plan tasks/lessons to challenge a common misconception.					
5 I know where to find out about common misconceptions.					

Analysis

- *Mostly 'regularly'/'often'*: If you are doing these practices regularly, I suspect this part of your assessment literacy is strong and you could consider the next section: 3.3 *Interpretation of student responses and appropriate interventions*. If you have a particular outlier in Table 3.1, then concentrate on the 'how to' sections related to that practice below.

- *Mostly 'sometimes'*: This indicates that you have some awareness of all these practices, but need to spend more time developing them. Select one you do least often and plan opportunities to address this using the 'how to' sections below.

- *Mostly 'rarely'/'never'*: This indicates that you need to spend some time developing all these features to improve your assessment literacy. Using these practices will help you to plan and make the most of learning opportunities through awareness of common misconceptions, misunderstandings, and mistakes.

Using the statements in the practice analyser (Table 3.1), select the numbers you wish to improve. Read the text and try the activities to help improve this area of your assessment literacy.

1 How to find out common mistakes

Mistakes are an important part of learning, but a teacher who is aware of the possible mistakes can be prepared to challenge and intervene when learners make those mistakes themselves. Alternatively, teachers can warn learners against making particular mistakes, with some guidance. Finding out common mistakes comes with experience, but there are ways to accelerate that process:

- Reflect on your own mistakes and experiences.

- Ask colleagues what they find their learners often get wrong.

- Research and apply some published ideas.

- Teach and reflect on your practice.

Own experiences

The common mistakes that learners make are often similar to the ones you might have made, or even still do. I still remember having trouble deciding on suitable scales for axes when drawing a graph, something I know learners have trouble with. Reflecting on what you found difficult when learning, or even what you are finding difficult to model or explain, will reveal common mistakes that are made in a particular topic.

Talk to colleagues

More experienced teaching colleagues and education professionals are often well aware of common mistakes that learners make in each topic they teach. Professional conversations with such colleagues will reveal mistakes you may not have experienced or anticipated.

You could ask the questions from the 'Consider' box above.

Internet research

The internet has a lot of information on common mistakes. Typing into a search engine 'Common mistakes in X' will generate webpages and resources for you to read and prepare with. 'X' can be 'Biology', 'Drama', 'English', 'Mathematics', for example, with the addition of the phase you teach, e.g. primary, secondary, etc.

Alternative phrases to search for include: learning deficits, misunderstanding, confusions.

Teaching and reflecting

When you teach, it is worth mentally noting or, if you can, physically noting any mistakes that arise and aim to pre-empt or challenge them in the future. Making notes on work schemes or lesson plans of mistakes that occur can be used the next time the topic is taught.

2 How to find out common misconceptions

As I explained above, misconceptions are a particular type of mistake. These have received a lot of academic interest, generating a lot of research, particularly in Science and Mathematics, but also other subjects.

Own experiences

Be aware that, as a teacher, you may still hold some key misconceptions. Common ones among graduates include in Biology that plants only have chloroplasts and no mitochondria, and the difference between fractions and decimals in Mathematics. In addition, you may have memories of finding out you had misunderstood something until a key moment challenged you. There is research interest in the misconceptions held by novice and trainee teachers.[7,8]

[7] **C. Counsell** (2011). Disciplinary knowledge for all, the secondary history curriculum and history teachers' achievement. *Curriculum Journal*, 22(2), 201–225.

[8] **H.O. Arslan, C. Cigdemoglu & C. Moseley** (2012). A three-tier diagnostic test to assess pre-service teachers' misconceptions about global warming, greenhouse effect, ozone layer depletion, and acid rain. *International Journal of Science Education*, 34(11), 1667–1686.

Talk to colleagues

Experienced colleagues will know what common misconceptions arise in their phase or subject. Often their lesson plans, resources, and activities will seek to challenge or address these misconceptions. Sharing ideas, experiences, and solutions makes it easier to tackle these issues.

Internet research

As with all internet searches, proceed with caution and evaluate the source before acting on the advice given. However, there are many reputable websites that include lists of common misconceptions for topics, particularly in the USA, Australia, and the UK. Some websites also offer ideas of how to challenge these misconceptions.

Try searching for the following using a search engine:

- school phase: primary/secondary/K12

- misconceptions/alternative conceptions/children's conceptions/children's ideas

- topic: Romans/cells/migration.

These searches should yield a variety of pages. Professional organisations for teachers often have lists of misconceptions to assist teachers.

Research literature

There is a lot of educational research literature on common misconceptions among different groups and age ranges. Often, the literature compares primary and secondary school children, school leavers and graduates, or makes international comparisons. These studies yield some fascinating similarities and differences, and can be applied to the classroom when teaching (see Research box 3.2).

Teachers do not always have access to research literature, but some educational journals make some articles available and many can be accessed via the website Google Scholar (scholar.google.com). Type into the search box similar key words to those in the general internet search (above).

There are also published books that detail common misconceptions in a particular phase or subject, which a bookshop or your local library could source for you (see Further reading).

Finally, professional organisations often have resources to support teachers. For example, for Science in the USA there is the National Science Teachers

Association (NSTA), and in the UK the Association for Science Education (ASE), as well as the Association of Teachers of Mathematics (ATM) and National Association for the Teaching of English (NATE).

Teaching and reflecting

A common feature of misconceptions is that they are hard to change, and often time is needed to help a learner to accept the new way of thinking (see Research box 3.2 below). Therefore, learners need challenging more than once and in a variety of ways.

3 How to plan to pre-empt or use mistakes in learning

It is essential that as a teacher you have good subject knowledge and are able to use that knowledge to plan and teach learners at a suitable level. Being able to respond to mistakes will improve learning. This is not necessarily a simple matter, as mistakes and misconceptions are due to a wide range of reasons and influences (see Research box 3.2). Here are some general approaches you can take to respond to mistakes.

Verbal responses

Having some verbal questions as part of your classroom patter will help you respond quickly and effectively. One approach is to tell a learner that they are wrong and have made a mistake. However, being wrong can cause a negative emotional response and there are more human ways to approach mistakes that will avoid these emotional barriers to learning. More effective is to engage with the mistake and facilitate the learner in rectifying it:

- How confident are you with that (answer)? Are you sure?

- How did you come to that (answer)? Explain that to me.

- What do you think of that (answer)?

Giving learners an opportunity to correct themselves can help them learn; sometimes they will say they haven't got a clue and at that point offering them the answer is the most humane thing to do. However, having a repertoire of alternative ways to explain the same concept can ensure that all learners understand.

4 How to plan to challenge misconceptions

Planning to challenge misconceptions has a particular approach. In most cases, you want to present learners with a situation where they can make a prediction and the actual outcome will be a surprise or at odds with their prediction. This is known as creating 'cognitive conflict'. It links to the desirable difficulties approach discussed in Section 2.4.

The four stages of challenging misconceptions are:

1. Probe prior knowledge.

2. Present cognitive conflict.

3. Provide a range of examples.

4. Revisit later on.

With particularly troublesome concepts or topics, teachers can plan lessons that address these four stages. The first three can be done within a lesson, but clearly the last stage must be planned to check knowledge and understanding.

There are many ways to probe prior knowledge, either directly or indirectly. Prior knowledge can be revealed through responses to questions, but is often effective when learners make and justify a prediction. Teachers asking learners what they 'think will happen if...' presents the opportunity for cognitive conflict. This is an event where what you think will happen, doesn't happen. It is at odds with your expectation; it may surprise or startle you. This exposes a gap in your own knowledge or understanding, creating cognitive conflict. Once that has occurred, the teacher needs to demonstrate to the learner that this event is not a one-off, but can be demonstrated in a variety of ways.

My favourite example is asking people to predict which ice cube will melt the fastest: one placed on wood or one placed on a metal surface. Most people predict that the one on wood will melt the fastest; others think it will make no difference. However, the one on metal will melt before your eyes. It creates great cognitive conflict and discussions about the nature of heat energy movement and temperature.

5 How to evaluate information about misconceptions

Mistakes and misconceptions have a number of influencing factors, particularly sociocultural and popular culture. So, although many misconceptions in Science and Mathematics are common internationally, there will be more localised misconceptions. For example, when I started teaching, learners rarely knew the word 'plankton', but once the cartoon *SpongeBob SquarePants*™ came into existence, learners knew the word but had a rather non-scientific understanding of the size and function of plankton in a food web. Similarly, an English teacher colleague was rather despairing of Baz Luhrmann's movie version of *Romeo and Juliet*, from which learners were recalling exploding petrol stations and gun fights in their exams. So, when reading and applying education research to your own practice, it is important to consider the context in which the studies were carried out.

Evaluating and applying literature

When reading research literature on learners' mistakes and misconceptions and how to challenge them, consider these four points:

- Where did the study take place?
- When did the study take place?
- Who was involved in the study?
- How applicable is it to your context?

As I have pointed out previously, some mistakes and misconceptions are often common among all learners, but others can be influenced by age, sociocultural factors, and popular culture factors. When considering whether the information in a study is relevant to your teaching and your learners, it is important to keep these ideas in mind. You need to assess the generalisability of the study.

Therefore, where the study took place is important. If it is in the same country as yours, it may be easier to apply; once you start to read studies from other countries, other factors come into play, such as language, local culture, and popular culture in that area. These could all impact the transferability of the findings. This is not to say that the study does not provide any value; it will just need to be treated with appropriate caution.

 Research

3.2 Research in misconceptions

Misconception research is predominantly in the STEM subjects, mostly because there is a set of accepted concepts that learners are required to understand. Researchers recognise that each misconception is a model of the world, supported by a framework of experiences and observations constructed by the learner over time. The model can't be changed easily because it is built on intuition, interpretation of empirical evidence, and folk wisdom. In order to change the existing model, the learner will first need to become dissatisfied with it. At the heart of this research has been the educational theory of constructivism, whereby the individual constructs meaning about the world around them, accepting or rejecting new information as they experience new ideas and phenomena.

In Science education, the late Rosalind Driver carried out a significant amount of work on the topic of misconceptions. This had a noteworthy influence on Science education in the late 1980s, and many of the ideas remain and are applied in curriculum design and lesson planning:

R. Driver, A. Squires, P. Rushworth and V. Wood-Robinson (1994). *Making Sense of Secondary Science: Research into Children's Ideas.* Abingdon and New York: Routledge.

The general consensus on the features of misconceptions finds that they:

- are often based on a limited focus

- focus more on transient changes, rather than steady-state, e.g. air pressure

- consider change through linear causal reasoning, e.g. difficulties with reversible changes

- are based on undifferentiated concepts, e.g. electricity, current, and power

- are context dependent.

As a teacher, it is useful when you come across a misconception, to consider how it came about. The above list helps to explain and also pre-empt possible misconceptions.

The method of challenging misconceptions is based on psychological thinking about the assimilation of new knowledge and ideas. It follows the jigsaw metaphor (see Section 1.3) of 'schemata', which are pockets of connected knowledge that can be connected with new information. This is based on the work of Jean Piaget, which has since been developed further due to research in cognitive psychology.

Challenging misconceptions is rarely a one-fix strategy. Often these are deeply held ideas that have worked for the learner their entire life. A teacher simply saying they are wrong will not be enough to change that mental model. Even when a learner appears to accept a concept, they may well revert sooner or later to their original model. Some researchers even argue that the original mental model is never really lost, and that the learner just learns to apply the new 'correct' model when needed.

The typical approach consists of four steps: find out what the learner thinks, present them with counter-evidence, apply that to a range of examples, and then use the new ideas later in another lesson:

1. Probe prior knowledge.

2. Present cognitive conflict.

3. Provide a range of examples.

4. Revisit later on.

Cognitive conflict is key here. Encouraging learners to realise that what they expect to happen is wrong will prime them to ask why. Most often they think they are being tricked in some way, but once they are over that, they can start to assimilate the idea as they see it used in a range of examples. For me, creating cognitive conflict is like organising a surprise: asking learners to predict what they think, then demonstrating something that is at odds with their expectation.

Research perspectives on misconceptions

The education theory used to understand misconceptions includes Piaget's ideas of cognitive conflict,[9] the theories of another educational psychologist, David Ausubel, about how learners organise knowledge,[10] and more recently desirable difficulties and deliberate mistakes for which neuroscience can offer some perspectives.[11]

The areas of research that have been of specific use to classroom and teacher education include:

- learner misconceptions in Science and Mathematics

- trainee teacher misconceptions in Science and Mathematics

- teachers' views of misconceptions in Science and Mathematics

- application to cognitive acceleration.

In the background, there has been much discussion about the term 'misconception', with alternatives being offered, such as alternative conceptions.

Application to progress

Awareness of learners' prior knowledge is the precursor to making progress; it gives us a starting point. If that starting point is at odds with what you want

---

9 **M. Chapman & M.L. McBride** (1992). Chapter 2: The education of reason: Cognitive conflict and its role in intellectual development. In C.U. Shantz & W.W. Hartup (eds) (1992). *Conflict in Child and Adolescent Development* (Cambridge Studies in Social and Emotional Development). New York: Cambridge University Press, pp. 36–69.

10 **D.P. Ausubel** (1980). Schemata, cognitive structure, and advance organizers: A reply to Anderson, Spiro, and Anderson. *American Educational Research Journal*, 17(3), 400–404.

11 **B. Carey** (2015). *How We Learn: The Surprising Truth About When, Where and Why it Happens*. New York: Random House.

the learner to learn, simply telling them they are wrong is not enough. Instead, demonstrating to them why it is wrong, giving them time to challenge their misconception and accommodate it, allows for deeper, longer-lasting learning.

 Discuss

- What are the reasons why learners make mistakes in your subject?

- Which mistakes can be remedied quickly and which may take longer to correct? Why?

- Are mistakes part of learning, or is it better to avoid making them?

3.1 Mistakes in the Art room

Rachel, the Art teacher we met in Part 1, says that artists can often take advantage of mistakes or 'happy accidents' as part of the creative process, but that a firm basis of knowledge and skills is required by young artists before adopting a more experimental approach. When her Year 9 (14–15-year-olds) class was studying pencil portraits, Rachel was able to use exemplars of previous portraits that illustrated the more common mistakes made by beginners. A discussion ensued in which Rachel was able to explain what was 'right' and, crucially, what was 'wrong' with each of the (unnamed) exemplars.

This discussion was really about training students to observe the face in front of them, rather than draw a face as they *think* it should be.

Eyes, and the position of the eyes within the oval of the human head, are a common problem. Students have to be taught that the eyes are placed about halfway between the chin and the very highest point of the head. A common problem is that the eyes are drawn too high up the forehead and too close to the hairline. Similarly, eyes are sometimes drawn with the iris and pupil as perfect, visible circles and the whites of the eyes without any shading. When you show students black and white photographs of eyes, they are able to see how much of the pupil and iris can really be seen, their shape and position, and the amount of shadow in the eye. Some students really enjoy drawing in the classic 'bloodshot' eye effect, and this rarely bears any relation to reality. Students' misconceptions need to be robustly challenged and they need to be taught to study the human face carefully before recording it accurately.

Hair is another area of common weakness: it is often drawn either in too much detail or with very little detail. Some students will try to draw every strand of hair (then will understandably become frustrated and resort to scribbling) and others might just block in the hair like a cartoon character. Rachel uses a range of famous portraits to show how hair can be portrayed, using pencil, pen, and paint.

Where the head is positioned on the paper and how large it is in relation to the page is another issue, with students sometimes drawing very small heads in the middle of a large piece of paper.

Measuring skills and an understanding of symmetry and proportion are necessary tools with which students need to be armed in order to successfully tackle this challenging topic. Once students have been made aware of common mistakes and misconceptions, and have the necessary skill set and understanding, they can adopt a more experimental and confident approach to the subject: an approach in which the 'happy accident' can perhaps be realised with confidence.

 Reflection

- What are the most common mistakes learners make in your phase/subject?
- How will you deal with mistakes or misconceptions?
- How will you pre-empt mistakes in your lessons?

 Further reading

To explore some of these ideas further, I recommend reading:

M. Allen (2014). *Misconceptions in Primary Science.* Maidenhead and New York: Open University Press.

R. Driver, A. Squires, P. Rushworth & V. Wood-Robinson (1994). *Making Sense of Secondary Science. Research into Children's Ideas.* Abingdon and New York: Routledge.

A. Hansen (ed.) (2014). *Children's Errors in Mathematics* (Transforming Primary QTS). London: Learning Matters.

J. Ryan & J. Williams (2007). *Children's Mathematics 4–15: Learning from Errors and Misconceptions.* Oxford: Oxford University Press.

J.H. McMillan (2018). *Using Students' Assessment Mistakes and Learning Deficits to Enhance Motivation and Learning.* Abingdon and New York: Routledge.

⊙ Also see

Part 1: 1.3 What are the features of a progress culture?

Part 2: 2.5 Teaching for progress

Part 3: 3.5 Knowledge of exam technique

3.6 Critical engagement with assessment theory, policy, and practice

3.3 Interpretation of student responses and appropriate interventions

Introduction

This teacher skill is focused on the decision-making for learners' next steps, based on their response to a question, task, or activity. Linking back to the discussions on learning pathways in Part 1, this section is concerned with the mental model of the subject that the teacher holds in their mind. Experienced teachers are expert at offering the next step for a learner to take to make improvement in their subject.

From the work on assessment for learning, one of the key findings was concerned with teachers and learners being able to perceive a gap between what the learner knows, understands, or can do and the desired knowledge, understanding, or skill for that particular stage of learning.[12] This gap is where the teacher intervenes to help the learner move forward; that is, make progress in their subject.

The assumption of this perception of a gap and the associated intervention is based on the professional knowledge of a teacher and an agreed pathway (or pathways) through a subject. As teachers become more experienced, they build this learning landscape in their mind and are able to spot where a learner is and what is likely to help them to get to the desired place. This is often summarised as:

---

[12] **P. Black & D. Wiliam** (1998). *Inside the Black Box: Raising Standards Through Classroom Assessment*. London: King's College.

- Where am I now?

- Where do I want to get to?

- How do I get there?[13]

This is analogous with the map metaphor, with starting points, destinations, and a variety of routes to take to get there.

Consider

- How do you decide the next step a learner should make in a situation in your classroom?

- Do you have a mental map of progress in your subject? What does it look like?

- Are all decisions based on making progress through the curriculum?

Analyse your practice

Use Table 3.2 to establish your current practice concerning how you interpret and respond to learners' responses.

Table 3.2: Practice analyser: Interpreting and responding appropriately to learners' responses

	Regularly	Often	Sometimes	Rarely	Never
1 I can identify what a learner knows, understands, and can do.					
2 I know where a learner needs to be, based on the curriculum, the age, and the stage of the learner.					
3 I can provide an appropriate intervention in response to a need.					
4 I can plan when to provide feedback.					
5 I give learners an opportunity to respond to feedback.					

[13] **P. Broadfoot, R. Daugherty, J. Gardner, W. Harlen, M. James & G. Stobart** (2002). *Assessment for Learning: 10 Principles. Research-based principles to guide classroom practice Assessment for Learning.* London: Assessment Reform Group. <www.aaia.org.uk/news/article/assessment-for-learning-10-principles> accessed 26 June 2019

Analysis

- *Mostly 'regularly'/'often'*: If you are doing these practices regularly, I suspect this part of your assessment literacy is strong and you could consider the next section: 3.4 *Knowledge of requirements of (statutory/ standard) assessments*. If you have a particular outlier in Table 3.2, then concentrate on the 'how to' section related to that practice below.

- *Mostly 'sometimes'*: This indicates that you have some awareness of all these practices, but need to spend more time developing them. Select one that you do least often and plan opportunities to address this using the 'how to' practices listed below.

- *Mostly 'rarely'/'never'*: This indicates that you need to spend some time developing all these features to improve your assessment literacy. Using these practices will help you to develop a mental map of progress in your subject, which you can use to identify and respond to learners' needs.

Using the statements in the practice analyser (Table 3.2), select the numbers you wish to improve. Read the text and try the activities to help improve this area of your assessment literacy.

1 How to identify what a learner knows, understands, and can do

Unfortunately, we cannot see into learners' brains to work out exactly what they know, understand, and can do. All identification is done via proxy, usually by what they say, draw, or write in response to an activity. However, teachers become very good at ascertaining what their learners know, understand, and can do by interpreting their responses to a specific task. This can be done by observation or active engagement through questioning.

Observation of learners

Teachers working with very young children or with children with special needs due to impaired communication or physical limitations are able to make assessment through observations, without any formal tests. These teachers watch their learners when they provide stimuli such as sounds, light, or touch. They are able to interpret the learners' response to a stimulus. Some learners can point to words or letters; others can use sign language to communicate. In all these situations, the teacher is a keen observer, using professional knowledge to interpret and respond.

Teachers who work in arts subjects or practical subjects can assess what learners know, understand, or can do through observation. Music teachers can listen to learners' compositions or playing of an instrument. Drama teachers can observe how a learner reads lines or uses their body in a performance. Physical education teachers can observe how learners playing a football game work together, use ball skills, and use strategy in their game.

How to improve observation skills:

- Find out what it is you are looking for. In a given activity, how will the knowledge, understanding, or skill manifest itself?

- Consider not just whether learners are demonstrating that knowledge, understanding, or skill, but also how well they are demonstrating it.

- Start to collect examples of good demonstrations of knowledge, understanding, or skills in this situation and use them as benchmarks or exemplars to model from.

Questioning learners

A key skill of a teacher is to question.

How to improve questioning skills:

- Plan your questions, aligning them with your learning intentions.

- Use open and closed questions appropriately: open questions to reveal general knowledge and concepts, and closed questions to reveal specific knowledge items.

- Use questioning to gauge knowledge and understanding and to guide thought processes.

There are lots of approaches to questioning. A good summary is in Jim Smith's book, *The Lazy Teacher's Handbook*.[14]

2 How to create a mental model of progress in your phase or subject

There are a variety of ways to help teachers create and develop a mental model of progress in their phase or subject. Depending on the subject being taught, the mental model will have different emphases. This links to the metaphors for progress. Below, I describe a map metaphor to help you understand a mental model of progress within a given topic.

---

[14] **J. Smith** (2017). *The Lazy Teacher's Handbook: How Your Students Learn More When You Teach Less*. New Edition. Carmarthen: Crown House Publishing.

Consider a geographical map that shows the key concepts and skills for a subject and has connections between them. Teachers will have an idea of the relative difficulty of each of these concepts and skills. This could be seen as a three-dimensional relief map with hills and mountains showing increasing difficulty, or maybe holes for misconceptions (see Section 3.2). Alternatively, the difficulty could be shown by contour lines, with steepness indicating increased difficulty. Maybe scattered around these mounds and mountains are little hazard symbols. These hazards include 'often confused with', 'difficult key words', 'mathematically challenging', and so on.

When an experienced teacher teaches a particular topic, they have a complex mental map of contours, links, and hazards that informs them how to approach the topic, often along with a good knowledge of the learner or learners being taught.

Activity

Improving your mental map of your phase or topic can be achieved through drawing mind-maps and asking yourself questions to improve your understanding of the terrain and potential hazards.

Try this:

- Take something you teach and identify the curriculum requirements for that topic.

- List the knowledge, understanding, and skills required for the topic.

Ask yourself the following questions:

- What are the key words, processes, concepts, and skills for this topic?

- How are this knowledge, this understanding, and these skills connected?

- Is there a hierarchy of sub-knowledge or sub-skills? Is there a progression pathway through increasingly demanding knowledge or skills?

- What are the common mistakes and misconceptions that learners can make in this topic?

- Is there more than one pathway to learning a particular concept or skill? What are they?

3.2 Case studies of teachers using the Mapping Exercise

 **Case study**

I have used this exercise with teachers in the same school and department. Here, I present two case studies of using the mapping exercise.

A particularly powerful approach involved working with teachers who had started their first job, and their mentors.

I asked the teacher and mentor to select a topic they were going to teach, then draw their own maps. Firstly, they write the key words and concepts on sticky notes, and then arrange the sticky notes into a progression map on a large piece of paper with links drawn between them. Next, the teachers add any notes about difficulty, common mistakes and misconceptions. At this stage, the mentor and teacher compare maps.

Usually the mentor's map has more content and is more detailed, as would be expected. However, the new teacher's key words and concepts are more aligned with the curriculum or examination specification.

Together, the mentor and teacher can discuss areas of strength and areas for development. This is an objective way to understand each other's assessment literacy in terms of progress, teaching, learning and assessment.

I carried the second case out with a whole Science department. They selected a topic that was coming up for their Year 10s: 'aerobic respiration'. They created their maps individually to start with. In this Science department there was a range of specialisms – Biology, Chemistry and Physics – and there were differences in teaching experience within the group: from newly qualified to over twenty years'.

This case revealed, very strongly, the difference between the novice and the expert teachers' assessment literacy, with far more detailed maps from the more experienced teachers. However, the interesting outcome was that even experienced teachers had less detailed maps if they were not Biology specialists. Revealing this to the Science department made them realise how much they could learn from each other, and the group resolved to do more joint planning as a result.

In these cases, both novice and expert teachers learned from the exercise. Novice teachers were able to see their strengths and areas for development. Using their maps, they knew to ask the right questions to the right people if they needed support. Teachers felt that it was a good exercise to help focus on areas for subject development, for example, if a topic is new to the teachers or the content is particularly difficult.

3 How to provide appropriate interventions in response to a learner's needs

Section 2.5 deals with this in some detail. As part of your repertoire as a teacher, you need to consider the best intervention for a learner at any given time. Sometimes this can be trial and error, but with more experience your professional judgement will improve. It is often a case not just of what to learn, but how to learn something.

Here are three examples of general approaches of interventions that can be added to your mind-map in appropriate places.

Contextualise

Often, making abstract and complex concepts more concrete and simple can help scaffold understanding. By taking a few steps back, you can check that the learner understands the basics, which can then be built upon. For example, analysing a poem may involve understanding linguistic devices; solving quadratic equations requires knowledge of algebraic functions; explaining osmosis requires an understanding of particle movement in diffusion.

Memorise

Helping learners to memorise can be achieved by using strategies such as tried and tested mnemonics for knowledge, *aides-mémoire* for spellings, and memory palaces[15] for more complex information. Introduce them to effective learning strategies including retrieval practice.

Practice

Share with learners how to practise exercises and develop self-testing strategies for developing knowledge and understanding.

4 How to plan to give feedback

Feedback is covered in detail in Section 2.5. Here, we will look at opportunities to apply these ideas to planning and your assessment literacy.

- When do you intend to give feedback? Instant or delayed? Why?

- How do you plan your lessons to allow time for feedback and response to feedback?

---

[15] **Oxford Education Blog** (2017). Memory palaces: What they are and how to use them. Available at: <https://educationblog.oup.com/secondary/english/memory-palaces-what-they-are-and-how-to-use-them> accessed 1 April 2019

- Do specific concepts and skills require specific feedback approaches?

- What type of feedback is appropriate for the situation: teacher, self, or peer?

5 How to give effective feedback

Strategies for giving effective feedback are given in Section 2.5. Here are some questions to help improve your assessment literacy.

- How do you decide the next step a learner should make in a situation in your classroom?

- Do you have a mental map of progress in your subject? What does it look like?

- Are all decisions based on making progress through the curriculum? Could other forms of progress be included?

 Research

3.3 The zone of proximal development and other theories

Many practices in the classroom can be understood and explained by sociocultural theories.[16] For this section of the book, the interpretation of student responses and appropriate intervention as part of a teacher's assessment literacy, Vygotsky's notion of the zone of proximal development (ZPD) is often used. A teacher recognising a learner's ZPD is able to put suitable interventions in place.

The ZPD is defined as the space between what a learner can do on their own and what they cannot do (yet). The ZPD is the space where someone, a more knowledgeable other (MKO) can bridge, support, or scaffold the learner. For me, it is the space where the teacher works to assist learning – the space for intervention.

Lev Vygotsky (1896–1934) was a Russian psychologist who was interested in the social aspects of learning. What we mean here, is that learning by individuals is strongly influenced by the people around them. As humans, we learn from our parents, our siblings, our peers, and our teachers. Learning can be understood as a social process where interactions between individuals lead to learning, often for both teacher and learner.

---

[16] **N. Mercer & C. Howe** (2012). Explaining the dialogic processes of teaching and learning: The value and potential of sociocultural theory. *Learning, Culture and Social Interaction*, 1(1), 12–21.

As well as the role of the MKO within the ZPD, Vygotsky emphasised the importance of language in learning, in terms of dialogic talk and the role of private speech in self-regulation.[17]

Limitations

Some academics point out that Vygotsky underplayed the role of culture; that is, he made generalisations about the role of language that do not account for cultural differences associated with language.

There are questions over the assumptions of the ZPD and the application to classroom practice. Vygotsky studied development and his theories have been applied to teaching and learning, which, although similar, have distinct differences. This has led to discussion over whether the applications are appropriate or necessary.

Developments from Vygotsky's ideas

The importance of language and particularly talk in learning has received significant attention and has a deep theoretical and practical basis in classroom research. Professor Neil Mercer has made significant contribution to this using dialogic talk based on neo-Vygotskian theories.[18] Dialogic talk is the scaffolded talk between pairs and groups of learners.[19]

Application to progress

The ZPD has become a metaphor for the Guy Claxton 'sweet spot' (see Section 1.2) where teachers can intervene. To be able to do this, a teacher must understand a learner's current knowledge, understanding, and skills; they must have an understanding of the next steps for learning and the resources with which to aid those next steps.

The importance of language in learning, particularly talk, is important when we consider that most subjects focus on listening, reading, and writing, with little opportunity to develop talk.

---

[17] **L.S. Vygotsky** (1978). *Mind in Society: The Development of Higher Psychological Process*. Cambridge, MA: Harvard University Press.

[18] **N. Mercer** (1994). Neo-Vygotskian theory and classroom education. *Language, Literacy and Learning in Educational Practice*, 92–110.

[19] **N. Mercer & K. Littleton** (2007). *Dialogue and the Development of Children's Thinking: A Sociocultural Approach*. Abingdon and New York: Routledge.

Discuss

- How do you think teachers' mental maps of their subject might compare?

- What would a trainee's mental map look like compared to a teacher with ten years' experience?

- What influences do you think might impact on teachers' mental maps?

- What might be the consequences for a teacher who does not have a mental map of their subject?

3.3 Interpretation and intervention in primary

 **Case study**

Observing a literacy lesson with Year 6 learners, I witnessed some very visible interpretation and intervention in the classroom. This case happened in real time, making sure each learner had their individual needs met. Sarah, their teacher, had carefully planned a short writing activity about the summer season. The learners were asked to write a paragraph that showed it was summer, without explicitly saying so.

The learners were given time to attempt the paragraph, followed by the teacher displaying some success criteria on the interactive whiteboard. The learners looked at each other's work and decided which areas they could improve. This covered four areas: use of alliteration, use of adjectives, use of connectives, and use of adverbials. Once the learners had decided which area they wanted to improve, they were given 20 minutes at a station in the room that had activities to improve that area of writing. Two of the stations were staffed by a teaching assistant who talked through the activities; the connectives and adverbial stations were supported by the teacher, but the learners were expected to work more independently using the resources.

This type of approach is often called differentiation. However, in the UK, this term is often associated with meeting the needs of those with learning difficulties. Although this was addressed in the lesson, the interventions were focused on the aspects of the activity that would improve it. The first task was effectively diagnostic, with the teacher helping the learners to interpret their response and identify appropriate interventions. Each station had two or three activities that learners could choose from, furthering the personalisation of the intervention.

For example, the 'Using adjectives' table had three activities. One was to read a short passage and highlight adjectives that represented summer; another was a word bank of adjectives from which the learner could choose words most suited to the task; the final activity used three photographs that represented summer and the learner was asked to write short descriptions of them using the adjective word bank.

This was a physical form of intervention, where learners moved to an area that would help them develop. They chose the activity they would find most useful at that station, and then there was the more subtle interpretation and intervention used by both the teaching assistants and the teacher. Through looking at a learner's first attempt at the paragraph, the adult could guide the learner to the most appropriate intervention activity; through questioning and discussion, the adults were able to encourage the learners to focus on particular aspects of the task.

Each learner had a go at two of the stations. At the end of the lesson, they were given time to improve their original paragraph. Some read these out, and they were diverse and individual, but all had improved their writing.

Sarah had used a variety of skills to plan this lesson. Her assessment literacy allowed her to identify common mistakes made in writing, the appropriate interventions for that class, and the use of a variety of resources (both human and physical). The richness of this was not only how the lesson was planned, but how the lesson was carried out: the unplanned interpretation and intervention that took place throughout the lesson, giving each learner a chance to progress.

 Reflection

- How do you decide the next step a learner should make in a situation in your classroom?

- Do you have a mental map of progress in your subject? What does it look like?

- Are all decisions based on making progress through the curriculum?

 Further reading

To explore some of these ideas further, I recommend reading:

S. Clarke (2005). *Formative Assessment in the Secondary Classroom*. London: Hodder Education.

W. Harlen (2014). *Assessment, Standards and Quality of Learning in Primary Education*. York: Cambridge Primary Review Trust.

Also see

This section also links to:

Part 2: 2.1 Models of progress

2.4 Teaching for progress

2.5 Feedback for progress

Part 3: 3.2 Knowledge of common mistakes, misunderstandings, and misconceptions

3.4 Knowledge of requirements of (statutory/standard) assessments

Introduction

If you have ever been through a change in examination system, or just taking on a new examination when teaching, you will know that it can feel quite daunting. I have often felt that I get better at teaching towards a particular paper or exam with time, even with the best preparation and intentions. The first classes to sit an exam for the first time may not do as well as those that sit it after a few cycles of teaching it.

Teachers who teach classes that are taking statutory tests need to have a thorough understanding of the test itself. Part of assessment literacy is to know the assessment itself inside out, in order to teach it as well as possible and give learners the best chances of success. Examinations are often what learners are progressing towards at the end of a teaching phase. However, as discussed in Part 1, this is just one aspect of the educational experience at school.

Research interest in this area is particularly scant, but there is some research on the concept of 'washback'; that is, either the positive or negative effect on teaching and learning in response to the assessment being taken (see Research 3.4 below). The issue of 'teaching to the test' is also significant and can have positive and negative effects on learning and attainment.

This section offers strategies to ensure that you fully understand the assessment that the learners will be taking, so that you can focus teaching and learning towards those outcomes. The next section, 3.5, explores exam technique, which is an even more finely tuned skill to be emphasised towards the time learners sit their examinations.

 Consider

- What do teachers need to know in order to help learners pass an examination?

- What are the advantages and disadvantages of teaching to the test?

- How much curriculum time should be devoted to preparing for examinations?

Analyse your practice

Use Table 3.3 to establish your current practice concerning knowledge of requirements of assessments.

Table 3.3: Practice analyser: Knowledge of requirements of assessments

	Regularly	Often	Sometimes	Rarely	Never
1 I know the content of statutory assessments my learners will face.					
2 I know the structure of statutory assessments my learners will face.					
3 I know how the data will be used from the statutory assessments.					
4 I know how to use the data from previous statutory assessments.					
5 I know the limitations of the statutory assessments my learners will face.					

Analysis

- *Mostly 'regularly'/'often'*: If you are doing these practices regularly, I suspect this part of your assessment literacy is strong and you could consider the next sections: 3.5 *Knowledge of exam technique* or 3.6 *Critical engagement with assessment theory, policy, and practice*. If you have a particular outlier in Table 3.3, then concentrate on the 'how to' section related to that practice below.

- *Mostly 'sometimes'*: This indicates that you have some awareness of all these practices, but need to spend more time developing them. Select one you do least often and plan opportunities to address this using the 'how to' practices listed below.

- *Mostly 'rarely'/'never'*: This indicates that you need to spend some time developing all these features to improve your assessment literacy. Using these practices will help you to plan and make the most of learning opportunities through knowledge requirements of statutory/standard assessments.

Using the statements in the practice analyser (Table 3.3), select the numbers you wish to improve. Read the text and try the activities to help improve this area of your assessment literacy.

1 How to improve knowledge of the content of statutory assessments

Most statutory assessments have an associated examination specification. Examination specifications are far more than a list of knowledge, content, and skills that need to be taught. They often include all the details of the administration of the exam, the weightings of marks, the content of different papers, and the rules and regulations associated with the examination.

As a teacher of the subject, an important part of your assessment literacy is to understand the knowledge, understanding, and skills required by the examination, often known as the content. These are the things you must teach and your learners must learn in order to be successful in the examination. Below, I describe two activities you can do to familiarise yourself with and implement a new specification.

Activity 1: Familiarising yourself with the content

The first step is to read through the content and any assessment criteria, so you know what is covered and how to cover it. The main areas to look at are:

- content to be assessed: knowledge, understanding, and skills

- aims and learning outcomes

- assessment objectives and how they relate to knowledge, understanding, and skills.

From this, you can start to understand the rationale, the scope, and what is included (and not included). Once you are familiar with the content, you are ready to sequence and plan.

Activity 2: Sequencing and planning

Depending on whether you like working with paper or computer screens, sequencing, planning, and timetabling can be creative processes that involve using your assessment literacy. These activities may not happen in this order, as they all are intertwined.

- *Sequencing*: Drawing on your own mental map (see Section 3.3) to help sequence the course and topics will help you put your assessment literacy to good use. Compare how your map and the assessment content compare. Identify issues with the sequencing or the combination of concepts or skills within a topic. You will need to consider which concepts and skills will need to be taught in a particular order.

    Note that if the examination is modular, you may be constrained to the order in which you teach. If the course is not well designed (sometimes they are not!), you may need to use some content earlier than it is assessed.

- *Planning*: When planning, you need to know when the teaching starts and when each part of the qualification is assessed. If it is a terminal exam, check how many papers will be taken and what each one covers. If modular, check when each section is tested.

    Consider also the difficulty of each section and how long it might take to teach it. Sometimes chunks of a specification can be easily accessed and learned; others need more time to take in and revisit. Again, using your mental map, you should be able to determine the common difficulties faced by learners on particular concepts and skills.

- *Timetabling*: Timetabling is often a constraint within schools, determining the number of hours per week you will be teaching the learners and over what period. When sequencing and planning, this needs to be kept in mind to ensure that there is time to teach and learn the full content, or make informed decisions about what to provide as independent study.

    See Case study 3.4 for an example of this.

2 How to improve knowledge of the structure of statutory assessments

Knowing how an assessment is structured will help you plan for teaching, practice, and revision.

Activity: Understanding assessment

Qualifications are often made up of different components. In languages, there is usually speaking, listening, reading, and writing. In Art, Music and Drama, there are often large components based on performance or producing an artefact of some kind. Subjects such as Science can have a practical part, while other subjects have a division between skills and content. Some exams have components that include coursework carried out throughout the course.

Navigating an examination specification includes taking these things into consideration. So, for this activity, find out the following.

- *Assessment weightings*: How is the exam divided into components? Is it just one paper that assesses everything? If so, what is the balance between skills and content, or literacy and numeracy content?

- *Administration*: How and when the examinations take place is important. Is there just one terminal exam, or several papers at the terminal exam? Is there a modular structure where particular units are tested at specific times? Is there coursework? When should it be done; what format does it take?

- *Structure of tests*: Some courses have different papers, depending on the difficulty of the content. Exams are often divided into low-, medium- and high-demand questions. However, some test papers are split into foundation and higher. The foundation paper covers low- to medium-demand questions, with a grade capped often at a grade C or equivalent. Higher papers usually cover medium- to higher-demand questions, with the lowest mark achievable being a grade C or equivalent. This will involve making some decisions about which learners sit which paper.

This knowledge and these decisions all make up a teacher's assessment literacy and in turn support progress of learners.

3 How to improve knowledge of how the data from the statutory assessments will be used

Knowing what data is generated and what it will be used for is necessary for understanding how high stakes a test is and the implications of getting specific grades or marks. For this, I will split assessments into government assessments and assessments for qualifications.

Government statutory assessments are often used to measure how well the population of learners is doing at a specific point in their education. For example, in England, 5–6-year-olds are tested on their reading using phonics; 10- and 11-year-olds are tested on their literacy and numeracy skills. These assessments are used to judge schools on their performance and often to judge teachers on their performance. For the schools and teachers, these assessments are high-stakes assessments, because they have an impact on a school's rating and sometimes on a teacher's pay and, either directly or indirectly, on their chances of being promoted. Ideally, these should be low stakes for the learners sitting them, but the results are often used to place learners in particular teaching sets and their marks are often used as the basis of a prediction about their success in school.

Assessments for qualifications are exams that learners sit at the end of their school career. They are high stakes for learners, because they will determine their next steps in education or their first steps into their career. However, in some countries these exams become high stakes for teachers, particularly if the results are used to judge the success of a school and the teachers' pay or promotion is linked to the exam results of the classes they teach.

Finally, there is always data from statutory assessment that can be used to benefit future teaching and learning. Raw data from classes can form the basis of reflection on, and decision-making about, future learning. The examination reports that are published can also be used to inform your assessment mind-map (see Section 3.2).

4 How to improve knowledge of using the data from previous statutory assessments

When statutory assessments take place, data is often available that can be used to inform future teaching and learning.

Activity

Taking a set of class-predicted grades and actual grades achieved can help you to understand how well learners have done and what you could learn from this.

Often, the class data can be made up of more than one paper or component that results in a final grade, so look at the array of results and ask:

- Which learners fell short of their target? Why?
- Which learners exceeded their target? Why?
- Which learners met their target? By how much and why?

Factors to bear in mind when analysing data include:

- How good is the target data?

- Is it a good predictor or poor predictor?

If the predictors are good, then:

- What factors led to those learners missing those targets?

- Was it something you could control as a teacher or was it something beyond your control?

Uncontrollable factors include:

- significant absence due to ill health or other personal reasons

- a particularly difficult exam paper, which is often adjusted for

- silly mistakes in answering questions/doing examinations.

Controllable factors include:

- deep and thorough understanding of the knowledge, understanding, and skills required by the specification

- learning more difficult concepts or skills

- being able to answer questions appropriately

- experience of past questions

- exam technique.

5 How to improve knowledge of the limitations of the statutory assessments

All tests have limitations, and being aware of those limitations will help you to ensure that your teaching, and your learners' learning, maximise their chance of success in the test.

Activity 1: Establishing the limitations of an examination

Examinations have several limitations based on how they are constructed and what they are assessing.[20] It is helpful for teachers and learners to understand the limitations. It is very rare for an assessment or examination to allow a learner to demonstrate their full range of knowledge, understanding, and

---

[20] **D. McAllister and R.M. Guidice** (2012). This is only a test: A machine-graded improvement to the multiple-choice and true-false examination. *Teaching in Higher Education*, 17(2), 193–207.

skills. In general terms, exams test very specific knowledge, understanding, and skills that are set out in the specification. Some typical styles of question examination, with more specific limitations, are as follows:

- *Multiple choice*:
  - Learners can often underestimate the difficulty of the questions.
  - Unless the learner has a deep understanding, distractor multiple-choice answers can be convincing.
- *Short answer*: These often require a specific answer and key word, so a detailed understanding of the exam specification is important.
- *Essay*:
  - Learners need to understand the boundaries of the question.
  - Despite the apparent openness of the question, the mark scheme will be very focused on a specific range of knowledge, understanding, and skills.
- *Performance in Art, Music, Sport, or Drama*: Specific knowledge, understanding, and skills are required to do the performance.

Activity 2: Managing changes in statutory assessments

When statutory assessments change, this effectively reduces a teacher's assessment literacy to zero in this part of the skill set. These changes can be stressful for teachers.

When assessments change you could try the following:

1. *Research*: Consult the examination board and attend meetings associated with the change.

2. *Conceptualise*: Use your research to conceptualise the way in which the specification should be taught and the focus of learning; that is, the balance of content and skills, content through skills, or skills through content.

3. *Predict*: Predict the types of questions that could be asked, the troublesome concepts and skills that will need to be addressed, and any novel knowledge, understanding, or skills required.

4. *Communicate*: Ensure that learners know the focus of the specification, your prediction, and the administration of the examinations (for example, the length of the exam, what it covers, the number and types of question, and where to answer them. This is covered in more detail in Section 3.5).

5. *Review*: After the first cycle of teaching and examinations is complete, review your teaching, the learning, and conceptualisation with respect to the first examination papers.

 Research

3.4 The washback effect

N.R. Elshawa, C.S. Heng, A.N. Abdullah & S.M. Rashid (2016). Teachers' assessment literacy and washback effect of assessment. *International Journal of Applied Linguistics and English Literature*, 5(4), 135–141.

The washback effect is any change that teachers or learners make to their actions based on the needs of an assessment, in this case high-stakes tests. Washback can either have a positive or negative effect on learning.

This paper is a review of the literature that was carried out by education researchers in Malaysia. It reviewed the relationship between teacher assessment literacy and the washback effect of assessment. Note that the main evidence base is from the university teaching context. However, I believe this has important insights for school teachers' assessment literacy, as I discuss below.

Positive effects of washback include both teachers and learners being able to prepare effectively for an assessment by being familiar with the format and assessment objectives. This knowledge and understanding is part of teachers' assessment literacy, which can have beneficial effects on learners' outcomes. The authors state, 'The level of assessment literacy that a teacher possesses can have direct effect on students' course achievement and learning' (p.135).

Negative effects include:

- 'teaching to the test', where there is a detriment to learning, such as use of rote learning at the expense of deep learning

- teachers only teaching what is required in the text at the expense of wider reading.

Conclusions

The authors conclude that teacher assessment literacy deserves more academic study as, although it appears important, it is under-researched. They emphasise that improved teacher assessment literacy will improve learner outcomes.

Application to progress

As part of the bigger picture of teaching and learning in school, this aspect of assessment literacy ensures that learners can maximise their success in an examination. This does not mean that it should dominate teaching and learning, but as part of the schooling system, examinations are the main measure of progress. Neglecting this would be a disservice to learners.[21] Teachers who have a well-rounded assessment literacy certainly need a deep understanding of the influence of assessments on their teaching, as well as ensuring that washback is positive rather than negative.

 Discuss

- What is the difference between the washback effect (see Research 3.4) and teaching to the test?

- What would positive washback and negative washback look like in your context?

- To what extent does this section improve your assessment literacy?

3.4 Teach to the test: A case of Mathematics

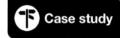 **Case study**

I had a discussion with a secondary Mathematics teacher that revealed how professional decisions about learning can be strongly influenced by the likely content of an examination. I use this discussion to exemplify the issues teachers face when examinations are imminent.

Towards the end of the course, Jo realised that there were only eight weeks of teaching time left for his Year 11 (15–16-year-olds) GCSE classes. There had been a series of 'snow days' (school closure when there is snow) and, although work is set for students to do at home, most are out sledging and the Mathematics exercises get overlooked. Jo said he was two topics behind and that he was making different decisions for each group he taught (he taught a middle set and a bottom set). The way the Mathematics GCSE paper was administered was that students who were likely to get a grade D or above sat the 'higher papers', and those who were likely to get a C grade or below sat the 'foundation papers'. Jo's middle set had about ten students

---

[21] **A. Green** (2007). Washback to learning outcomes: A comparative study of IELTS preparation and university presessional language courses. *Assessment in Education*, 14 (1), 75–97.

ready for the higher papers and the other 20, plus his bottom set, were sitting the foundation papers.

At this stage, Jo felt he had to teach to the test. He had to look at the examination, use his knowledge of what content and skills were classified as 'higher' and what was classified as 'foundation'. He also pulled on his knowledge of the types of question that come up, the likelihood of a question appearing, and which paper it would appear in. Using this knowledge, Jo carefully planned the lessons so the students covered only what they needed to know for the exams. Usually, Jo taught in a more open way, for the enjoyment of numbers and patterns, adding interesting anecdotes and problems to contextualise and enhance interest in the subject. Now, he had to pare right back to the skills and knowledge required to pass the test; not only that, but to pass the test to the learners' target grades.

Although there were revision lessons planned for the six weeks leading up to the examinations, Jo knew he had to complete these topics. For the remaining lessons he planned using textbooks, specific exercises, and then relevant past exam questions, so that those doing higher papers had different questions and exercises from those doing foundation papers.

Interestingly, Jo was able to decide not to cover certain parts of the topics, as he realised that they were what he called 'low-gain knowledge', where from experience he knew that they were unlikely to come up in the exam, or at least, if they did, they rarely had many marks associated with them. Based on the fact that his students were unlikely to get A or A* grades, these decisions could be made.

This case study illustrates the tensions with regard to personal philosophy of teaching, learning, and progress when it comes down to the need to pass an exam. Jo had been using his assessment literacy and pedagogical content knowledge throughout the course to pre-empt mistakes, challenge misconceptions, and to interpret responses and intervene appropriately. However, it was his knowledge of the examination structure and experience of previous years that allowed him to make decisions on what and how his students should study when time was short.

Reflection

• What will you find out in order to help learners pass an examination?

• To what extent will you teach to the test?

• How much curriculum time will you devote to preparing for examinations?

Also see

This section also links to:

Part 2: 2.4 Teaching for progress

       2.5 Feedback for progress

Part 3: 3.2 Knowledge of common mistakes, misunderstandings, and misconceptions

       3.5 Knowledge of exam technique

3.5 Knowledge of exam technique

Introduction

Part of being successful in examinations is knowing *how* the exam works and *how* to respond to the exam questions. An aspect of teachers' assessment literacy is for them to understand those requirements, share them explicitly with learners, and provide learners with opportunities to practise these techniques.

One of the debates about using this knowledge is *when* to share it with learners. Should it be shared from the start of the course in a 'drip-drip-drip' approach, or should it be shared as part of revision in the few months leading up to the examination? This question is addressed in Research 3.5, which looks at work in the field of cognitive science.

In Section 3.4, we looked at the washback effect and the impact of understanding the requirements of an examination on the outcomes for learners. This section, too, is an essential part of creating positive washback. Again, this is just part of the whole repertoire of teacher assessment literacy.

Consider

- What is the main advice that you give to learners who are sitting exams?

- How much influence do you think knowledge of exam technique has on learners' performance in an exam?

- Could you sit an exam and be successful without considering exam technique?

Analyse your practice

Use Table 3.4 to establish your current practice concerning exam technique.

Table 3.4: Practice analyser: Knowledge of exam technique

	Regularly	Often	Sometimes	Rarely	Never
1 I know the types of questions asked in these examinations.					
2 I know the types of responses required by the assessors or examiner.					
3 I know the common mistakes made by learners in these examinations.					
4 I know techniques that can gain credit or marks from assessors or examiners.					
5 I give learners opportunities to try past exam questions in the styles they will experience in the examination.					

Analysis

- *Mostly 'regularly'/'often'*: If you are doing these practices regularly, I suspect this part of your assessment literacy is strong and you could consider the next section: 3.6 *Critical engagement with assessment theory, policy, and practice*. If you have a particular outlier in Table 3.4, then concentrate on the 'how to' section related to that practice below.

- *Mostly 'sometimes'*: This indicates that you have some awareness of all these practices, but need to spend more time developing them. Select one you do least often and plan opportunities to address this using the 'how to' practices listed below.

- *Mostly 'rarely'/'never'*: This indicates that you need to spend some time developing all these features to improve your assessment literacy. Using these practices will help you to plan and make the most of learning opportunities through knowledge of exam technique.

Using the statements in the practice analyser (Table 3.4), select the numbers you wish to improve. Read the text and try the activities to help improve this area of your assessment literacy.

1 How to improve knowledge of the types of questions asked in exams

Each exam has a particular style of questions or tasks. In addition, they will have a particular style of expected answer (see approach 2, below).

If you have access to previous exam papers, which many examination boards provide, these can be used to identify the ways in which questions are asked. Question-types may include:

- multiple choice

- matching exercises

- short-answer questions

- longer-answer questions

- extended response

- essay

- performance

- product.

Activity

- Collect a series of past exam papers.

- Sort them into the types of question that are asked.

- Select some questions as exemplars for use in class.

Also look at the proportion of the examination that is made up of each question type. See approach 2, below.

2 How to improve understanding of the questions and responses required by exams

I use the word 'question' here, but it could be another type of task or an activity to carry out. Most exam specifications provide mark schemes with exemplar or past papers. It is important to see how learners can best gain marks.

- For multiple-choice questions, particularly those marked electronically, how important is it to tick a box or completely fill it with pencil? What colour pen or pencil should be used? How do you correct a mistake?

- In calculations, how many marks are available for showing the working out and how many marks for the actual answer? Can you still get marks if you get the question wrong? Are marks awarded for the use of the correct units?

- In essay questions, are marks given for an initial plan? If so, how many? Are marks given not only for what is written, but how it is written? For example, are marks awarded for structure, spelling, punctuation, and grammar and, if so, how many?

- For longer answers, including essays, how is the mark scheme structured? Is it criteria-based, with a 'best-fit' model for gaining marks, or does the learner get marks for each point mentioned? The style of answering these questions is quite different.

Activity

- Collect a series of past exam papers and mark schemes.
- Look at each type of question and the types of responses required.
- Select some questions and their mark scheme as exemplars for use in class.

Some examination boards provide exemplar materials and additional guidance for learning how to answer their questions.

3 How to improve understanding of the common mistakes learners make in exams and how to avoid them

To improve your knowledge of common mistakes that learners make in your phase or subject, it is necessary to use examiner reports to keep your assessment literacy up to date. If you have not done this before, it is worth using as many relevant examiner reports as you can source. If you do consult these from time to time, it is worth doing this systematically each time a group of learners sits an examination. Adding this knowledge to your scheme of work will extend your assessment literacy mental model, and will provide concrete examples of exam questions that have caused particular difficulties.

Activity: Using examiner reports

- Source examiner reports from the past 3–5 years.

- Read the reports and summarise them.

- Identify common topics that learners find difficult.

- Identify common general mistakes.

- Add these difficulties and issues to your scheme(s) of work.

- Collect examples of exam questions that address specific difficulties and place them within your resource bank.

4 How to improve learners' techniques to gain credit or marks in exams

This approach is linked to approaches 1 and 2 above. Learning the specific techniques is important, in order to maximise the chance of gaining marks.

It may be that certain topics require specific responses, particularly on a key word or subject convention level. For example:

- In Chemistry, it is important that learners use chemical formulae symbols correctly. Common mistakes include capitalising both letters of an element symbol, e.g. CU not Cu for copper, or using a superscript number instead of a subscript number, e.g. H^2O not H_2O.

- In GCSE History, the analysis of the usefulness of evidence is an important skill. It requires a clear understanding and application of concepts such as 'bias' and 'reliable'.[22]

- In high-school Art examinations, a common issue is poor composition, where the composition is cheesy, boring, too simple, or unbalanced.[23]

---

[22] **Oxford Education Blog** (2018). What can we learn from the 2018 AQA GCSE history 9–1 examiner reports? Available at: <https://educationblog.oup.com/secondary/what-can-we-learn-from-the-2018-aqa-gcse-history-9-1-examiner-reports> accessed 2 April 2019

[23] **Student Art Guide** (2018). The top 10 mistakes made by art students. Available at: <https://www.studentartguide.com/articles/top-10-mistakes-by-art-students> accessed 2 April 2019

5 How to give learners opportunities to try past exam questions

Now that you have tried all these approaches for really understanding exam technique, you are ready to support your learners in developing theirs.

Activity

- Give learners opportunities to try past exam questions in the styles they will experience in the examination.

- Give learners a mark scheme to show them how the examiners will mark that paper.

- Discuss with learners how best to gain marks for specific questions.

- Encourage learners to reflect on what they have learned about how to answer exam questions successfully.

Finally, use exemplar questions and their mark scheme as and when it is relevant to a particular topic area. Just attempting one question will enable learners to understand the knowledge, understanding, and skills required for that topic, as well as the skills required to attempt that question.

 Research

3.5 Revision using cognitive science approaches

Knowing how to revise effectively can have significant improvement in attainment. Rereading and highlighting notes is an ineffective way of revising. However, experiments using neuroscience and cognitive studies have recently revealed the most effective ways to revise. These have been summarised in a very readable book by Benedict Carey, which is supported by a wide range of educational research evidence.[24]

The key aspects relevant to revision are:

- *Owning*: Making the material your own. Rework it using mind-maps, knowledge organisers, or other ways of reorganising information.

- *Spacing*: Rather than long revision sessions, do it 'little and often', taking regular breaks. Aim for 20-minute intensive sessions, rather than sessions lasting several hours.

---

[24] **B. Carey** (2015). *How We Learn: The Surprising Truth About When, Where and Why it Happens.* New York: Random House.

- *Retrieving*: Self-test. Make flash cards or written quizzes. Test yourself, checking the answers. Keep doing it until you get them all correct; then do it some more.

- *Mixing*: When revising several topics or subjects, mix up your revision. Rather than one topic one day and another the next, study different topics throughout the day.

Limitations

Cognitive science is an emerging field in education and there have been obstacles to its becoming part of education practice.[25] Much cognitive research is laboratory based and may not be ecologically valid for classroom situations.

Cognitive science approaches are seductive and need to be critiqued appropriately, and at least trialled in a range of contexts. They can be seen as reductive and focused purely on cognitive processes, ignoring motivational issues and the sociocultural aspects of the classroom ecology.

As with all statistical results, cognitive science techniques work for a significant proportion of learners, but not all learners. One size does not fit all. How can we ensure that all learners make progress?

In relation to progress

Progress in the sense of learning the curriculum and attainment in examinations can be optimised by using a range of techniques beyond normal methods of revision. Teaching learners these skills will indeed aid their progress. As we learn more about neuroscience and cognitive aspects of learning, we can become more sophisticated at teaching how to learn more effectively and efficiently.

 Discuss

- What are the general and specific strategies for improving exam technique in your phase and subject?

- What can you do to improve your knowledge of exam technique?

- To what extent will this knowledge help learners make progress?

---

[25] **D. Ansari & D. Coch** (2006). Bridges over troubled waters: Education and cognitive neuroscience. *Trends in Cognitive Sciences*, 10(4), 146–151.

3.5 Improving exam technique in GCSE Geography

 **Case study**

Nathan was taking his first GCSE class and was keen to make sure both he and his learners were as well prepared for the GCSE exams as possible. In order to understand the types of questions that would come up and the types of answers that were expected, Nathan took three actions.

First, he collected a selection of past exam papers and mark schemes. Then, he read the online examiners' reports. Finally, he created guidance for his students on how to approach each question.

As a result, he identified the types of question that are asked and, using the mark scheme, he was able to understand the best way to gain marks. Two examples are shown below.

- Longer answers for 4 or 6 marks occur in the middle of each paper and require a particular structure to best ensure that students achieve the marks. Students get a mark for making a point and then another mark for developing that point. For example, if they are asked to explain the effect of volcanoes on global warming, they need to make a point that 'ash reflects the sun's rays' and develop the point by adding 'reducing the temperature of the lower atmosphere'. This needs to be repeated to cover the main points and elaboration of the points.

- In contrast, some exam questions involve the use of case studies where printed material such as maps and texts are provided, with questions linked to the material. These are usually extended-answer questions, for which learners can gain between 6 and 8 marks.

  According to the mark scheme, the marks are gained from first identifying relevant facts from the case-study material and then expanding on those facts using the geographical knowledge applied to those facts.

Nathan also came up with some general points from his research, which included:

- Spelling and grammar matter. Most answers require the correct spelling of key words, and longer answers require correct punctuation and grammar.

- Be specific. Use data or specific terms whenever you can. General or vague answers do not get awarded marks.

- Read the question carefully. Examiners report that marks are lost through giving the incorrect response to the question. Pay attention to stem words in questions: Describe, Explain, Justify.

Using this information, Nathan made a page of general tips to help learners gain, or avoid losing, marks. He then spent ten minutes per lesson on each type of question the learners were likely to come across, using more specific guidance. This way, the learners had content knowledge as well as developing 'exam technique'. Nathan also used the information from examiners' reports to enhance his teaching, addressing particularly troublesome areas at the time of teaching. He was able to make these points in a timely way, and not just during revision towards the examination at the end of the course.

Reflection

- How will you prepare learners who are sitting exams?

- What would you consider to be the features of good examination technique for your context?

- How do you think your knowledge of examination technique contributes to your assessment literacy?

Also see

This section also links to:

Part 2: 2.4 Teaching for progress

2.5 Feedback for progress

Part 3: 3.2 Knowledge of common mistakes, misunderstandings, and misconceptions

3.4 Knowledge of requirements of (statutory/standard) assessments

3.6 Critical engagement with assessment theory, policy, and practice

Introduction

Being critical of theory, policy, or practice is in essence questioning: asking what is being done, why it is being done, what are the advantages and disadvantages, what are the implications of doing it in the way it is being done, and finding another, improved way.

If you imagine theory, policy, and practice as a triangle, they all influence each other (Figure 3.3). They all are entwined, with changes in one leading to changes in another. For example, a policy change that moves from modular examinations to terminal examinations will have different theoretical underpinnings and will result in changes in practice (see Case study 3.7).

Figure 3.3: The theory, policy, practice triangle

Critical engagement with theory, policy, and practice involves understanding three different modes of reflection:

- personal reflection
- professional reflection
- critical reflection.

Personal reflection is a response to a professional situation that is entirely a recognition of your own feelings as a person. For example, a school may change the marking policy and you have an emotional response to this. It may be relief, enthusiasm, and excitement, or it could be irritation, annoyance, and anger. These are your personal responses, usually feelings. They are valid and important. Managers need to recognise these to help manage changes of policy. These are the first reactions, which are usually easy to recognise.

Professional reflection is based on more pragmatic and philosophical foundations. These may overlap with emotional personal reflections. If the marking policy changes will mean less time spent marking for you and more uniformity across the school, these are practical professional reflections. If the marking policy changes are welcome because they align more with your views on feedback, you will be able to articulate this. These are based on your professional values.

Critical reflection is engagement with evidence beyond the personal and beyond the professional. It takes into account the 'education knowledge base' and contextualises the change in marking policy within that framework. For example, if the marking policy moved from weekly marking to monthly marking, but with more automatically marked online quizzes, critical reflection would question the reasons, assumptions, and outcomes of this policy. You may find that a research review shows that indeed regular marking of work has little or no impact on learning, but less frequent, more detailed marking can improve outcomes. You may also find that regular quizzing using spacing and interleaving techniques improves memory and, therefore, attainment in exams. However, you may also be able to question that research, whether it is applicable to your context. You might also question whether teachers doing less marking but learners spending more time in front of a computer screen is beneficial to the learners; there may not be research or an evidence base yet to answer that.

In assessment, there are a number of underlying assumptions that can cause differences in professional opinion. Here are some of the debates:

- Should assessment be done to, or done with, learners?

- Is high-stakes assessment damaging to teachers and learners?

- Are teacher assessment judgements valid and reliable?

- What should be the balance between formative and summative assessment in lessons?

- Is learning to remember detrimental to the enjoyment of the subject?

> ## 🗨 Consider
>
> - Do you know the purpose of every assessment strategy you use?
> - Do you know the advantages and disadvantages of different assessment tools and strategies you use?
> - Can you critique assessment theory, policy, and practice?

Analyse your practice

Use Table 3.5 to establish your current practice in understanding and critiquing assessment theory, policy, and practice.

Table 3.5: Practice analyser: Critical engagement with assessment theory, policy, and practice

	Regularly	Often	Sometimes	Rarely	Never
1 I know what assessments I use and why I use them in the classroom.					
2 I read research regarding assessment theory.					
3 I can apply assessment theory to practice.					
4 I can critique assessment policy.					
5 I can critique assessment practice.					

Analysis

- *Mostly 'regularly'/'often'*: If you are doing these practices regularly, I suspect this part of your assessment literacy is strong. You may wish to use this exercise in supporting colleagues with improving their assessment literacy. If you have a particular outlier in Table 3.5, then concentrate on the 'how to' section related to that practice below.

- *Mostly 'sometimes'*: This indicates that you have some awareness of all these practices, but need to spend more time developing them. Select one you do least often and plan opportunities to address this using the 'how to' practices listed below.

- *Mostly 'rarely'/'never'*: This indicates that you need to spend some time developing all these features to improve your assessment literacy. Using these practices will help you to understand and critique assessment theory, policy, and practice.

Using the statements in the practice analyser (Table 3.5), select the numbers you wish to improve. Read the text and try the activities to help improve this area of your assessment literacy.

1 How to improve knowledge of assessments and why they are used

Most experienced teachers know which assessments they use and why they use them. Whether or not the learners will be sitting a statutory examination in their current year of study or in the future, this will affect what is being taught.

In the case of an exam year, teachers will have a detailed understanding of the examination content, the requirements, and the style. These statutory or qualification examinations often become the reason you are teaching. There is clarity, even if no choice, in which assessments will be used. It is likely that you will be supporting learners towards the exam using techniques discussed in Sections 3.4 *Knowledge of requirements of (statutory/standard) assessments* and 3.5 *Knowledge of exam technique.*

Informal examinations such as 'low-stakes' quizzes, end-of-unit tests, and formative assessment activities have more importance concerning teacher decision-making and professional reflection. There is a range of assessment activities that take place, from teacher judgement to carefully constructed topic tests.

Activity

- Select a class you teach or have recently taught.

- List all the assessment activities that you have used with them over a school year.

- For each assessment activity:

  - describe its particular purpose

  - categorise whether you have used it summatively or formatively (or both)

  - decide whether it is fit for purpose and whether you can improve the assessment.

For example, in Year 7 Geography, the teacher listed the activities in a table (Table 3.6).

Table 3.6: Assessing the purpose of assessments

List of assessment strategies	Purpose	Fit for purpose?
End-of-term tests x 3	*Used to track progress in topics taught. Provides a grade for the term. Summative. Encourages all learners to revise.*	Yes. Questions should be reviewed regularly. How comparable are the test results?
End-of-year test x 1	*Summarises retention over a year of selected topics*	Yes
Weekly quizzes	*Self-assessment knowledge checks, useful for teacher too*	Yes
Exit tickets with lesson objective questions	*To inform planning next lesson*	Could be improved, but useful for planning
Homework questions	*To consolidate classroom learning*	Not all learners do this. Time consuming to mark. What alternatives could we use?

2 How to read research regarding assessment theory

Assessment theory can sound a bit daunting, but you only need familiarity with the key concepts and principles of assessment to be able to understand assessment more deeply. In the activity in approach 1 above, you will have reflected on your own practice and considered specifically the assessments you use, their purpose, and whether they are fit for purpose. By reading about assessment theory, you will be able to interrogate your own practice more deeply, understand the advantages and disadvantages of specific assessment strategies, and make informed decisions about assessment policy and practice.

Activity 1

Read about assessment theory. It sounds dry, but there are some accessible books out there that can get you engaged with the principles and key concepts. Read one or both of these books, both of which have been influential on my understanding of assessment:

- **P. Black** (1998). *Testing: Friend or Foe? Theory and Practice of Assessment and Testing.* London and New York: Falmer Press.

  This was my first introduction to the theory of assessment. It tackles complex issues such as reliability and validity in an accessible way for an interested teacher. There are also chapters on what to test, how to assess, and teacher/learner roles in assessment. This is a great introduction for classroom teachers, from which to undertake further reading of more technical or academic books.

- **W. Harlen** (2007). *Assessment of Learning*. London: Sage.

This book has influenced my thinking a lot through my doctorate and assessment projects, particularly with regard to the place of the learner within assessment. This is a practical book with many examples from the UK and around the world. It challenges some of the (still) current ideas of whether assessments are done to, or done with, learners.

When reading these or similar texts, keep an eye out for the key concepts and debates listed in Table 3.7.

Table 3.7: The key concepts and debates in assessment theory

Concepts	Debates
Purposes of assessment	Using tests for accountability
Types of assessment	Impact on learning
What to assess	Impact on learners
How to assess	Testing good/testing bad
Validity and reliability of assessments	Assessment as a science or social science
Teacher judgement	Is there a theory of assessment?

When reading these texts, you may wish to organise your thoughts under these headings or make a mind-map to help conceptualise the ideas. It is always helpful, I find, to relate the more challenging concepts to my own practice, to help make sense of them. For example, you could look through a test paper and analyse it for validity and reliability.

3.6 Reliability and validity  Case study

In the research and use of assessments, two areas of assessment that are often poorly understood are the terms 'reliability' and 'validity'.

Reliability

When referring to reliability of assessment, we are talking about how dependable they are. Weather forecasters will often forecast rain with a percentage, giving an indication of how dependable the information is. Do we know how dependable our assessments are?

No assessment is 100% reliable, but some are better than others. If we do not know how reliable a test is, we cannot be sure of our inferences. To continue with my weather analogy, if the weather forecast in my area is for rain at a 10% chance, I am less likely to check I have an umbrella than I am if the chance is 90%.

Many factors affect reliability, and various tools can be used to assess the reliability of tests. In general terms: the longer the test, the more reliable it is. Careful wording of questions, clarity, and appropriate reading age improves reliability. Reliability is also affected by how the test is marked and moderated, learner factors such as how well prepared students are, and when the test takes place (morning, afternoon, weather conditions).

A test with low reliability will also have low validity.

Validity

No assessment is valid. Instead, the inferences generated from the assessment information determines its validity. Is the inference valid? Are you using the assessment information appropriately? This means that how the information is being used makes it valid or not. It comes down to the purpose of the assessment and whether the inferences made from that assessment are in line with that purpose.

The two aspects of this are making sure that the assessment tests what it intends to test, and ensuring that the information from the assessment is used appropriately and usefully.

For example, a foreign language test might be intended to test verb endings. However, if the questions only test the present tense, it is not valid to infer that the learner knows how to use all verb endings. In addition, if the words used in the test are not age appropriate (they may be too difficult or irregular), then the test is invalid for specifically testing verb endings, as results will be hindered by irrelevant factors.

 Further reading

P. **Black** (1998), *Testing: Friend or Foe? Theory and Practice of Assessment and Testing,* London and New York: Falmer Press.

D. **Christodoulou** (2016), *Making Good Progress? The Future of Assessment for Learning,* Oxford: Oxford University Press.

Activity 2

Next, you may wish to explore a particular researcher's work more deeply. Note that I have kept this list to academic researchers in the field of assessment. In Research 3.6, I summarise their work, provide an example of their work in books, and make links to their key academic papers.

- Choose a researcher who interests you.

- Read some of their work.

- Reflect on it in relation to your own practice.

 Research

3.6 Research in assessment theory and practice

Assessment is as hot a topic in the academic world as it is in schools and the offices of policymakers. As with much in education, it is not a precise natural science, rather a social activity that has underpinning values, attitudes, and philosophies. All these have influenced my own assessment literacy. I am presenting this as a short history of assessment for learning, from my perspective.

There is no doubt that the real starting point for me was the publication of a small pamphlet in 1998 called *Inside the Black Box* by Paul Black and Dylan Wiliam.[26] I didn't come across this until the early 2000s, when there was a big movement towards Assessment for Learning (AfL). I was teaching at the time and became very interested in formative assessment, not just in my own subject, but in others as well. At around that time, the findings of a significant school-based project were summarised by Paul Black, Christine Harrison, Clara Lee, Bethan Marshall and Dylan Wiliam in a book called *Assessment for Learning: Putting it into Practice*.[27] Schools around the UK and in other parts of the world were starting to put formative assessment into policy and practice.

Once I started my doctorate in classroom assessment, I first read and critiqued the original Black and Wiliam paper on classroom assessment.[28]

---

[26] **P. Black & D. Wiliam** (1998). *Inside the Black Box: Raising Standards Through Classroom Assessment*. London: King's College.

[27] **P. Black, C. Harrison, C. Lee, B. Marshall and D. Wiliam** (2003). *Assessment for Learning: Putting it into Practice*. Maidenhead and New York: Open University Press.

[28] **P. Black & D. Wiliam** (1998). Assessment and classroom learning. *Assessment in Education: Principles, Policy & Practice*, 5(1), 7–74.

I had also published a range of Science formative assessment activities that were widely used in secondary Science lessons as a means of assessment.[29] However, I was starting to see that these activities were not used in the formative way I had intended. Two papers hit a nerve with me when I was reading about this, the first by Beverley Marshall and Jane Drummond, which exposed the fact that teachers were doing formative assessment 'to the letter' or 'in the spirit'.[30] Their research showed that some teachers were only acting out parts of formative assessment, rather than actually having any deep understanding of the approach. If you like, it became 'performative assessment' – just to meet the perceived expectations of policy. Then, Shepherd's paper on the culture of classroom assessment got me interested in classroom culture[31] – a focus on the behaviours, practices, beliefs, and attitudes of teachers and learners, and their interaction.

A decade after the first Black and Wiliam paper, several reflections and reviews were produced to assess formative assessment and the assessment for learning movement. There is little doubt that the original research has had huge impact on policy and practice around the world, as well as in academia. Black and Wiliam rightly praise their own research,[32] but also recognise some of the issues with the concept of Assessment for Learning (AfL) and its application.

It was a growing concern that AfL was not being used as well as it could be in schools, and this led Dylan Wiliam to write *Embedded Formative Assessment*.[33] Several issues about the definition, application, and lack of theoretical underpinning were raised in a much-cited paper by Randy Bennett.[34]

Several attempts at applying and developing theory to AfL have produced interesting discussions, papers, and books. Quite early on, John Gardner collated some theoretical perspectives on formative assessment.[35] There was also some interest in motivational theories and the application of Carol

---

[29] **A. Grevatt** (2005). *Badger Levelled Assessment Tasks: Year 7*. Stevenage: Badger Learning.

[30] **B. Marshall & J. Drummond** (2006). How teachers engage with assessment for learning: Lessons from the classroom. *Research Papers in Education*, 21(02), 133–149.

[31] **L.A. Shepard** (2000). The role of assessment in a learning culture. *Educational Researcher*, 29(7), 4–14.

[32] **P. Black & D. Wiliam** (2003). 'In praise of educational research': Formative assessment. *British Educational Research Journal*, 29(5), 623–637.

[33] **D. Wiliam** (2011). *Embedded Formative Assessment*. Bloomington, IN: Solution Tree Press.

[34] **R.E. Bennett** (2011). Formative assessment: A critical review. *Assessment in Education: Principles, Policy & Practice*, 18(1), 5–25.

[35] **J. Gardner** (ed.) (2006). *Assessment and Learning*. London: Sage.

Dweck's growth mindset theories.[36] However, there was, lurking in the background, some other significant work on formative assessment that drew on sociocultural theory, by John Pryor and Harry Torrance, with a focus on primary schools. They had produced a book,[37] a paper that put forward their theory,[38] and some work building upon that by Barbara Crossoaurd, who had worked with Scottish teachers on formative assessment practices.[39] These sociocultural theories helped me to understand, explain, and apply assessment policy and practice, and the complexities therein. The research, the debate, and the associated policies and practices continue to play out.

3 How to apply assessment theory to practice

There can be a perceived gap between educational research and educational practice. To start out relating theory to your practice, you may wish to use books that have already summarised the theory for you. For example, this book by Susan Swaffield is a useful start:

S. Swaffield (ed.) (2008). *Unlocking Assessment: Understanding for Reflection and Application*. Abingdon and New York: Routledge.

This is a collection of evidence-based discussions about assessment, with reflection exercises and further reading suggestions. It will take you deeper into assessment debates and issues.

Additionally, you can look at research reviews, which bring together current research into one article, or at meta-analyses, which concentrate usually on exclusively quantitative studies. If you have access to and wish to read original research papers, the following activity should help you to navigate and make sense of them.

Activity

Select a research paper to read and use the following questions to guide you. It's best to read a research paper three times: first, just to get the feel of the

---

[36] **C.S. Dweck** (2007). *Mindset: The New Psychology of Success*. New York: Random House.

[37] **H. Torrance & J. Pryor** (1998). *Investigating Formative Assessment: Teaching, Learning and Assessment in the Classroom*. Maidenhead and Philadelphia, PA: Open University Press.

[38] **J. Pryor & H. Torrance** (1997). Formative assessment in the classroom: Where psychological theory meets social practice. *Social Psychology of Education*, 2(2), 151–176.

[39] **J. Pryor & B. Crossouard** (2008). A socio-cultural theorisation of formative assessment. *Oxford Review of Education*, 34(1), 1–20.

181

paper; second, with more general questions; and, finally, to consider more deeply whether it is applicable to your own practice.

General questions when reading educational assessment research

- What's it about? What is the research question? What's the problem?

- How was it done? What type of methods have been used?

- What data did they get? Is it transparent? Do you have access to all the relevant data?

- What did they conclude? Are the conclusions based on the evidence?

- Where does it fit? Which educational theory(ies) does it build upon?

- What's new? What is the contribution to knowledge?

Questions about application to my own practice

Something called 'ecological validity' can be useful to consider when finding research papers that may help. That is, how close to your own classroom context is the research?

- When was the research carried out?

- In which country?

- In what type of school?

- What age were the learners?

- Over what period of time was the study carried out?

- What was done or used?

- Could it be repeated in my classroom?

- How would I do it in my classroom?

As a result of reading educational research, you may wish to make small or large changes to your practice.

4 How to critique assessment policy

In professional situations, you may find that educational policy changes mean that you have to carry out particular practices even if you do not want to.

There are two types of policy that teachers are subject to: education authority or national government education policies, and local school policies (that is, policies that are put together by a school's management, often in response to the first type).

Very few politicians have any experience or understanding of education or assessment beyond their own school experiences, or maybe that of their children. Educational policy is often written by civil servants, again whose level of expertise is often low. However, some governments take on advisers who do have expertise, but will have a political filter on what they choose to take forward.

Activity

Ask the following questions about assessment policy:

- What is its purpose?
- What is the change for?
- How will learners benefit?
- What are the short-term benefits and disadvantages?
- What are the long-term benefits and disadvantages?
- What are the implications on practice?
- What are the assumptions behind the change?
- Do the changes have any basis in assessment theory?
- What changes in practice will there need to be?

A more recent addition to Paul Black's *Testing: Friend or Foe?* is a book by Gordon Stobart, who tackles some of the big issues with different types of test and testing, and offers an alternative:

G. Stobart (2008). *Testing Times: The Uses and Abuses of Assessment.* Abingdon and New York: Routledge.

5 How to critique assessment practice

Critiquing assessment practice can be a critical reflection of your own practice or of practices that are recommended before you decide to try them in the classroom.

Non-researchers often rely on the perspectives of educational researchers, but there is a growing voice of teachers who are embracing evidence-informed practice. They are questioning their practice and their school policies, and reading educational research and applying it critically. Case study 3.7 demonstrates how practice can be interrogated, questioned, and explained.

Activity

Look at an assessment practice in your lessons or a policy within your school. Ask the following questions:

- Why do I do this?

- Does it promote progress?

- How well does it promote progress?

- Which learners benefit most?

- Are any learners disadvantaged?

Examples of critiques of assessment, testing, and progress include:

J. Bower & P.L. Thomas (eds) (2016). *De-testing and De-grading Schools: Authentic Alternatives to Accountability and Standardization.* New York: Peter Lang.

W. Mansell (2007). *Education by Numbers: The Tyranny of Testing.* London: Politico's Publishing.

 Discuss

- How can learning theories help you to support the progress of your learners?

- What are the tensions between theory, policy, and practice in your context?

- How important is a critical perspective for a classroom teacher?

3.7 Verbal feedback stampers　　

This is a case of the wrong practice being implemented due to a misunderstanding of policy, when in some schools in England teachers were asked to 'stamp' learners' books with an inked stamper that said 'Verbal feedback received'. This practice arose from school management feeling that they needed to monitor how and when feedback was given, based on what they interpreted from Ofsted reports (the school inspection organisation in England).

The practice was supposed to encourage verbal feedback, but also to 'capture' or document when verbal feedback was given. Part of being critical about assessment practices is to question them. Why are they being used? What benefit do they have on teaching, learning, and assessment? Is this a good use of teaching and learning time? Who benefits from the practice?

One example I have seen involved the teacher ensuring that over two one-hour lessons, she spoke to every learner at least once. The teacher looks at a learner's piece of work and gives some verbal feedback. At this point, the learner's exercise book is stamped with the verbal feedback stamp and the learner is then expected to write down that feedback and respond to it. This, it seemed to me, defeats the object of verbal feedback: it becomes written feedback. I have yet to see any research that shows this has any benefit to learning beyond what normal written feedback would achieve.

The main point here that it is a performance for accountability. It demonstrates a complete lack of trust of teachers by their senior leaders. I know that verbal feedback happens all the time in classrooms on a whole-class level, in small groups, or individually. Good teachers use their professional judgement to decide which type of feedback is most effective. School leaders, under pressure to meet what they perceive as the demands of Ofsted, make decisions that they believe will help demonstrate that they are 'doing verbal feedback'. However, the doing does not show it is effective. A stamp will not improve that effectiveness; in fact, it is a costly distraction. The schools pay money for these stamps to be made, some even specially designed to have the school's and teacher's name on them.

To me, the verbal feedback stamper is the epitome of the culture of performance and accountability in schools: teachers performing for their managers, the managers performing for their local authority or for what they think Ofsted want. In this culture of what Warwick Mansell has called 'hyperaccountability',[40] teachers and their managers end up making extra work for themselves, even losing sight of the purpose and value of education. In response to some of these practices that are created due to lack of trust and feeling of high accountability, Ofsted have even produced a myth-busting webpage to try to counter some of the misinformation.[41]

---

[40] **W. Mansell** (2007). *Education by Numbers: The Tyranny of Testing*, London: Politico's Publishing.

[41] **Ofsted** (2015). Guidance: Ofsted inspections: myths. Available at: <https://www.gov.uk/government/publications/school-inspection-handbook-from-september-2015/ofsted-inspections-mythbusting> accessed 19 March 2019

Reflection

- What is the purpose of every assessment strategy you use?
- What are the advantages and disadvantages of different assessment tools and strategies you use?
- Can you critique your own assessment policy and practice?

 Further reading

To explore some of these ideas further, I recommend reading:

C. Brown (2013). *Making Evidence Matter: A New Perspective for Evidence-informed Policy Making in Education*. London: IOE Press.

J. Gardner, W. Harlen, L. Hayward & G. Stobart (2010). *Developing Teacher Assessment*. Maidenhead and New York: Open University Press.

A. Moore (2012). *Teaching and Learning: Pedagogy, Curriculum and Culture*. 2nd edition. Abingdon and New York: Routledge.

A. Moore (2014). *Understanding the School Curriculum: Theory, Politics and Principles*. Abingdon and New York: Routledge.

A. Pollard, J. Collins, M. Maddock, N. Simco, S. Swaffield, J. Warin & P. Warwick (2005). *Reflective Teaching: Evidence-informed Professional Practice*. 2nd edition. London: Continuum.

D.A. Schön (1987). *Educating the Reflective Practitioner*. San Francisco: Jossey-Bass.

 Also see

For understanding progress towards your examinations:

Part 3: 3.4 Knowledge of requirements of (statutory/standard) assessments

Summary

Through Part 3, I hope I have shown the importance of teacher assessment literacy in enabling learners to make progress within their phase and subject. Assessment literacy is often a neglected part of teacher training and, although it can be developed with experience, there are several strategies that teachers can use to accelerate and consolidate their knowledge and understanding of assessment in their subject and phase.

The aspects I chose to concentrate on were two holistic approaches to the phase and discipline that will improve assessment literacy of the more general parts of teaching and learning. Two sections focused on a narrower view of progress based on success in statutory examinations. The final section supports the critical reflection of assessment practices within schools and of statutory examinations. Together, I expect these will improve teacher confidence in selecting and using assessment strategies that will in turn aid learner progress.

Final thoughts

This book has focused on three aspects of progress within schooling.

- First, it has interrogated what progress could mean and actually means within education. This raises philosophical questions about the purpose of schools and allows you to reflect upon the reasons for teaching and the purpose of education.

- The second part focuses on a range of aspects of progress in school: models of progress, measuring progress, communicating progress, teaching for progress, and feedback and intervention. By exploring these aspects and offering a range of existing strategies, theoretical perspectives, and case studies, I hope you will have been able to interrogate your own practice and make professional judgements on where to improve and trial in your practice.

- Finally, I have tried to bring together the key aspects of improving teachers' assessment literacy, so that you can continue to support the progress of all the learners you teach.

This book represents the coming together of many aspects of my own professional experiences, practice-based research, and academic study. During this, it has raised many questions for me, as well as consolidating and reshaping my knowledge and understanding. At the minimum, I hope this has raised questions that you, as teachers, don't often have the time or opportunity to contemplate, and informed your knowledge and understanding of some aspects of assessment practices that can provide a holistic approach to the progress of all learners in education.

Index

bias, cultural 42

Bjork, Robert 107

Black and William paper 179, 180

Bloom, Benjamin 75, 86

Bloom's taxonomy 75–7, 78, 80

revised 75–7, 78–80

Boaler, Professor Jo 64

Brown, G T L 127–8

building on concepts 54–5

'building learning power' 35

C

CAME (Cognitive Acceleration through Mathematics Education) 111

Cameron, William Bruce 88

Canadian aboriginal groups 43

Carey, Benedict 168

CASE (Cognitive Acceleration through Science Education) 111

case studies

assessment 177–8

chemistry 55

exam technique 170–1

feedback 184–5

language 57

in primary literacy 63–5, 150–1

mapping exercise 146

mistakes 139–40

teaching tensions 66

teaching to the test 161–2

catchment area 42

checking books 118

chemistry

exams 167

Key Stage 3 81–2

learning pathways 81–2

Progress in 55

child development 49, 53, 56

children, special needs 143

China, culture in 44

Chinese values 26

Christodoulou, Daisy 59, 69, 94, 95, 178

class systems 27–8, 42

classroom culture 101, 180

Claxton, Guy 35, 36, 149

'climbing a ladder' model 53, 54–7, 60, 66, 68–9, 83–5

CLT (cognitive load theory) 107, 109–10

cognition defined 102

Cognitive Acceleration

through the Arts 111

through Mathematics Education (CAME) 111

programmes 111

through Science Education (CASE) 111

'cognitive conflict' 111, 135, 137, 138

cognitive development 55–6

cognitive load

extraneous, germane, intrinsic 110

theory (CLT) 107, 109–10

The publishers would like to thank the following for permissions to use their text:

Ruth Ashenden, Teacher of English, Robertsbridge Community College for a quotation. Reproduced with kind permission.

Australian International Academic Centre PTY. Ltd. for excerpts from "Teachers' Assessment Literacy and Washback Effect of Assessment" by Niveen R. M. Elshawa, Chan Swee Heng, Ain Nadzimah Abdullah, Sabariah Md. Rashid, published in *International Journal of Applied Linguistics and English Literature*, Vol. 5(4), p.137, 2016. Licensed under a Creative Commons Attribution 4.0 International License.

Badger Publishing for Tables 2.4, 2.5 from *Badger Key Stage 3 Science. Levelled Investigation Tasks* by Andrew Chandler-Grevatt, Badger Publishing, 2006, p.6; and *ACE Science: Science Tasks with Learning Ladders: Chemistry Homework Book* by Andrew Chandler-Grevatt, Badger Publishing. 2014, S4, Task 4. Reproduced by permission of Badger Publishing.

Bloomsbury for an excerpt from *Philosophy of Educational Research*, 2nd edition by Richard Pring, Continuum Publishing, 2004, p.15, copyright © Richard Pring, 2004. Used by permission of Bloomsbury Publishing Plc.

Crown House Publishing for a quotation from "What is Progress?" by Will Ord, published in *Progress* (Best of the Best) eds Isabella Wallace and Leah Kirkman, Crown House Publishing, 2017, pp.65-71. Reproduced with permission.

Department for Education for excerpts from '2011 Teacher Standards for England', https://www.gov.uk/government/publications/teachers-standards, pp.10, 12; and 'The National Curriculum'. https://www.gov.uk/national-curriculum, © Crown Copyright 2011, 2013.

Elsevier for an excerpt from 'Teacher assessment literacy in practice: A reconceptualization' by Yueting Xu, Gavin T.L. Brown, published in *Teaching and Teacher Education* by Elsevier, August 2016, copyright © 2016 Elsevier Ltd. All rights reserved.

ETL Project for excerpts from 'Threshold concepts and troublesome knowledge: Linkages to ways of thinking and practising within the disciplines 2003', *Occasional Report 4. Edinburgh: ETL Project*, University of Edinburgh, http://www.etl.tla.ed.ac.uk/docs/ETLreport4.pdf, accessed 4 April 2019, pp.1, 4-5. Reproduced by permission.

Incorporated Society of Musicians for an excerpt from "The National Curriculum for Music: A revised framework for curriculum, pedagogy and assessment in key stage 3 music" by A. Daubney & M. Fautley 2019, copyright © 2019 Incorporated Society of Musicians, Dr Alison Daubney and Professor Martin Fautley. Reproduced by permission.

Richard McFahn for Figure 2.3 'An example pathway from History' by Richard McFahn, August 2017, redrawn from https://www.historyresourcecupboard.co.uk/dont-tell-interpretations-difficult-key-stage-3/ (accessed 22/05/2019). Reproduced with permission of the author.

Danielle Musselwhite, Teacher at Southwater Junior Academy for a quotation. Reproduced with kind permission.

Pearson Education, Inc. for Tables 2.2, 2.3 adapted from *A Taxonomy for Learning, Teaching, and Assessing: Pearson New International Edition: A Revision of Bloom's Taxonomy of Educational Objectives*, Abridged Edition, by L.W. Anderson, D. R., Krathwohl, P. W., Airasian, & B. Samuel, Longman, 2001, Table 12.3, p.204. Reprinted by permission of Pearson Education, Inc., New York, New York.

Phi Delta Kappan for an excerpt from 'Assessment literacy' by Rick J. Stiggins, Phi Delta Kappan, Vol. 72(7), 1991, pp.534-539. Reproduced by permission.

Becky Prior, Professional Tutor and Teacher of Science at Robertsbridge Community College for a quotation. Reproduced with kind permission.

Routledge for Figure 2.4 from *Student thinking and learning in science: perspectives on the nature and development of learners' Ideas* by Keith S. Taber, Routledge, 2014, p.208. Permission conveyed through Copyright Clearance Center, Inc.

Taylor & Francis for excerpts from 'Curriculum coherence and national control of education: issue or non-issue?' by William H. Schmidt, Richard S. Prawat published in *Journal of Curriculum Studies* by Taylor & Francis, December 2006; and 'Learning progressions and teaching sequences: a review and analysis' by Richard Duschl, Seungho Maeng, et al, published in *Studies in Science Education* by Taylor & Francis, September 2011. Rights managed by Taylor & Francis.